100 BIRDS
TO SEE BEFORE
YOU DIE

For Mum and Dad, who bought me my first binoculars, not knowing where it would lead.
DAVID CHANDLER

To my children Emily and Samuel, hoping that they will see some of the treasured birds in this book.
DOMINIC COUZENS

Thunder Bay Press
An imprint of the Advantage Publishers Group
10350 Barnes Canyon Road, San Diego, CA 92121
www.thunderbaybooks.com

ISBN 13: 978-1-59223-958-0
ISBN 10: 1-59223-958-7

Printed in Dubai.

1 2 3 4 5 12 11 10 09 08

Text and design copyright © 2008 Carlton Publishing Group

Project Editor: Gareth Jones
Copy Editor: Liz Dittner
Senior Art Editor: Lucy Coley
Designer: Vicky Rankin
Picture Researchers: Steve Behan, Stephen O'Kelly
Production: Lisa Moore

100 BIRDS TO SEE BEFORE YOU DIE

THE ULTIMATE WISH LIST
FOR BIRDERS EVERYWHERE

DAVID CHANDLER & DOMINIC COUZENS

THUNDER BAY
P · R · E · S · S

San Diego, California

Contents

The Golden Bowerbird (*Prionodura
newtoniana*) (page 148) is found in
the rainforests of Queensland, Australia,
above 700 meters (2,300 feet). The
world's smallest bowerbird, it builds
the largest bowers of all.

The Eurasian Hoopoe (*Upupa epops*) (page 108) is a striking bird with its barred back and wings, and remarkable fanned crest.

The Monserrat Oriole (*Icterus oberi*) (page 58) is a rare species threatened more by a volcano than by humankind.

Foreword

Before You Die: the title is merely a device. Open the book and it's all about living, not dying—about wild birds as a glorious celebration of life.

When I first heard that this book was in the works, I was dubious. Of course I knew that the authors, David Chandler and Dominic Couzens, were first-rate authorities on birds, but it seemed they had taken on a monumental challenge. With some 10,000 species of birds in the world, how could they settle on just 100 to feature? Now that the book is here, however, I'm happy to say that it is a spectacular success.

Just look at the diversity in these pages. These birds run the gamut from the world's largest (Common Ostrich) to the smallest (Bee Hummingbird). They include creatures that are unbelievably gorgeous (I'iwi, Resplendent Quetzal, Blue Bird-of-paradise) and others that just look weird (Hoatzin, Southern Brown Kiwi) or practically ugly (Shoebill). They include beautiful songsters (Common Nightingale), talented mimics (Superb Lyrebird), and awful noisemakers (Capuchinbird). They will stretch almost anyone's concept of the variety of birdlife.

Do these 100 birds all qualify for the honor of inclusion here? Absolutely. Are there others that might have made the cut? Well, yes: about 9,900 of them. That's the thing: start looking closely and every bird is phenomenal in its own right. Consider the plucky little House Sparrow, boldly taking advantage of its human neighbors all over the world. If I were visiting Earth from another planet, this adaptable upstart would top my most-wanted list. Virtually everyone reading this book has seen it already, so it's not in these pages. But it could have been.

That is the genius of *100 Birds to See Before You Die*. Chandler and Couzens made their selection with such thoughtful criteria that we can see how practically any bird might qualify. The Woodpecker Finch might seem utterly drab, until you realize that it is making and using its own tools. The Oilbird might just look like a bloated nightjar, until you find out that it flaps about in the dark eating fruit and using sonar to navigate through its roosting caves. Arctic Tern with its remarkable migration, Smith's Longspur with its overactive love life, Maleo building its own incubators—every bird has its own amazing story. In a delightful paradox, by narrowing their spotlight to these 100, the authors have demonstrated that every bird around the globe is worth seeing.

Just one complaint: this book should have come with a warning label, because it's certain to increase one's desire to travel. Wonderful birds live all over the world, and to see them, that's where we must go. By the time I was 10 years old, already an avid birder in Kansas, I had seen one of the species in this book—Scissor-tailed Flycatcher. Now, after years of pursuing birds on all seven continents, I have seen close to 70 of those listed here—but that leaves many fabulous experiences still ahead, and this inspiring volume has got me planning my next trip. Whether it leads you to travel by airliner or by armchair, let this book take you along on a celebration of the birds that enrich both our world and our lives.

Kenn Kaufman

Introduction

In one way or another, every bird species is remarkable. This makes selecting just one percent of the world's 10,000 or so species as the ones "to see before you die" a tricky task. Our aim has been to profile 100 of the world's most extraordinary birds. Some of the species included are extraordinarily rare, but this is not a book that's primarily about rarity, and most of the included species are of little conservation concern. Rather, our approach has been to take a much more rounded look at the planet's avian diversity and to create a wish list that celebrates the wonder, beauty and amazing lifestyles of the world's avifauna.

Narrowing the list to just 100 species was challenging enough, but ranking the chosen few, from "least must-see" (of the "top" one percent that is!) to what might be the world's "most wanted" species was something else. The birds are arranged in reverse order, with number 100 at the front of the book, counting down to the treasure of treasures at the back. There was method in the ranking and each species was allocated a point score against 11 different criteria (see page 214). This provided a (mostly) subjective assessment of their beauty and visual impact, their behavior, their conservation status and how hard they are to see.

Every species account aims to capture the bird's essence and to convince the reader that it is worthy of its place in the book. We have also included summary information, a distribution map and, of course, some stunning photographs. The taxonomy and English names that we have adopted are those of *Birds of the World, Recommended English Names* (Gill and Wright, 2006). The maps provide an indication of where and when a species may be seen (see key below), and where a range may be hard to spot, arrows have been used to make the reader's life a little easier! For "Conservation status" we have used 2007 IUCN Red List categories.

Neither of us are foolish or arrogant enough to believe that this book is a definitive statement on the world's 100 best bird species. To do so would be to invite trouble and a mountain of correspondence that we'd prefer to avoid! No doubt there will be missing species that you think should be in here, and some that are included that you think could be bettered. But whatever your opinion of the final selection, all of the birds that grace these pages are fantastic creatures. For one reason or another, and sometimes for several reasons, they are all great birds to experience.

Enjoy the book. May it fuel your passion for birds and birdwatching. Let it whet your appetite for some avian adventures. Then, whether close to home or in distant lands, get out there and live the adventure.

David Chandler and Dominic Couzens

Map Key

- Breeding
- Non-breeding
- Resident
- Nomadic
- Resident/Nomadic

Opposite: The nest of Sociable Weaver (*Philetairus socius*) (see page 30)

100. Arctic Tern *Sterna paradisaea*

An incredibly well-travelled migrant

Size: 33–36 cm (13–14.2 inches).

Distribution: Breeds in northern hemisphere, mostly at higher latitudes; winters in Antarctica.

Habitat: Breeds mostly on and around low-lying coasts, sometimes inland, including beaches, islands (inshore and in lakes and lagoons), meadows, peat moss, bogs, rough grassland and heath; winters around pack ice and at sea.

Classification: One of 100 species in the family Laridae, and one of 34 in the genus *Sterna*.

Population and conservation status: Estimated at 1 million birds. Least Concern.

Breeding system: Monogamous, mostly colonial.

Nest and eggs: Shallow scrape. 2–3 eggs, one brood.

Incubation and fledging: 22–27 days. 21–24 days.

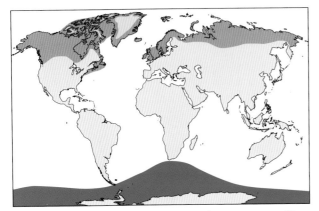

During its lifetime, an Arctic Tern might migrate 1 million kilometers (650,000 miles), flying almost pole to pole, and back again, year after year, for decades. Many breed within the Arctic Circle, some within 800 kilometers (500 miles) of the North Pole. When breeding is done, the birds begin an astonishing migration, to spend the "winter" around the Antarctic pack-ice. The northern winter is the southern hemisphere's summer, so Arctic Terns see more daylight in their annual cycle than any other animal. Birds from different parts of the range have longer or shorter journeys, but a bird ringed in North Wales was recovered off Australia, over 17,500 kilometers (11,000 miles) away. This is a fairly long-lived species—a ringed bird survived for nearly 34 years, and some may live even longer.

Birds breeding from Canada east to northern Siberia use the Atlantic as their primary flyway. Those west of the Atlantic head towards Europe or Africa, joining the Atlantic "freeway" perhaps off northwest Europe, or taking a more southeasterly course towards Africa. Those on the European side of the Atlantic fly around western Europe towards West Africa, mostly over the sea. Most continue towards South Africa, then onwards towards their frozen goal, catching a ride on a westerly wind to ease their passage. Others cross the Atlantic from West Africa and follow the South American coast, and some take a more easterly route from South Africa over the Indian Ocean towards the Antipodes. Arctic Terns breeding from Alaska to eastern Siberia track the Pacific coast southwards on their journey to their winter quarters.

The seas around the pack-ice are good feeding areas and wintering birds spend 3–4 months there before their northbound journey in the first days of March, with most European birds more or less reversing their southbound route. Some do things differently though, heading north over the Indian Ocean, passing Somalia and then flying high overland, perhaps thousands of meters above the surface.

Birds reach their breeding grounds between the beginning of May and late June. Arctic Terns breed with the same partner year after year. Pairs spend the winter apart, however, so must re-find each other every spring. Most don't breed until they are at least three years old, while a few pairs benefit when unpaired three-year-olds assist with incubation and sometimes with feeding the chicks.

Small fish account for most of this bird's diet. They will take fish offal, too, as well as molluscs, crustaceans (including krill) and insects. They eat midges in Finland, and are known to take berries, earthworms, caterpillars and bread. Piracy may be employed on occasion, with Atlantic Puffins (*Fratercula arctica*), Black Guillemots (*Cepphus grylle*) and Horned Grebes (*Podiceps auritus*) among their victims. More often though, they are a piracy victim, and Common Terns (*S. hirundo*) and skuas (*Stercorarius* spp.) are the pirates.

Time on the breeding ground is kept short, the Antarctic-bound voyage starting between July and September. So fond are Parasitic Jaegers (*Stercorarius parasiticus*) of harassing Arctic Terns for food though, that the terns may have unwelcome travelling companions for a substantial part of the journey.

99. Western Grebe *Aechmophorus occidentalis*

The striking star of the "rushing ceremony"

Size: 51–74 cm (20–29 inches).
Distribution: Parts of United States, Canada and Mexico.
Habitat: Breeds mostly on large freshwater lakes and marshes with plenty of marginal vegetation; winters mainly at sea, and in coastal bays and estuaries.
Classification: One of 21 species in the family Podicipedidae, and one of two in the genus *Aechmophorus*.
Population and conservation status: Estimated at 130,000 birds. Least Concern.
Breeding system: Monogamous.
Nest and eggs: Pile of vegetation, which floats, secured to nearby plants, or sits on lake floor or sunken branch. 3–4 eggs, one brood.
Incubation and fledging: 21–28 days. About 70 days.

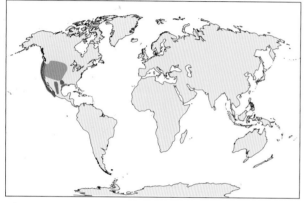

The Western Grebe is one of the world's larger grebes. It is strikingly marked (though not colorful), with a long, daggerlike bill. Unlike some grebes, it is often seen in large flocks, specifically with other Western and Clark's Grebes (*A. clarkii*), the only other grebe in its genus. Western is a colonial breeder, the bigger colonies containing thousands of nests, though some birds nest in smaller colonies or even as lone pairs. It is a gregarious species in the winter, too, and flocks may be seen around the American Pacific coast from Canada to Mexico.

This bird is famed for its performance of the "rushing ceremony", one of the world's most elaborate examples of avian courtship behavior, making this a species well worth seeking out. It takes two (or more) to "rush", and the performers could be a female with one or a few males, or two males. A typical ceremony begins with two-note advertising calls. Western Grebe colonies often include Clark's Grebes (from 1886 to 1985 the two were regarded as conspecific), and the rushing ceremony is sometimes performed by a mixed-species pair. Visually the two species are similar, but their advertising calls are different—two notes for Western, one for Clark's. Step two is "ratchet pointing". With much

of the body submerged and the head held low, the crest comes into action, the tail is raised and the bill points towards the co-performer, to the accompaniment of a rough, clicking, ratchet call. There could be some "dip-shaking" too, in which a bird immerses its bill and the front of its head in the water before lifting it out and shaking it from side to side. The climax is the rush itself. The two stars of the show rise up and practically walk on water, almost vertically, side by side, as far as 20 meters (72 feet). They don't call, but their pattering feet provide plenty of sound to go with the visual spectacle. Finally, they give in to gravity and dive.

The Western Grebe is mainly a piscivore that feeds by diving. While fish make up over 80 percent of its diet, there are records of invertebrates and even a salamander being taken. They eat feathers too, which are ingested during preening; the feathers clump together in the stomach, where they may protect the bird's innards from sharp fish bones. This species, with Clark's Grebe, has an unusual neck structure akin to that of herons (Ardeidae) and Anhingas (*Anhinga anhinga*) that enables the bill to be thrust forward, perhaps for spear fishing, but exactly how it is used is not understood.

The bill does appear to be a serious weapon, however. Westerns are thought to spear unwelcome visitors from underneath and have probably killed Mallard (*Anas platyrhynchos*) and Red-necked Grebe (*Podiceps grisegena*).

The breeding colony may well be a mixed species community. In addition to Clark's Grebe, a Western Grebe's neighbors may include Franklin's Gull (*Larus pipixcan*), Forster's Tern (*Sterna forsteri*) and Black-necked Grebe (*P. nigricollis*). Intriguingly, Western Grebes are flightless after returning to their breeding areas, their pectoral muscles becoming too weak for flight. The situation is remedied when new flight feathers are grown, but clearly you don't need to be able to fly to rush!

98. Common Nightingale *Luscinia megarhynchos*

A plain-clothed virtuoso of the avian world

Size: 16.5 cm (6.5 inches).
Distribution: Breeds from western Europe and northwest Africa eastwards into Asia; winters in Africa.
Habitat: Scrub, woodland, hedgerows, orchards and similar places; often near water; likes open areas as well as cover in habitat.
Classification: One of 294 species in the family Muscicapidae, and one of 11 in the genus *Luscinia*.
Population and conservation status: 8.5–23 million birds in Europe. Least Concern.
Breeding system: Monogamous.
Nest and eggs: Cup of grass and leaves with softer lining, on or near ground. 4–5 eggs; southerly breeders have second brood.
Incubation and fledging: 13 days. 11 days.

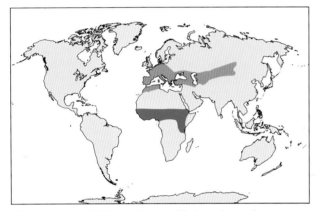

The Common Nightingale is unlikely to be at the top of anyone's "must see" bird list. Visually, there is nothing too remarkable about this species—a bird that can be hard to see, keeping itself hidden in thick cover. But the Nightingale experience is not about seeing—it is about hearing, and this bird qualifies for inclusion by dint of its voice alone. Its song has a quality that few other species can match, a voice that takes control of the airspace, full, rich, loud, explosive, sometimes piercing and highly varied. It is a voice that has inspired poets and musicians, including Beatrice Harrison, a cellist, whose performance with the Nightingale singing in her garden was broadcast live on BBC radio in 1924, to the delight of a huge listening audience.

The song is made up of short phrases and pauses, with one studied bird blasting out 400 phrases in an hour, from a soundbank of 250 or more different phrases—that is one phrase and a pause every nine seconds. Each phrase consisted of 5–20 sound-units from 600 in this bird's auditory armory.

Despite its name, the Common Nightingale doesn't just sing at night, but it does seem to sing with different intent during daylight hours. Its nocturnal performances tend to be delivered from a single perch: this is the male doing his utmost to impress females. In contrast, the male moves around during his briefer, less impressive daytime performances—typically, this is the male doing his best to keep other males at bay. Singing is not restricted to breeding territories. Birds on migration have been known to sing and Nightingale song can be heard in their African wintering areas too, where territories are held, though the song does seem to be gentler and quieter than the full-blown version and is sung mainly during daylight hours.

Males return to their breeding areas a little ahead of the females, the oldest birds arriving first and probably reclaiming their previous year's territory. Song is used to defend the territory, though conflicts may escalate to chasing and fighting. This is a monogamous species that normally changes partners from one year to the next, though last year's partner may be breeding nearby. In southern areas, where two clutches are laid, the female may take sole charge of the second clutch, or may mate with a second male, her former partner having left with the first batch of young.

When breeding is done, the Africa-bound migration begins, European birds leaving from late July to September. Hefty fat deposits are required to fuel the journey—a weight increase in excess of 50 percent over a 15-day period has been documented. Birds from the west of the range winter in a belt stretching right across Africa, while birds from the east head mostly for East Africa.

The Common Nightingale is primarily a ground-feeder, with ants and beetles as favorite food items. Other invertebrates are also taken, as well as berries.

The photos on these pages won't sell this species to you. A good quality sound recording is needed to really do justice to this brilliant bird.

97. Bar-headed Goose *Anser indicus*

A sky-high migrant and "spiritual pilgrim"

Size: 71–76 cm (28–30 inches).
Distribution: Breeds in China, Central Asia and Mongolia; most winter in India.
Habitat: High altitude (4,000–5,000 meters/13,000–16,500 feet) wetlands for breeding;
low altitude wetlands in winter.
Classification: One of 161 species in the family Anatidae, and one of seven in the genus *Anser*.
Population and conservation status: Estimated at 52,000–60,000 birds in 2002. Least Concern.
Breeding system: Monogamous, colonial.
Nest and eggs: Shallow, made from plant material; ground-nesting, or in marshland or tree. 4–6 eggs.
Incubation and fledging: 27–30 days. Around 53 days.

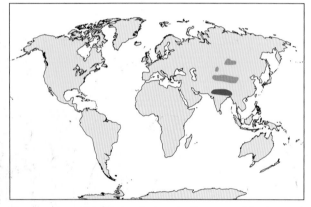

You won't see this bird at its best in Europe or North America, where it is common in wildfowl collections, and may escape to a feral existence. To fully appreciate the wonder of this species you need to see it where it is meant to be: on its mountain plateau breeding grounds perhaps or, even better, migrating high over the Himalayas.

Bar-headed Geese are colonial breeders. Some are ground-nesters, others nest in marshland and some, unusually for geese, build their nest in trees. At the end of the breeding season most head south to the north of India or to neighboring countries. Their route takes them right through the Himalayas, and sometimes over Mount Everest. A flying height of over 10,000 meters (33,000 feet) has been claimed. There are alternative, lower altitude routes and no one knows why the Bar-headed Goose opts for such a tough migration, though it has been suggested that this may be an ancient route, one that has been used since before the mountains were that high, and that as the world's highest mountains were formed, the geese gradually adapted to the increasing physiological demands of their journey.

Being in the 6-mile-high migration club is challenging. At this altitude there's two-thirds less oxygen than at sea level, the wind can exceed 320 kilometers (200 miles) per hour and it can be very, very cold. Despite all this, or perhaps because of it, the Bar-headed Goose can complete its migration of over 1,600 kilometers (1,000 miles) in just one day. Its wings are large and under its own steam these birds can hit 80 kilometers per hour (50 mph)—with a good tail wind, much higher speeds are possible. The strong winds are a mixed blessing. The birds can navigate through crosswinds, but if the wind is too strong and in the wrong direction, departure is delayed, and if the ride is too bumpy, smoother air must be sought or the flight abandoned until conditions improve.

Getting oxygen out of "thin air" and into the muscles where it is needed requires special equipment, especially to sustain flapping flight. Bird lungs are a lot more efficient than those of mammals and the hemoglobin of a Bar-headed Goose enables it to get more oxygen from "thin air" than a typical bird could. The oxygen-loaded blood is then moved quickly along capillaries, well into the muscles where the oxygen is put to work. Flapping produces heat and down feathers provide insulation to make the most of it—it is vital that the wings should not become too ice-laden. Given the nature of their migration, it is perhaps not surprising that in India their epic journey has been compared to a spiritual pilgrimage.

After spending the winter in a more hospitable southern landscape, the geese head north again, braving the elements like few other birds. Life on the northern breeding grounds is not without hazard. There are bird and mammalian predators to contend with, and in May 2005 some fell victim to avian influenza—178 were found dead at Qinghai Lake Nature Reserve in China. Hopefully, this will be no more than a blip for this remarkable pilgrim that appears out of thin air!

96. Vermilion Flycatcher   *Pyrocephalus rubinus*
A vermilion eye-catcher

Size: 13–14 cm (5–5.5 inches).

Distribution: Southern United States, Central America and much of South America.

Habitat: Open areas including cultivated land, grassland, scrub, savanna, desert, clearings and wooded areas, frequently near water.

Classification: One of 432 species in the family Tyrannidae, and one of two in the genus *Pyrocephalus*.

Population and conservation status: Estimated at around 2 million birds. Least Concern.

Breeding system: Probably monogamous.

Nest and eggs: Loose cup in a horizontal tree or bush fork; building materials include twigs, grass, lichens and other plant material, kept together by spider's silk, with a softer hair and feather lining. 2–3 eggs, 1–2 broods.

Incubation and fledging: 13–15 days. 13–15 days (longer in Argentina).

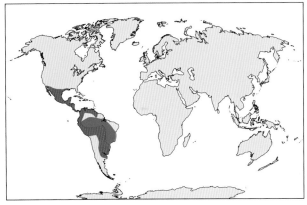

Tyrant flycatchers are not, on the whole, the most eye-catching of birds and pose a good few identification challenges. South America's Many-colored Rush Tyrant (*Tachuris rubrigastra*) may be more colorful, but for sheer color audacity the bright plumage of a male Vermilion Flycatcher is hard to beat. For the most part, when you see one, you know what it is. This is a bird that can provide a quick and sure identification, an eye-catching species to encourage the novice Neotropical birder.

This is not currently a species of any global conservation concern. It has a reasonably large range and can be almost impossible to miss but, surprisingly, its biology is not that well understood.

Vermilion flycatchers appear to be monogamous. The male's plumage is striking enough, but he doesn't rely solely on pigments when there is a female to woo; being red is not enough. He puffs up his breast feathers, lifts his crest and ascends with fluttering flight up to 20 meters (65 feet) or more, singing as he rises. His song flight rises and falls through the airspace, wings quivering as he traces out a more or less circular route, and tells all who can hear of his presence and intentions. It is a performance that impresses birders, and

presumably other Vermilion Flycatchers too. These birds will also sing from trees and bushes, especially in the morning, though they will sing at any time, and have even been heard serenading during the hours of darkness.

The male seems to play a major role in choosing a nest site. His "nest-site-showing" is simple enough—when he has found a would-be nest site he quivers his wings over his back, makes the "chatter call" and acts out some gentle nest-building moves. When the decision is made, the female probably builds the nest, and mating may take place during the building phase. The male may arrive with an impressive insect in his bill and mating will occur with the insect either still in his bill, or passed to his partner. The female incubates the eggs, and may find herself incubating an Icterid too—both Shiny and Brown-headed Cowbirds (*Molothrus bonariensis* and *M. ater*) have parasitized this species.

Feeding is simple enough. A suitable perch is found, perhaps on a fence line or fence post, and prey is either dropped onto on the ground or chased and caught in midair. It seems that Vermilion Flycatchers eat nothing but arthropods, including spiders and insects. When there is a beehive nearby, a Vermilion Flycatcher may take more than its fair share. Not everything that it swallows is put to use, though—the unpalatable parts are regurgitated in pellet form.

While most populations are not migratory, many from the north of the range head south for the winter, and those at the southern end move north.

Much has been made of the vibrancy of the male's plumage. This is, in fact, a species with a number of sub-species. In the male, the differences are primarily in the intensity of their color, although *obscurus*, a Peruvian race, has a high proportion of melanistic birds (*cocachacrae* also has some). For some, this is a sought-after race, but for most, surely it is the classic male that sets the pulse racing.

95. Siberian Rubythroat *Luscinia calliope*

A popular but wayward migratory stray with a superb song

Size: 14–16 cm (5.5–6.3 inches).
Distribution: Breeds mainly in Siberian taiga; also Mongolia, Korea, Japan and China; migrant, wintering Southeast Asia, Taiwan and Philippines.
Habitat: Breeds in dense vegetation in taiga zone.
Classification: One of 294 species in the family Muscicapidae, and one of 11 in the genus *Luscinia*.
Population and conservation status: Not recorded. Least Concern.
Breeding System: Monogamous.
Nest and eggs: Loosely constructed cup or domed nest on the ground. 4–5 eggs.
Incubation and fledging: Unknown, probably 13–14 days. Unknown.

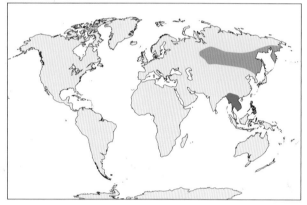

Never write off small brown birds: a little modesty of plumage can hide bundles of charisma, and this is certainly true for one of the jewels of the Eurasian taiga, the Siberian Rubythroat. With the male's startling appearance, a fine song, and an intriguing tendency to wander off its normal migratory route, the Rubythroat is the sort of bird to thrill any birder with a soft spot for travelling waifs.

It also frustrates them. The brown plumage fits well with the bird's infamous retiring, skulking habits. The Siberian Rubythroat feeds mainly on the ground, on flies and beetles, and it so happens that the very midst of a bush will often suit its foraging needs, keeping the bird out of sight in the shade. When breeding and, especially in the winter when it can disappear for hours into bamboo thickets, it can be hard to coax into view, driving birdwatchers to distraction. When it does move it will either flit low to the ground, or make a few Robinlike hops to the next thicket.

But of course that glittering red throat, together with the bold white stripes on the head, mean that the merest glimpse will suffice to identify the male. And unsurprisingly, this is as true for the birds themselves as it is for birdwatchers.

Rubythroats are highly territorial, and display their red throats to best effect when singing, often from the treetops, the colorful "badge" acting as an accompaniment to the vocal signal. And what a song it is, full of rich, fluty phrases, odd scratchy sounds and imitations of other local birds. It has been admiringly compared to the famed Common Nightingale (*Luscinia megarhynchos*) (see page 15), although this is an exaggeration—it is a much more fitful and less confident effort. There is one similarity, however: in common with Nightingales, Siberian Rubythroats often perform all through the night.

The season is short in the taiga zone, many Rubythroats arriving in May, or even June, and departing at the end of August. For breeding they select territories away from deep forest, preferring more open areas, including birch/willow scrub and boggy patches. The nest is made on the ground, out of the very softest materials available, and the more elaborate constructions actually have a roof and a side-entrance. Young Rubythroats hatch into comparative luxury.

Owing to their demanding schedule, almost as soon as they fledge the youngsters must begin their journey down to the wintering grounds that cover a broad swathe of Southeast Asia. As they set off you might expect them to take a bearing south, but normally they travel east first, often for many hundreds of kilometers, to avoid crossing the highest Himalayas and adjacent ranges below the taiga. Even so, they have still been seen at 4,000 meters (13,000 feet) on migration, so this strategy doesn't always work.

Indeed, part of the Rubythroats' charm is their propensity for going off course. Sometimes they overshoot south to Peninsular Malaysia, but more often they go too far east or west, turning up as great rarities both in western Europe and in Alaska. Here these sprites transform birding days and delight birders—if they can catch sight of them, that is.

94. Magnificent Frigatebird *Fregata magnificens*

A pirate of the Caribbean . . . and elsewhere, too

Size: 89–114 cm (2.9–3.7 feet); wingspan: 217–244 cm (7.1–8 feet).

Distribution: Mostly around tropical seas of American Pacific and Atlantic coasts; some off West Africa.

Habitat: Feeds mostly at sea; builds nest in mangroves or shrubs on islands or adjacent coast.

Classification: One of five species in the family Fregatidae and the genus *Fregata*.

Population and conservation status: Estimated at 200,000 birds. Least Concern.

Breeding system: Monogamous, colonial.

Nest and eggs: Platform of sticks in tree or bush. One egg.

Incubation and fledging: 40–50 days. 20–24 weeks.

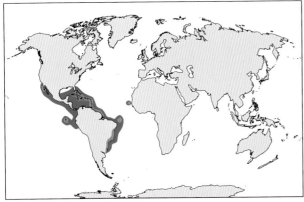

The Magnificent Frigatebird is the biggest of the frigatebirds, with very long wings and a long scissor-like tail. Frigatebirds, or Men-of-war, are infamous for their acts of piracy, but the reality is that most of their food is acquired much more legitimately.

Fish are the main food of the Magnificent Frigatebird, especially flying fish. Squid are also taken, as are young turtles, the eggs and chicks of seabirds, jellyfish and offal. Once prey is spotted, an airborne frigatebird gently reduces its altitude, perhaps circling on the way and hovering, then grabs its prey with a downward and backward movement of its head and long, hook-tipped bill. Its speed and agility is such that it can take flying fish from midair, as the fish leap to avoid capture by hunting tuna or dolphins. It will pick small turtles off beaches, and plunder eggs and chicks from nests—even the nests of other frigatebirds.

Female Magnificent Frigatebirds seem more piratical than the males, who probably focus their piracy on taking nest-building materials from other frigatebirds. The females, however, harass other seabirds for food, forcing them to give it up by "playing" with their victim's wings or tail and disturbing their in-flight equilibrium. Their pace and maneuverability are such that they can grab the ejected food before it reaches the sea. In some areas, this species harasses people too, taking fish from fishermen as they carry their catch up the beach.

A frigatebird's bones are proportionately lighter than those of any other bird, accounting for less than 5 per cent of its weight. For its size, this is a lightweight bird (about 1.1–1.6 kilograms (2.4–3.5 lb) with around 25 percent of its weight being flight muscle and another 25 percent its plumage). The huge wingspan gives it impressive flying skills; its small feet and legs make walking and swimming very difficult however, and its feathers have little waterproofing.

Male Magnificent Frigatebirds gather at the breeding grounds before the females arrive. The spectacle of the males displaying with wings open, inflated throat pouches and bills aimed towards heaven can be seen from quite a distance and lures in females. The sight of a female moves things onto head- and wing-trembling, with sound effects as the male shakes his bill on his drumlike throat pouch.

Just one egg is laid, typically in a nest of sticks, in a mixed seabird colony. Incubation can take around 6–7 weeks, followed by up to 5½ months before the young frigatebird has fledged. Care for the youngster continues for another 5–7 months, making for a breeding season that is so long that successful females can breed only every other year. But it doesn't stop the male—he abandons his mate and chick about 14 weeks after hatching and is thought to pair with another female before his first chick is fully independent, making it possible for the male to breed annually—no other species is known to have males that breed every year, while females do so every other year. Intriguingly, twice as many females are produced as males and the male death rate is higher, supporting this scenario.

93. Angel Tern *Gygis alba*

An ethereal beauty with one of the world's most incongruous nest sites

Size: 25–30 cm (10–12 inches).

Wingspan: 76–80 cm (30–31.5 inches).

Distribution: Pantropical, on islands.

Habitat: Well vegetated islands and islets in tropical seas.

Classification: One of 100 species in the family Laridae, and the sole member of the genus *Gygis*.

Population and conservation status: Over 100,000 pairs. Least Concern.

Breeding system: Monogamous; loosely colonial.

Nest and eggs: None. One egg.

Incubation and fledging: 28–32 days. 60–75 days.

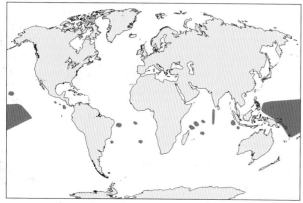

Where else could a bird like this exist but on a tropical island, a place of perfect sunshine, coral beaches, palm trees and travellers' tales? With its spotless white plumage and eponymous angelic expression, the Angel Tern could be made for its habitat, where its ethereal image happily fits the dreams of wide-eyed tourists. This is a bird straight out of a holiday brochure.

Dreamily gorgeous it might be, but the Angel Tern is very much flesh, blood and feathers. Found throughout tropical seas, it subsists on an unglamorous diet of fish and squid, which it catches by dipping down and snatching them from the water surface—not for an Angel the more routine, unsubtle style of plunge diving practiced by most terns. It will also deftly field fish that are in flight themselves, jumping out of the water to escape predators beneath the waves. Many of the items recorded in the diet of the Angel Tern are among those sea creatures that migrate to the surface at night and retreat deeper by day, suggesting that this predator's most productive fishing takes place at dawn and dusk. And although it is usually seen in inshore waters, it will commonly forage over the deep oceans far from land.

Apart from its photogenic looks, the Angel Tern's other eyebrow-raising feature is its quite extraordinary, highly precarious nest site. Rather than construct any kind of platform for breeding, the Angel Tern simply lays an egg onto the surface of a branch of a tree, often in the canopy at dizzying heights of 20 meters (65 feet) or more. The host limb, which is usually horizontal, can be as little as 8 centimeters (3 inches) wide, although 10–13 centimeters (4–5 inches) is more typical. And although the birds will choose a knot-hole or small depression for their precious egg, and will often do a bit of gardening before laying, such as scratching out loose bark with their feet, their strategy is invariably risky. Strong winds routinely blow eggs and young down; the young have strong claws to help them hold onto their natal branch, and occasionally attempt to clamber up again, but with limited success.

Nevertheless, such a site usually assures safety from predators, and Angel Terns are, as a result, confident sitters, often remaining on the nest even when people are a meter or two away. When coming and going, they maneuver themselves a good deal more carefully than most other birds, falling away backwards to leave, so that their genetic investment should not be dislodged.

If all goes well and the egg hatches, one of the adults is on duty to brood the youngster assiduously for the first 10 days of its life, and make sure it doesn't wander. Meanwhile, the foraging parent brings in fish, often 5–6 at once, carried crosswise in the bill; the youngster deftly takes them one at a time, like pieces of meat on a kebab. It takes some 60 days before the youngster can leave the nest, but once its dangerous early days are past it can enjoy a good life expectancy: Angel Terns have been known to live to the age of 17 years.

92. Rock Ptarmigan *Lagopus muta*

A triumph of avian design, and the world's most northerly wintering landbird

Size: 33–38 cm (13–15 inches).

Distribution: Northern hemisphere; circumpolar with some populations further south.

Habitat: Mountain tops and stony/rocky tundra, including areas at sea level in the far north, and over 1,700 m (5,600 feet) in the Alps.

Classification: One of 176 species in the family Phasianidae, and one of three in the genus *Lagopus*.

Population and conservation status: Not recorded, common in some areas. Least Concern.

Breeding system: Monogamous, sometimes polygynous.

Nest and eggs: Shallow, sparsely lined scrape near bush or rock. 5–8 eggs.

Incubation and fledging: 21–24 days. About 10 days.

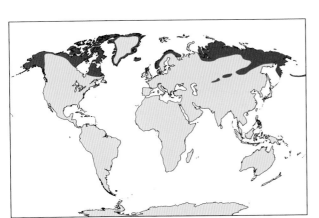

The Rock Ptarmigan is a brilliant feat of ornithological design. It is a bird of hostile environments, of cold, wild, windswept places. It is not exclusively a bird of high mountaintops—at high latitudes especially, it is found at low altitude, even at sea level, and is a bird of the cliffs around the Barents Sea.

This bird is well adapted to the cold. Surprisingly perhaps, it does not have large numbers of true down feathers, but the feathering is dense, and in the winter the contour feathers have an extensive aftershaft to provide essential extra insulation. In the summer, the aftershaft is much shorter. The duvetlike properties of the bird's winter plumage seem to be further enhanced by air chambers in the barbules, which may also serve to make the white plumage appear even more snowlike.

Walking on snow can be energy-sapping. To make the most of hard-won calories, the Ptarmigan's feet work like a pair of snowshoes. The legs and toes are feathered, more so in winter than in summer. The dense feathering, coupled with long toes, and claws that are much longer in winter, serves to spread the load, making snow-walking much easier.

The Rock Ptarmigan must be a contender for "best camouflaged bird". Its plumage changes through the year, mirroring its surroundings. This is made possible by "more molts than most"—the Rock Ptarmigan has three molts in its annual cycle, instead of the more usual two. Molt patterns vary across the species' range to maintain the habitat match of the cryptic plumage: in Scotland and on Amchitka Island in the Aleutians, where snow cover is briefer, the third molt starts later and doesn't replace all the browner summer feathers with white ones.

Across their range, Rock Ptarmigans eat a wide variety of plant material, the composition depending on what is available locally. Crowberry (*Empetrum* spp.) is the main food item on Amchitka, and heather (*Calluna* spp.) and bilberry (*Vaccinium* spp.) are important in Scotland. Twigs, buds and catkins are eaten, with Dwarf and Downy Birch (*Betula nana* and *B. pubescens*) and Dwarf Willow (*Salix herbacea*) being key winter food sources for Icelandic birds. Finding food is not always easy and may require digging through the snow. Spitzbergen Rock Ptarmigans are unique within the species and genus: to cope with frozen snow, when food is nearly impossible to come by, they rely on fat deposits which may be around one-third of their weight. Living off their fat they can survive for 10 or more days without eating.

Monogamy seems to be the norm for Rock Ptarmigans, although polygyny has been reported and may be more common in the high Arctic. The parental workload lies mainly with the female, the male leaving to molt before there are chicks to look after.

Despite its extreme survival skills, there is uncertainty about the future for this cold-niche species. The full effects of climate change on its habitat, and therefore on the bird itself, are yet to be seen. Time will tell whether it can adapt fast enough to survive, or sufficient suitable habitat still remains.

91. Roseate Spoonbill *Platalea ajaja*

The most colorful of all the spoonbills—a beauty from a distance

Size: 68.5–86.5 cm (27–34 inches).

Distribution: South and Central America, southern United States, Caribbean.

Habitat: Coastal, sometimes inland; ponds, marshy areas and mangrove swamps.

Classification: One of 33 species in the family Threskiornithidae, and one of six in the genus *Platalea*.

Population and conservation status: Estimated at 100,000–250,000 birds. Least Concern.

Breeding system: Monogamous, colonial.

Nest and eggs: Stick platform with lining of softer plants, in reeds, shrub or a short tree. 2–3 eggs, one brood.

Incubation and fledging: 22 days. About six weeks.

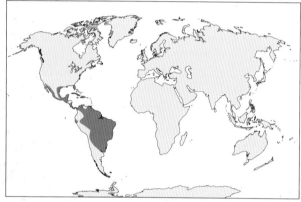

Most birdwatchers want to see a spoonbill, and this is certainly the most colorful (all of the other species are mostly white). The pink and red coloration of mature individuals, coupled with the long spoonlike bill, make for a good-looking bird that's easy to identify, although some people maintain that Roseate Spoonbills look at their best when viewed from afar. Viewed at close quarters, however, the baldness of the adult (like no other spoonbill) may well change your mind about that far-off impression of beauty.

The bird's bill is probably its most curious feature and the reason so many people want to see one. Its prime use, of course, is in feeding, though it has other functions too. A feeding bird plods through the water, normally in depths of no more than 12 centimeters (5 inches). In deeper water much of the body may be submerged and the head and neck may be completely underwater. Its spatulate bill is kept ajar and is moved from side to side, slicing through the water and closing whenever it touches a food item. In this feeding mode, touch is key to finding food, although prey may be located visually at other times. And when the food is found, be it a fish, prawn, shrimp or insect, it is the spoon that does

the grabbing, though the rest of the bill may well help the bird "feel" food. Food that is unwieldy, or packaged in a tough exoskeleton, may be given a thorough shake, or bashed on something hard to force an entry. Some vegetation is eaten, too. Roseate Spoonbills feed both diurnally and nocturnally, sometimes flying over 60 kilometers (37 miles) from the colony to find food.

Breeding colonies may be single species, or more diverse, with perhaps herons or egrets (Ardeidae), ibises (Threskiornithinae), Wood Storks (*Mycteria americana*) or cormorants (Phalacrocoracidae) nesting nearby. The bill is also important in courtship and breeding behavior. To win a partner, a male finds somewhere suitable to nest and proclaims "male seeks female" by shaking twigs with his bill and moving his head up and down. As things proceed, the male will present sticks to the female—heads dip up and down, bills are stroked and criss-crossed and sticks are shaken. If this goes well, the stick is passed to the female and built into the nest, which is not always sited where the courtship began. Mating is preceded by the male and female using their bills jointly to shake the same twig, and during the act itself he grips her bill in his, shaking both of them. The Roseate Spoonbill's display repertoire also includes a certain amount of bill clattering when one bird takes over incubation from the other.

Historically, this species has suffered at the hands of feather collectors, either directly, or because of disruption in mixed colonies when nearby egrets were targeted. Today, Roseate Spoonbills may have to contend with predation from Raccoons (*Procyon lotor*) or Turkey Vultures (*Cathartes aura*), and fire ants may take their toll on very young birds. Thankfully though, this pinkest of spoonbills is not of global conservation concern.

90. Sociable Weaver *Philetairus socius*

A neighborly species with an extraordinary communal nest

Size: 14 cm (5.5 inches).
Distribution: Southern Africa.
Habitat: Open, arid country with scattered trees.
Classification: One of 45 species in the family Passeridae, and the sole member of the genus *Philetairus*.
Population and conservation status: Not recorded. Least Concern.
Breeding system: Monogamous, but changes partners between broods.
Nest and eggs: Enormous communal grass structure, resting on branch. 2–6 eggs, laid in chamber.
Incubation and fledging: 13–14 days. 21–24 days.

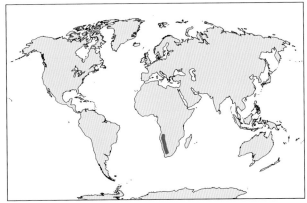

You don't have to be a large bird to build a large nest. It so happens that the world's largest avian breeding structure is not built by a bird of prey, or a stork or some other giant, but by the relatively tiny, sparrow-sized Sociable Weaver. It is a collective effort, for sure—more like a block of apartments than a single exclusive residence—but the very scale of the construction is quite extraordinary: the nest may be as much as 4 meters (13 feet) tall, 7.2 meters (23 feet) across, weigh a ton and provide homes for more than 500 birds at a time. Some nesting blocks may survive multiple generations of weavers, and remain active for over 100 years, as long as the bough on which they are built does not break under the weight, which it sometimes does. It is truly workmanship on a grand scale.

Sociable Weaver colonies are very much part of the landscape in which they are found, the arid, barren hinterland of the western half of southern Africa. From a distance they make an extraordinary, conspicuous sight, giving the trees in which they are built a swollen and bizarre look. In recent years the birds have found telegraph poles an ideal substitute (see above), and as a result have managed to increase their range.

Although many members of the weaver family are renowned for their skill and subtlety in knotting and threading, Sociable Weavers are not in the same class as some, using the principle of stuffing material, rather than coaxing art out of it. The roof of the block is constructed first and the birds then simply push some stems inward from the bottom and create a space for the bell-shaped nesting chamber, which is then lined with feathers and other soft material. It is not especially complicated but, as far as the nest itself is concerned, it works perfectly. Owing to its great size, the nest remains cool during the fearsome heat of summer and is a warm refuge when it is cold outside, insulating the birds from extremes of weather. The birds inhabit the nest all year round and roost within it. The buildings, indeed, are a great draw for other birds besides the builders themselves; African Pygmy Falcons (*Polihierax semitorquatus*) rely on them completely in this part of their range, "renting" blocks of up to four chambers for their breeding quarters, and other tenants include Rosy-faced Lovebirds (*Agapornis roseicollis*) and Familiar Chats (*Cercomela familiaris*). Some of these hangers-on use the nest simply as a roost site.

The Sociable Weaver certainly lives up to its name. Not only do birds pack together for breeding, but absolutely everybody contributes to the maintenance of the nest. Material may be added by any bird at any time, and rains often trigger a frenzy of building work. Furthermore, this collective attitude also stretches to feeding the young, because many pairs are aided in their provision of insects to the nestlings by a small team of helpers, often youngsters that have not yet begun to breed. With so many birds crowded together, it seems churlish to waste the opportunity of a helping hand.

89. Indian Vulture *Gyps indicus*

One of three Asian vultures that have suffered a massive and rapid population decline

Size: 92 cm (3 feet).

Distribution: India and Southeast Pakistan; sedentary.

Habitat: Open places around people, from villages to cities, and woods; uses cliffs and ruins for nest sites.

Classification: One of 242 species in the family Accipitridae, and one of eight in the genus *Gyps*.

Population and conservation status: Estimated at fewer than 10,000 birds. Critically Endangered.

Breeding system: Monogamous, colonial.

Nest and eggs: Stick and straw platform on ledge. One egg.

Incubation and fledging: 45+ days. About 90 days.

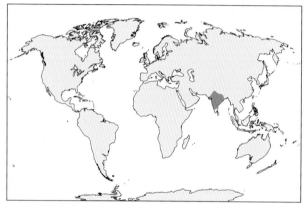

Vultures are well known as nature's binmen, and play a vital role in clearing up carrion. Clearly, a reduction in vulture numbers could lead to an increase in uncleared carrion and, therefore, in India, in the number of stray dogs, which could be rabid. Where vultures are part of the system, removing them can have serious public health consequences. The Indian Vulture was a common species, but something went wrong, and numbers dropped by over 95 percent in just three years in the late 1990s.

This was not the only vulture species in trouble. Two other Asian vultures were also in rapid decline: the White-rumped Vulture (*Gyps bengalensis*) and the Slender-billed Vulture (*G. tenuirostris*), which until relatively recently was considered a subspecies of Indian Vulture. Millions of vultures died and all three species are now classified as Critically Endangered. When the crisis first emerged, a viral infection was thought to be the culprit, but we now know that this was not the problem.

Indian Vultures are carrion eaters, feeding mainly on dead cows. Their eyes are sharp and when a soaring vulture sees its next meal, a crowd of willing diners soon gathers. An airborne vulture is not just looking for carrion—it will have its eyes on other vultures too, and when one descends to eat, others follow to join a mealtime that can be both noisy and messy. But it was the carrion that was the problem: cattle were being given diclofenac as a painkiller. This may well ease pain in cattle, but when vultures ate meat from an animal that had been given the drug the meal was lethal, killing the birds by dehydration and kidney failure, and it was estimated that 10 percent of the carcasses contained the lethal medication. Other factors may also have played a part in the decline, but diclofenac has been identified as the big killer.

Much conservation effort has been directed at the Asian vulture crisis. A vulture-friendly alternative to the drug has been promoted to the veterinary world and in 2006 the Indian government outlawed veterinary diclofenac.

Ordinarily, Indian Vultures build a stick and straw nest on a cliff, or perhaps on a ruined building, often nesting in colonies. They don't breed until they are five years old, and when they do they lay just one egg. Clearly, now that diclofenac has been banned, things look brighter for this species, but with their slow breeding rate it will take some time for the population to recover. A helping hand is being provided by BirdLife International (through the Royal Society for the Protection of Birds and the Bombay Natural History Society) an organization that has been instrumental in establishing captive-breeding programmes to aid the recovery of Asian Vulture stocks. By 2007, the first captive-bred vulture chick had hatched (a White-rumped Vulture).

For a time, it looked as though the Indian Vulture and two of its congeners could have been going the way of the Dodo (*Raphus cucullatus*) and the Passenger Pigeon (*Ectopistes migratorius*). There is hope now, but it will be a long time before this most utilitarian of species is as common as once it was.

88. Red-billed Scythebill *Campylorhamphus trochilirostris*

A small brown bird with an amazing body design

Size: 22–28 cm (8.7–11 inches).

Distribution: Northern half of South America.

Habitat: Mainly open forest and woodland.

Classification: One of 51 species in the family Dendrocolaptidae (recently subsumed into the family Furnariidae), and one of five in the genus *Campylorhamphus*.

Population and conservation status: Not recorded. Least Concern.

Breeding system: Monogamous.

Nest and eggs: Shallow cup placed inside a cavity. Two eggs.

Incubation and fledging: Both unknown.

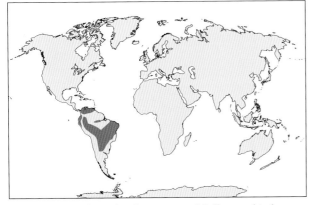

What do you do with a long, curved bill two-thirds the length of your body—except pose for photographs like this? The answer, as far as the splendid Red-billed Scythebill is concerned, is to use it to probe deep into holes and crevices among the limbs of trees and bamboo in tropical South American forests. There lurks a rich fauna of soft-bodied invertebrates, especially spiders and beetle larvae, which are harder to reach for short-billed competitors. The length of the bill enables the owner to probe further than the rest, and its curvature enables the bird to poke around through holes more efficiently and comfortably than it could with a straight bill. All in all, the rewards are plentiful for a bird with so daring a body-plan.

The Red-billed Scythebill is very much a specialist, and not just as a hunter that probes. It is also a highly adapted tree-climber, a member of the woodcreeper family, roughly ecologically equivalent to the tree-creepers of Eurasia and North America. It forages by climbing up vertical stems and branches in a series of upward hops, and for this purpose has extremely strong thigh muscles to power its climb and long, curved claws

for gripping. The woodcreeper tail is also unusual, specially stiffened to hold the bird's weight when it rests, the denuded tips of the tail feathers curved inwards to add to the grip. It is thus a bird that lives in the vertical, a bird for which normal crosswise perching would be strange.

Red-billed Scythebills are found in a variety of forest habitats, where they are normally encountered among flocks of small insectivores travelling through the trees. Their niche is quite distinct; they eschew the high canopy in favor of the understorey, and they spend most of their time among clumps of epiphytic plants (especially bromeliads), moss and tangles of vines— just the sorts of places where a long bill would be useful. On the whole they tend to be found singly.

Members of the woodcreeper family are famed among South American birds for their loud songs, which are frequently uttered only at dawn, and may be the very first voices of all to respond to the lightening sky at daybreak. The Red-billed Scythebill is no exception, and its spirited trills are typical. Some males are known to have at least two songs, one fast and one slow, and there is a great deal of variation among birds from different parts of the bird's wide range.

Apart from this, not much is known about the Red-billed Scythebill. Males and females appear to form stable pairs, and only a few nests have been found so far—these have been made inside a hollow trunk, or in broken-off stumps. The nest itself is a cup of leaves and other vegetation, but one would imagine that the process of actually constructing the nest must be something of a challenge. A long bill can be a competitive advantage, but it does have its disadvantages, too.

87. Common Cuckoo *Cuculus canorus*

A dastardly character

Size: 32–34 cm (12.6–13.4 inches).

Distribution: Europe and Asia; North Africa and the Middle East; winters in Africa and Southeast Asia.

Habitat: Farmland, woods, uplands, scrub, heathland and reed beds; not found in major conurbations; African wintering habitats include savanna and woods.

Classification: One of 144 species in the family Cuculidae, and one of nine in the genus *Cuculus*.

Population and conservation status: Estimated at 8.4–17 million birds in Europe. Least Concern.

Breeding system: Probably promiscuous; brood parasite.

Nest and eggs: Lays in nest of host species. Averages 9 but up to 25, each one normally laid in a different nest.

Incubation and fledging: About 12 days. 17–21 days.

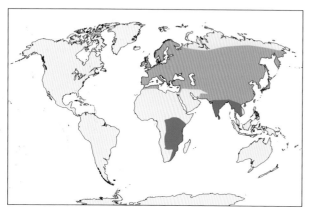

Many people welcome the Common Cuckoo's distinctive call as a sure sign of spring. Freshly arrived birds will have just completed a long migration after spending the northern winter way down in Africa. That this bird is a brood parasite is well known, though some of the details of its brutal breeding strategy are not common knowledge. Typically, Common Cuckoos put little effort into defending a territory and there may be a number of males and females operating on the same patch. All the males are interested in all the females and a single female will mate with more than one male, and lay her eggs in different nests, so both sexes spread their genetic investment throughout the area—they certainly don't put all their eggs in one basket.

Common Cuckoos parasitize many more species than they are normally given credit for—over 100 throughout Europe. In the UK, their main victims are Meadow Pipit (*Anthus pratensis*), Dunnock (*Prunella modularis*) and Reed Warbler (*Acrocephalus scirpaceus*) but in other parts of Europe Garden Warbler (*Sylvia borin*), Brambling (*Fringilla montifringilla*), Redstart (*Phoenicurus phoenicurus*) and Pied Wagtail (*Motacilla alba*) are targetted, among many other species.

Female Common Cuckoos (which can be rufous, as above) are species-specific parasites; a Common Cuckoo could be a Reed Warbler specialist for example, placing every one of her eggs (or the majority of them) in Reed Warbler nests. The eggs, generally marked to mimic those of the host, are reinforced to protect them during "elevated deposits", and just one egg is left in each nest. Finding a nest is not easy, but by careful observation, normally from a perch or sometimes in flight, nesting areas are located. To pinpoint the nest, Common Cuckoos move into the general area and watch the potential host's behavior—the closer the cuckoo is to the nest, the stronger the response from the host.

Typically, a Cuckoo lays her egg into an incomplete clutch. She holds onto the edge of the nest with her strong legs, removes an egg with her bill, and replaces it with one of her own. It is all over very quickly—she can be away in under 10 seconds, taking the host's egg with her and then eating it, if she hasn't already done so. When her egg hatches, the alien nestling completes the massacre, pushing out eggs or young. Any young that somehow manage to survive are likely to be smothered by the young Cuckoo, leaving the invader as the sole nestling.

Common Cuckoos feed primarily on caterpillars, even those of hairy species or those whose coloration suggests that they are best left alone. Harmful caterpillar hairs may subsequently be coughed up in pellets and from time to time the gizzard lining is disposed of in the same way. Where there is a rich food source Common Cuckoos may gather, especially during migration, when tens may forage in a relatively small area. They also seem to use their wings as beaters, to knock caterpillars out of trees before eating them.

This is not a rare species, but it is more often heard than seen. Despite its cruel breeding behavior, this is a bird that most birdwatchers like to see.

86. Paradise Tanager *Tangara chilensis*

A tropical beauty, amidst tropical beauty

Size: 12–14 cm (4.7–5.5 inches).
Distribution: Amazonia.
Habitat: Lowland tropical forest and second-growth forest.
Classification: One of 395 species in the family Thraupidae, and one of 50 in the genus *Tangara*.
Population and conservation status: Not recorded. Least Concern.
Breeding system: Monogamous.
Nest and eggs: Cup made up of moss placed high in the canopy. 2–4 eggs.
Incubation and fledging: 13–17 days. Unknown.

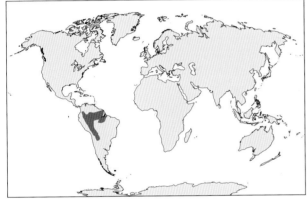

The Paradise Tanager epitomizes the extravagant luxuriance of its habitat, the lowland tropical rainforest of the Amazon basin. It embodies, perhaps, our collective idea of what every jungle bird ought to look like, with its outrageous scheme of bold colors, lavished with iridescence. It is the sort of bird a child might dream up in a flight of fancy.

Yet the Paradise Tanager is actually a reasonably common bird of the Amazonian canopy and edge. Indeed, when you come across one, you are likely to come across several, since this bird likes to move through the forest canopy with others of its kind, sometimes 10 or more. Its general sociability extends further than this; groups of Paradise Tanagers often act as part of the nucleus for the mixed species flocks of the upper storey, that are so much a part of the neotropical rainforest scene. These flocks often contain a hundred or more birds of diverse species, many of them stunningly colorful, and the birds spend much of the day moving rapidly from one tree to another, feeding in somewhat slapdash fashion before moving on. Every flock is a bonanza for a visiting birder, providing a giddy and glorious exercise in identification skills. Another

related species, the Green-and-gold Tanager (*Tangara schrankii*), is almost always seen in these flocks in company with the Paradise Tanager.

Despite its comparative abundance, the Paradise Tanager's lifestyle is not particularly well known. It takes fruit, berries and invertebrates on its wanderings through the canopy, but there are few specific details to separate it ecologically from some of its relations. Furthermore, only a few Paradise Tanager nests have ever been found, and such basic knowledge as the time the nestlings take to fledge has not yet been determined. Nests are notoriously difficult to find in mature rainforest, especially in the canopy, where most tanagers build. One Paradise Tanager nest described in 1989 was 31 meters (102 feet) above ground, hidden by leaves! It was a small cup of moss supported in a tree fork, and one of its somewhat unexpected components turned out to be a stringy fungus.

In common with most other tanagers, only the female Paradise Tanager builds the nest, although the male often stays nearby for moral support. Interestingly, however, when the pair visit the nest, either to build or to feed the young, they are sometimes accompanied by other species, including Green-and-gold Tanagers (*Tangara schrankii*) and Green Honeycreepers (*Chlorophanes spiza*). These birds are close associates, permanent co-members of their particular canopy flock, but this does seem to be taking sociability a bit too far!

Like many rainforest birds, the Paradise Tanager sings a special song at dawn that is not repeated for the rest of the day. Tanagers are not the world's greatest songsters, however, and the Paradise Tanager's effort has been rendered as a mere "chak-zeet". However, its usual high-pitched contact calls, chirpy "zee" notes, are a pleasant message that a flock of these gilded beauties is on the way.

85. Snowy Sheathbill *Chionis albus*

A true Antarctic oddity and hanger-on at seabird colonies

Size: 34–41 cm (13.4–16.1 inches).
Distribution: The Antarctic Peninsula and some outlying islands, plus southern South America in winter.
Habitat: Various coastal habitats.
Classification: One of three species in the family Chionidae, and one of two in the genus *Chionis*.
Population and conservation status: Estimated at 10,000 pairs. Least Concern.
Breeding system: Monogamous.
Nest and eggs: Simple cup in a natural crevice. 2–3 eggs.
Incubation and fledging: 22–28 days. 50–60 days.

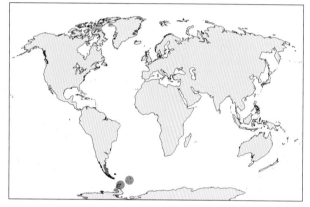

If you are fortunate enough to set eyes on a wild Snowy Sheathbill, you can be sure that you have reached the edge of the world. For this peculiar white character, ugly though it may be, is a member of the only bird family entirely confined to the Antarctic and sub-Antarctic region. Neighboring penguins (Spheniscidae) may be more famous for their allegiance to the ice, but these can also be found at the Equator; sheathbills are the real southern deal.

They might be totemic, but sheathbills are also the dustbin birds of their world. To say that their diet is varied would be the most delicate way to put it. Usually found hanging around colonies of seabirds or seals (Phocidae), they consume such insalubrious delights as placentas, nasal mucus straight from its source, feces, feathers, carrion, and blood from wounds and scabs. Revolting as this sounds, the sheathbills perform the important task of cleaning up after messy colonial animals. They are highly opportunistic and also somewhat nerveless. After all, when you have such a diet, manners hardly enter into it, and sheathbills can muster the temerity to steal milk from suckling seals, and to snatch regurgitated matter from the mouths of unsuspecting penguins, siphoning the mixture away from chicks, the intended recipients. They also steal unguarded eggs and predate small penguin chicks. In a place where the only alternative is to scoop algae off marine rocks on the shore, all types of rich food are a bonus.

Snowy Sheathbills, indeed, cannot breed without access to the appropriate active colonies of Adélie Penguins (*Pygoscelis adeliae*), Chinstrap Penguins (*P. antarcticus*), cormorants (Phalacrocoracidae), Weddell Seals (*Leptonychotes weddellii*) and Southern Elephant Seals (*Mirounga leonina*), and their reproductive schedule follows that of their hosts. In season, the sheathbills divide up each colony between pairs, each one patrolling, for example, 40–300 nests or birthing areas of their hosts. There is intense competition for these territories, and in any given year up to 40 percent of the population will be unable to settle down at all. Inevitably, the dominant birds win, and it has been shown that sheathbill status is correlated to the size of a given individual's bill.

Despite their striking dependence on colonies of marine animals, Snowy Sheathbills are not really seabirds at all. They don't have webbed feet, they don't swim and they are not exceptional fliers: they are, in every sense, hangers-on to the marine scene. However, their adaptation to their extreme climate is authentic enough. They have strong legs and feet, and their dense white outer plumage conceals a thick layer of down.

Even so, the chill of the Antarctic winter is just a little too intense for Snowy Sheathbills, so they migrate to the relative mildness of southern South America after breeding. Despite their rather short wings, they fly well and it is thought that they make the 800-kilometer (500-mile) flight across the Drake Passage in a single flight, unless, as sometimes happens, they hitch a lift on a floating iceberg for a short respite.

84. Greater Flamingo *Phoenicopterus roseus*

A shimmering pink spectacle

Size: 120–145 cm (3.9–4.75 feet).
Wingspan: 140–165 cm (4.6–5.4 feet).
Distribution: Discontinuous—Southern Europe, Africa, West Asia, Central Asia and the Middle East.
Habitat: Large lakes/lagoons with shallow, saline or very alkaline water; mudflats, salt pans and sandbanks.
Classification: One of six species in the family Phoenicopteridae, and one of three in the genus *Phoenicopterus*.
Population and conservation status: Estimated at 800,000 birds. Least Concern.
Breeding system: Monogamous, colonial.
Nest and eggs: Tapering mud pile capped with a shallow depression. One egg.
Incubation and fledging: 27–31 days. 65–90 days.

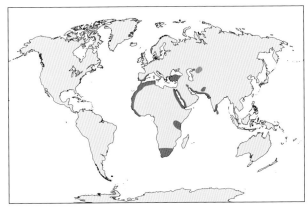

There was a time when Greater Flamingo included two sub-species: *ruber* in the New World, and *roseus* in the Old World. Here, these two taxa are treated as separate species, Greater Flamingo and American Flamingo (*P. ruber*), with the former occurring in the Old World.

Flamingos are remarkable birds. Their legs are very long with minimal feathering, making deep-water wading possible. The feet are webbed, so if the water is too deep for wading, swimming is an option. The webbed feet also spread the bird's load when it walks on soft mud. Their necks are long too, and as a group their legs and neck are proportionately the longest in the bird world.

Their famous coloring comes from the algae which are eaten by the flamingos, or by other animals that the flamingos subsequently feed on. The color is ingested as carotenoid pigments, which are transformed by enzymes into flamingo pink. The Greater Flamingo is one of the paler species, being more pinkish than pink, and may look quite pale. As well as plant material, Greater Flamingos eat a range of invertebrates including brine shrimps (*Artemia* spp.), copepods and chironomids. They feed by sweeping

their head through the water, or with head, and perhaps neck, submerged, sometimes using their feet to disturb the mud so that prey items are easier to find.

Flamingos are "baleen birds", having a bill that has been likened to the filtering equipment of baleen whales. The filter is a series of hair-covered lamellae with gaps of about 0.5 millimeters (0.02 inches) between them, which set the lower limit for food size. When the bill is closed there is a gap of 4–6 millimeters (0.16–0.24 inches) between the two mandibles and, because the bill is bent, this gap is roughly the same right to the tip. The tongue works in the gap, pumping water through the bill, and the gap sets the upper size limit for food entering the filter. Where Greater and Lesser Flamingos (*Phoeniconaias minor*) coexist, direct competition for food is avoided as Lessers have a finer filtering mechanism and take much smaller food items.

Water levels appear to play an important role in determining where and when Greater Flamingos breed. In East Africa there may be a pause of several years followed by a few years of breeding, averaging one attempt every other year. They are monogamous and nest colonially, with records of 200,000 pairs at a colony in India. Typically, the nest is a tapering mud structure capped with a shallow depression for a single egg. Both male and female play a part in incubation, though neither has a brood patch. There is much vocal communication between the emerging chick and the adults, which probably helps with mutual recognition in a busy colony. Both parents secrete a special milk for the chick, which is nutritionally similar to the milk produced by mammals, and which the chick obtains from its parent's mouth.

After 10 days or so, the young flamingo becomes part of a large crèche, where it remains for the next few months before gaining full independence.

83. Ruff *Philomachus pugnax*

A flamboyant dandy when dressed for display

Size: Male 26–32 cm (10.2–12.6 inches), female 20–25 cm (7.9–9.8 inches).
Distribution: Breeding range mostly in northern Europe and Asia; winters in Africa, southern Asia, Middle East and Europe.
Habitat: Breeding habitat includes damp or wet meadows, wetlands and tundra with small lakes and marshland; muddy edges of water bodies. Wintering areas include marshland, plains and rice or wheat fields.
Classification: One of 91 species in the family Scolopacidae, and the sole member of the genus *Philomachus*.
Population and conservation status: Estimated at 2 million individuals. Least Concern.
Breeding system: Polygynous.
Nest and eggs: Shallow depression with lining of leaves, grass and stems. 3–4 eggs.
Incubation and fledging: 20–23 days. 25–28 days.

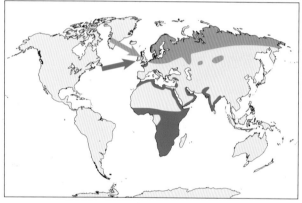

Ruffs are unusual waders. There is a big size difference between the genders, and a male in display plumage looks very different from the females that he is out to impress, and different also from most of the other displaying males. Ear-tufts and a ruff are *de rigueur* for a displaying male. These exotic adornments come in different colors and some birds wear them decorated, perhaps with spots, streaks, bars or vermiculations, while others wear them plain. There is a huge variety, but it seems that any one bird is quite likely to don the same display plumage year after year.

Ruffs are promiscuous, particularly the males, who assemble at leks to court and mate with visiting females. Here, 5–20 males, sometimes as many as 50, gather, each defending a small court within the arena. Lekking sites are traditional, and some have hosted this annual spectacle for decades, or even a century. Males at the lek may be "independent" or "satellite" males. Independent males are those that hold territories in the arena (independent "residents"), or those that might do so and perhaps have one somewhere else (independent "marginals"). Independents are feisty birds; satellites tend to be more peripheral and much less aggressive. Interestingly, in some regions at least, independent males wear predominantly dark display plumage and satellites wear white. If a bird has black ear-tufts, it is definitely an independent, and if all adornments are white and the ruff or ear-tufts are unpatterned, it is a satellite.

Before the sun rises there are independent males at the arena, the residents being the first in position. Fly-by females are welcomed with a wing-quivering greeting ceremony and at its most frenetic the performance includes birds jumping up into the air ("flutter jumps") and perhaps a hovering display. Males defending the most centrally located courts, and those that display most fervently, are frequently victorious with visiting females. A minority of the males do most of the mating, and over 50 percent of females raise a brood that more than one father has invested in.

Satellites may be tolerated because they help to lure in females. These non-territorial males do manage to mate, and can be as successful as independents, and certainly more so than marginals. Not surprisingly, males play no part in incubating or rearing the young.

The Ruff's high-energy breeding season is fuelled by an insect-based diet, flies and beetles being particularly important. Invertebrates are eaten at other times of the year, too, and sometimes amphibians, fish, rice, other seeds and other plant material.

It is not that difficult to see a Ruff, but most of the Ruffs that birdwatchers see don't look like the ones in the photo. Normally, it is the less dramatic plumages that are encountered—those that look like a different species. Seeing a male dressed for display can be much trickier, and is something that some birdwatchers never manage. That's the one to see before you die.

82. Tufted Puffin *Fratercula cirrhata*

The funkiest puffin in the world

Size: 36–41 cm (14.2–16.1 inches).
Distribution: Breeds around islands and coasts of northern Pacific and Bering Sea; winters at sea.
Habitat: Pelagic; nests mostly in burrows in turfed slopes and stack-tops.
Classification: One of 23 species in the family Alcidae, and one of three in the genus *Fratercula*.
Population and conservation status: Estimated at 2.4 million individuals. Least Concern.
Breeding system: Thought to be monogamous; colonial.
Nest and eggs: Chamber lined with vegetation and feathers, in burrow. One egg.
Incubation and fledging: 42–53 days. Average 49 days.

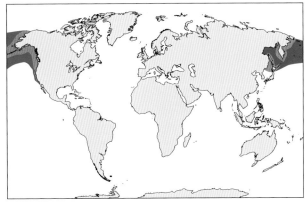

Puffins are the "clowns of the seas", and a Tufted Puffin in breeding plumage, with its long, down-curled tufts, is perhaps the most clownlike of any of them. This is an easy bird to identify—it is big, has a massive bill and lacks the white underparts of both of its congeners, the Atlantic Puffin (*F. arctica*) and the Horned Puffin (*F. corniculata*). In breeding plumage its white face, remarkable bill and yellowish tufts make this a very distinctive species.

A Tufted Puffin may not breed until it is at least five years old. The bill can give some idea of the age of a bird: juveniles have noticeably smaller bills than adults, with no cere at the base of the upper mandible. As the bird matures, the shape of its bill is gradually modified and its size increases. The bill is grooved, and the grooves provide clues to the owner's age. After a year, there is just a suggestion of a groove. Within another year, the groove is clearly there, and becomes more pronounced over the following 12 months. Birds with two pronounced grooves are between three and four years old, and three or more grooves indicate a bird that is at least five years old. In breeding plumage the bill is orange, with a yellowy-green cere at the head end of the

upper mandible. There is no cere in the winter plumage and the bill is less brightly colored.

The feet and bill are used to excavate a nest burrow, which can be over 2 meters (6.5 feet) long, though sometimes Tufted Puffins commandeer premises from a Pigeon Guillemot (*Cepphus columba*) or Rhinoceros Auklet (*Cerorhinca monocerata*). Not all nests are in tunnels; some are tucked away in hard-to-get-at nooks and crannies, perhaps on a rocky beach or cliff. This provides better protection from hungry Arctic Foxes (*Alopex lagopus*) who, on St. Paul Island at least, seek out Tufted Puffins rather than other, commoner auks. Tufted Puffins may also fall prey to Snowy Owls (*Bubo scandiacus*) and Bald Eagles (*Haliaeetus leucocephalus*), and gulls may take eggs or chicks. Colonies vary in size, with the biggest, on Egg Island, numbering over 160,000 birds.

At the beginning of the breeding season, birds congregate on the sea, where much courtship and mating takes place. Courtship occurs on land too, and both parents take turns in incubating the single egg. About 13 weeks after the egg is laid, if all has gone well, the young puffin leaves its parental care behind and heads out to sea, normally at night.

Tufted Puffins are "pursuit divers" with a particular fondness for fish and squid, although their feeding behavior is not fully understood. It has been suggested that zooplankton could be an important food for adult birds, but little is known about their winter sustenance.

Our understanding of their migratory movements is also limited: they are thought to spend the winter a long way out at sea, and frozen northern waters must force high-latitude breeders to move south. Clearly, there are still things that we don't know about this comical auk. But one thing is for sure—this bird is definitely worth a look.

81. White-throated Dipper *Cinclus cinclus*

A hardy passerine that goes for a dip

Size: 18 cm (7 inches).
Distribution: Patchy—from western Europe to parts of Asia, plus northwest Africa.
Habitat: Fast-flowing upland rivers and streams.
Classification: One of five species in the family Cinclidae and the genus *Cinclus*.
Population and conservation status: Estimated at 330,000–660,000 in Europe. Least Concern.
Breeding system: Monogamous.
Nest and eggs: Domed outer made of grass, leaves and moss, with cup inside, in hole or on ledge, normally very near water. 4–5 eggs, 1–2 broods.
Incubation and fledging: 12–18 days. 20–24 days.

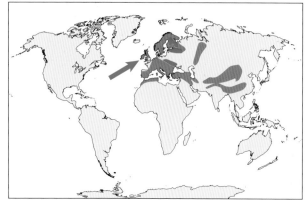

The White-throated Dipper is essentially an upland species, a bird of bubbling, rocky waterways, at ease both beside the water and under it. It is a bird that swims (without webbed feet) and upends, and will take itself underwater from midair, a boulder, the water's surface or simply by walking in and immersing itself. However they enter the water, dippers go in with their head pointing upstream and use their wings and legs to get around under the surface.

Most of their food is found on the river bottom, typically in depths of less than 1 meter (3 feet). When they reach the bottom, White-throated Dippers walk along the river bed, fanning their tails, and "flying" in more turbulent conditions. As they walk, they look for prey under pebbles. Caddisfly larvae and mayfly nymphs are particular favorites, though shrimps, beetles, snails and fish are also taken. Small prey is swallowed in situ, while larger, more challenging items are dealt with at the surface. Dives can be frequent and normally last just a few seconds (though dives of over 20 seconds are possible), with even briefer, sometimes split-second, surface interludes between the dives.

Most caddisfly larvae live in protective cases made of stones, snail shells or bits of plant. With White-throated

Dippers about, the cases are of limited value, and their softer, edible contents may be removed by a "Song Thrush and anvil" impression at a nearby rock. Not all feeding is submarine—airborne waterside insects, a dragonfly or mayfly perhaps, may be grabbed in a brief flycatching flight, and stones and other hideaways may be overturned by a dipper in "Turnstone" mode.

The White-throated Dipper is a hardy species, though cold weather may force it to move to lower altitudes or to the coast. Some north-European birds move southeast for the winter, travelling up to 950 kilometers (600 miles), while others stay put and may continue their underwater feeding even when the river is covered in ice (see opposite).

Dippers are densely feathered to help keep the water out and their temperature up. Their plumage is waterproofed with oil from a large preen gland, and when submerged their nostrils are covered with a special membrane and their eyes protected by a "third eyelid", the nictitating membrane. Good eyesight makes underwater foraging much easier and, like cormorants, dippers can change the shape of the lenses in their eyes to achieve clear underwater vision. "Flying" through water is very demanding and, not surprisingly, a dipper's flight muscles are substantial.

Dippers are monogamous and defend a territory all year round. Winter territories may be different from breeding territories, with male and female typically defending a different stretch of waterway. The domed nest is usually built on a wall, bridge or similar structure, but nest boxes may also be used.

The bobbing, or dipping, behavior that gives the bird its name is widely used in dipper communication, including courtship and in response to a threat. Dippers blink as they bob and may dip up and down around 50 times a minute.

To see this remarkable little passerine, head for the hills!

80. Musician Wren *Cyphorhinus arada*

One of Amazonia's best and most unusual songsters

Size: 12.5–13 cm (4.9–5.1 inches).
Distribution: Amazonia.
Habitat: Humid tropical rainforest.
Classification: One of 80 species in the family Troglodytidae, and one of three in the genus *Cyphorhinus*.
Population and conservation status: Not recorded. Least Concern.
Breeding System: Monogamous.
Nest and eggs: Sphere with funnel-shaped neck, placed on branch low down. Two eggs.
Incubation and fledging: Both unknown.

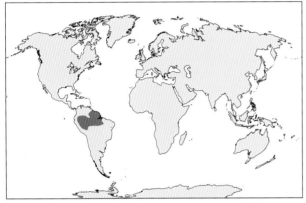

Birding in the Amazon rainforest is often as much an aural as a visual experience. Throughout the day, and especially at dawn and dusk, the jungle is often a theater of disembodied voices, each tantalizingly invisible and out of reach, reverberating through the foliage. As in most parts of the world, these songs and calls are very much the realm of the expert, many of them sounding similar to the untrained ear, in this chaos of biodiversity.

However, there is one Amazonian voice that cuts through all the frustration of the confusing dawn chorus. It is a sound so pure and unusual that it is immediately recognizable. It is also a ditty so surreal and utterly charming that, when you first hear it, it is difficult not to laugh. This sound is made by a small bird of the forest floor and undergrowth, the aptly named Musician Wren.

The song is not easy to describe. If the bird is a musician, then it sounds like a flautist practising scales; if anything else, it is like a person cheerily whistling as they meander through the chores of the day. It is quite fast, and between the fluty scales the Musician Wren interposes some delightful gurgling sounds to embellish the performance.

Much as it is pleasing to listen to, the song of this wren carries a serious message, as do all bird songs. Birds sing to delineate territory and attract a mate—the staple tasks of life. Among Neotropical wrens, however, there is something of a complication: their songs are usually performed in duet, both male and female equally tuneful. Although there is some doubt over whether the songs are always duets among Musician Wrens, recent work on a related species suggests that, where they occur, the duets are statements of togetherness. The female tends to start the phrase, and the male breaks in to confirm that she is paired up; if the female sings unaccompanied, the community knows that she is available.

These birds are as difficult to see as they are easy to hear, spending their lives on or close to the forest floor, where they feed on arthropods such as caterpillars and beetles unearthed from the litter. They sometimes follow swarms of ants to snap up the creatures fleeing the column, but more often they simply search fastidiously through the leaves. In typical wren fashion, they construct a domed nest out of grass and leaves, adding a small funnel-shaped "lobby" by the entrance hole. It is usually placed above ground in a small understorey shrub, and is extremely well concealed, as it must be.

In common with many small passerines in this rich forest, Musician Wrens live stable lives. They probably remain as a pair for life, and stay in the same territory for the duration; if a group of more than two is observed, it will invariably be a family party. Longer-lived than their temperate equivalents, they have a lower reproductive rate: a clutch of two eggs is all that they rear at a time.

79. Scissor-tailed Flycatcher *Tyrannus forficatus*

A pretty tyrant flycatcher with a very impressive scissor-tail

Size: 19–38 cm (7.5–15 inches), Only about 11 cm (4.3 inches) without tail.

Distribution: Breeds mostly in Texas, Oklahoma and Kansas; winters in Central America, some in southern Florida.

Habitat: Breeding range includes grassland, savanna, scrub and farmland with scattered trees, towns, parks and roadsides; wintering habitats are damper.

Classification: One of 432 species in the family Tyrannidae, and one of 13 in the genus *Tyrannus*.

Population and conservation status: Estimated at 7.9 million birds. Least Concern.

Breeding system: Monogamous.

Nest and eggs: Cup, made mostly of plant material; rough outer, finer lining; may incorporate man-made materials. 4–5 eggs, occasionally three or six, normally one brood.

Incubation and fledging: Average of 14–15 days, longer in cold weather. 14–17 days.

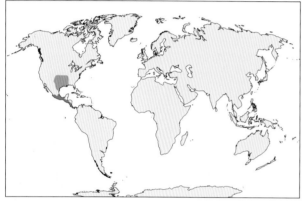

If you are not used to seeing Scissor-tailed Flycatchers, and perhaps even if you are, spotting one by the roadside can be quite a distraction. Wires, fences and trees are favorite perches for this tyrant flycatcher, and provide good starting points for some stylish aerial hunting. A bird in aerial flycatching mode will chase after prey for as much as 60 meters (200 feet), though often much less, and will do it with panache. This is a very eye-catching bird and, with the similar Fork-tailed Flycatcher (*T. savana*) of Central and South America, is quite different from most *Tyrannus* flycatchers. Indeed, neither of these species was even thought to be in this genus until relatively recently. Scissor-tails are currently believed to be closely related to Western Kingbirds (*T. verticalis*), with which they are thought to have hybridized, as well as their more Neotropical look-alike.

Flycatching seems to be this bird's main feeding method, but not all of the predatory flights are directed at flying insects. In one study, over 80 percent of the targets were sitting on vegetation, an unusually high proportion for a kingbird species. Scissor-tails will also feed on the ground, or may "flycatch" prey off the ground, perhaps grabbing prey from a hover. Grasshoppers, crickets and beetles are their main food, though many other insects are also taken, as well as spiders. A foraging Scissor-tail will often go back to the same perch at the end of the flight, eating smaller catches on the way and dealing with chunkier victims at the perch—a large catch may need to be crushed and bashed before being fit for consumption. This is not a solely insectivorous species. While it is not gregarious in the breeding season, flocks can be seen around migration or during the winter months, eating seeds or berries. Normally, Scissor-tailed Flycatchers feed during daylight, but there are reports of opportunistic birds feeding at night on insects attracted to streetlights.

The tail is remarkably long, the male's averaging almost 50 percent longer than that of the female. Tail length varies: males range from about 14–26 centimeters (5.5–10.2 inches) long, females from around 11–19 centimeters (4.3–7.5 inches). Birds with longer tails also have longer wings. It is also known that the tail length of an individual bird may vary from one year to the next and it seems that males with the longest tails may mate with the longest-tailed females. While some females have longer tails than some males, within a pair the male always has the longer of the two.

Courtship is impressive—during the male's display flight the tail opens and closes like a pair of scissors, and a particularly keen male may win a mate by doing backflips in midair. The female builds the nest and incubates the eggs. Normally, there is just one brood, but if things go wrong, a replacement clutch will be laid, sometimes up to four times in one season. The incubation period varies, and the young are fed by both parents. By October at the latest the relatively short journey south has begun.

78. Superb Fairywren *Malurus cyaneus*

One of Australia's best-known and best-loved birds, with a highly unusual lifestyle

Size: 15–20 cm (5.9–7.9 inches).

Distribution: Southeast Australia.

Habitat: Open woodland and bush; cultivation, gardens.

Classification: One of 28 species in the family Maluridae, and one of 13 in the genus *Malurus*.

Population and conservation status: Not recorded. Least Concern.

Breeding system: Live as pairs, but both sexes may be promiscuous.

Nest and eggs: Domed structure of grass and rootlets, placed low down in dense vegetation. Usually three eggs.

Incubation and fledging: 14 days. 10–14 days.

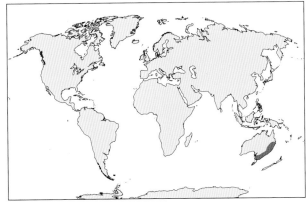

Neither fairies nor wrens, these delightful and colorful birds—members of a quite distinct Australasian family – are among the most popular birds in their native land. Their extraordinary bright, metallic colors, their unusual shape (kangaroolike long legs and a long tail), and their general abundance, make them familiar backyard characters. Although small and cover-hugging, they are extremely inquisitive, and the sound of birdwatchers "pishing" is usually enough to bring them into view.

In common with a high proportion of Australian birds—higher than anywhere else in the world—Superb Fairywrens live in cooperative family groups in a permanent home territory. This means that, when you see one Fairywren, there are usually at least two or three others nearby, and they will be the same individuals that you may have seen previously in the same location. Each territory is inhabited by a stable pair, who remain together for life, and they are accompanied by offspring from previous years; these offspring will help with any current breeding attempt, bringing food to the nestlings and fledglings. Birds in a given territory will naturally know each other very well, and all members of the family can be enlisted

to help should the family estate be threatened by intruders.

If this gives the impression of a wholesome family-based life, the reality is somewhat different. Underneath the veneer of respectability lies a darker side, which was first exposed when some researchers in Canberra, Australia's capital city, performed DNA tests on the chicks in Superb Fairywren nests. They were astonished to discover that a mere 24 percent of the chicks carried DNA from the father that was feeding them and was the mother's permanent partner; no fewer than 76 percent were the product of elicit extra-pair copulations out of territory. Bearing in mind that the male and female remained in the territory together despite this tension, this was an extraordinary revelation.

What apparently happens is that, during the female's fertile egg-laying period, she routinely makes her way in the predawn darkness each morning to a neighboring territory, in search of sex. In case this sounds like unbridled promiscuity, it is not just any average male with which the female has her tryst. Some males, it seems, are born superior. They molt from a dull winter plumage into the brilliant iridescent blue much earlier than the rest, and spend the prebreeding months flaunting this plumage to nearby females, making regular visits and displaying. The displays include fanning the colorful feathers, flying off with head high and tail down (the "sea-horse flight") and even bringing a gift of yellow flower petals. The incumbent male sometimes makes no attempt to chase away such an intruder, despite the likelihood of what will follow later in the season.

Nobody is quite sure why Superb Fairywren females exhibit such high levels of extra-pair copulation, far higher than for other small birds. It may be just for good genes or to ensure sexual compatibility. The one sure thing is that, even among familiar birds, appearances can be deceptive.

77. Woodpecker Finch *Camarhynchus pallidus*

A tool user and one of Darwin's finches

Size: 15 cm (6 inches).
Distribution: Galápagos Islands including Santa Cruz, San Cristóbal, Isabela, Pinzón and Santiago.
Habitat: Varied—includes Scalesia forest (Santa Cruz), humid highlands, dry lowlands and agricultural zone.
Classification: One of 395 species in the family Thraupidae, and one of six in the genus *Camarhynchus*.
Population and conservation status: Not recorded, but uncommon in parts of range. Least Concern.
Breeding system: Monogamous.
Nest and eggs: Domed with side access. 2–3 eggs.
Incubation and fledging: About 12 days. 13–15 days.

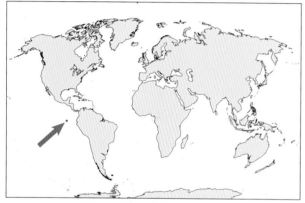

Over 170 years ago, HMS Beagle's grand tour took it to the Galápagos Islands. The ship's naturalist was Charles Darwin, who went on to controversy as well as great scientific acclaim. His name remains familiar as the man behind *On the Origin of Species*, a foundation for modern evolutionary theory. In *The Voyage of the Beagle* Darwin wrote: "Seeing this gradation and diversity of structure in one small, intimately related group of birds, one might really fancy that from an original paucity of birds in this archipelago, one species had been taken and modified for different ends."

The birds Darwin was writing about are known as the Darwin's Finches, though this name was never used by him and did not, in fact, enter popular usage until the 1940s. Today, 14 species of Darwin's Finch are recognized. All are found on the Galápagos Islands, with the exception of the Cocos Finch (*Pinaroloxias inornata*) of the Isla del Cocos, 700 kilometers (435 miles) from the Galápagos. The finches are similar in plumage, but differ in bill shape and size, and also in feeding behavior.

There are no true woodpeckers on the Galápagos islands, leaving a niche that the Woodpecker Finch has ingeniously filled. As both a tool-maker and a tool-user, this bird is one of the more unusual finches, and one that consequently has become well known. A hungry Woodpecker Finch locates its insect prey, perhaps a beetle larva, by some careful listening while checking out a tree branch. If it can hear a munching larva, it may use its bill for excavation, to get nearer to the prey. Its bill would look out of place on a woodpecker (Picinae), but seems perfectly adequate for the task. Woodpeckers, though, have long tongues to help them extract their prey from tricky places, a tool the Woodpecker Finch is not naturally endowed with. So it improvises, using a leaf stem, twig, or most famously an *Opuntia* cactus spine to make a meal of a nutritious insect, typically a fairly large one, that otherwise would elude it. The bird takes care to choose a tool that is a good size for the specific extraction challenge, perhaps trying a range of options before making the final selection, and sometimes shortening it to better suit it to the task. The tool is held in the bird's bill, stuck into the hole and manipulated, with the aim of spearing the larva. If necessary, the tool is popped into another hole or secured under a foot while the hole is enlarged. The end result, if successful, is a bit like a cocktail stick with a treat on the end!

The Critically Endangered Mangrove Finch (*C. heliobates*), a congener, uses twigs and leaf stems in a similar way, but it is the Woodpecker Finch that is famed for its use of cactus spines. This may be what it is known for, but it is not its only feeding method. Where there is plenty of food that is easy to find, tools are hardly ever used. But in arid areas, in the dry season, when finding food is much more challenging, tool use is much more frequent. So, to see this bird at its best, that is the time to visit the Galápagos!

76. Montserrat Oriole *Icterus oberi*

A resilient and much-loved oriole living on the edge

Size: 20–22 cm (7.8–8.7 inches).
Distribution: Montserrat, Lesser Antilles.
Habitat: Forests.
Classification: One of 106 species in the family Icteridae, and one of 30 in the genus *Icterus*.
Population and conservation status: Estimated at 200–800 birds. Critically Endangered.
Breeding system: Monogamous.
Nest and eggs: Hanging, woven basket. 2–3 eggs per brood.
Incubation and fledging: About 14 days. About 13 days.

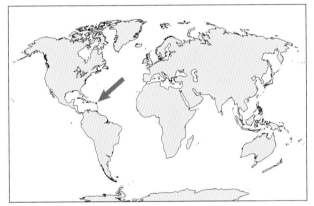

The Montserrat Oriole is an attractive Icterid, endemic to the island of Montserrat in the Lesser Antilles. It is a species that has never had a large range, but now has a tiny range of around 16 square kilometers (6 square miles); the whole island is only just over 100 square kilometers (38 square miles). It survives in only two areas, with a small population numbering no more than about 400 pairs. No other endemic birds are found on the island—this black and yellow dazzler is Montserrat's national bird, and a species that local people take pride in. Until fairly recently, however, relatively few birdwatchers were aware of its existence. All that changed in the 1990s when the Montserrat Oriole hit the ornithological headlines.

Montserrat is volcanic, and in 1996 the Soufrière Hills volcano erupted, and was still active over 10 years later. The best places for the Oriole were destroyed—volcanic activity demolished over 60 percent of the bird's habitat, and the remaining forest has to contend with huge amounts of ash, which wrecks Oriole nests, makes arthropod prey harder to locate, and may damage the health of surviving birds.

A Montserrat Oriole's nest is an impressive affair, a woven basket dangling from, typically, a *Heliconia* leaf. Both fresh

and ageing leaves are shunned—a middle-aged leaf is the nest site of choice. Other plant species are used too, but the bird's attachment to the *Heliconia* is a boon to scientists, who have little problem locating nests. This makes studying the species easier, but early research struggled when Orioles, unaware of the intruders' good motives, removed the plastic color rings that betrayed their identity. Aluminium color rings were then used, taking away any hopes of avian anonymity.

The breeding season is fairly protracted, running from March to August. During this time, if all goes well, a pair may raise two broods. When things go wrong, a determined pair might lay as many as five clutches as they struggle to bring new Orioles into a volcanic world. When successful parents are intent on raising more young, the previous brood may be forced to leave home just two weeks after fledging, though at other times they may be looked after for several months.

No one knows what the future holds for Montserrat's sole endemic bird species. The bird has more than volcanoes to contend with. Pearly-eyed Thrashers (*Margarops fuscatus*) and Black Rats (*Rattus rattus*) like to dine at oriole nests and can have a significant impact, and adverse rainfall patterns can reduce both the number of adults and the number of young raised.

But there is hope. Much research has already been done by BirdLife International through the Royal Society for the Protection of Birds, its UK partner. There are plans to establish a protected area for Montserrat Orioles and, as an insurance package, a captive breeding programme has been set up at Jersey Zoo by the Durrell Wildlife Conservation Trust. Results so far are encouraging. But perhaps most importantly, local people care about their national bird. It is not the end of the road for the Montserrat Oriole—there is still time to see this resilient black and yellow endemic.

75. Harlequin Duck *Histrionicus histrionicus*

A handsome whitewater champion

Size: 38–51 cm (15–20 inches).
Distribution: Northern hemisphere; breeds mostly at high latitudes across Europe and Asia with some in North America; most wintering areas are further south.
Habitat: Breeds on fast, turbulent upland streams and rivers; winters on rough seas around rocky coasts.
Classification: One of 161 species in the family Anatidae, and the sole member of the genus *Histrionicus*.
Population and conservation status: Estimated at 190,000–390,000 birds in 2002. Least Concern.
Breeding system: Monogamous.
Nest and eggs: Well-hidden scrape with grass, leaves and twigs, down lining. 5–7 eggs.
Incubation and fledging: 27–29 days. About 60–70 days.

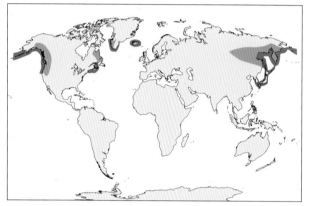

There are well over 100 duck species in the world and, while beauty may be in the eye of the beholder, the Harlequin must be high on the shortlist of the world's best-looking ducks. The males have design-studio looks, with their blue-grey ground color, russet flanks and head stripe and striking black-and-white markings. As is the case with many birds, to our eyes at least, the females are less attractive.

The European breeding population is estimated at between 4,000 and 10,000 pairs, all of which are in Iceland or Greenland. In this regional context its small population makes it a species of conservation concern. Elsewhere, however, it can be very common (the Aleutian Islands are particularly good for this species) and in a global context the Harlequin Duck is currently of little concern to conservationists.

Harlequins seek out wild water. They are white-water champions, undeterred even by waterfalls. No other duck of the northern hemisphere feeds in the bubbling torrents of cold, upland water of the Harlequin's breeding areas. Ecologically, this bird fills a similar niche to South America's Torrent Duck (*Merganetta armata*) and New

Zealand's Blue Duck (*Hymenolaimus malacorhynchos*). It is a diving duck *par excellence*—it can enter the water from midair, walk on the riverbed and return to midair straight from its submarine antics. Most of its food is found by diving, often from the water's surface, though Harlequins will take food from near the surface too. When feeding, they spend a lot of time underwater, with only three- to five-second intervals between dives of around 15 seconds. Their diet seems to be surprisingly lacking in vegetable material, with insects and insect larvae providing much of their breeding season sustenance. Winters are spent on rough seas where wave-tossed Harlequins feed mainly on crustaceans and molluscs. Their tough waterscape takes its toll—broken bones are not uncommon in the life of a Harlequin Duck.

Courtship takes place mostly on the sea and, despite the handsome plumage of the male, is more vocal than visual. Some head-nodding takes place, where the head traces an oval form on a horizontal plane. While its courtship may hold little of visual interest, compared to many other sea ducks, its high-frequency vocalizations are very unusual, and have resulted in the alternative names of "Sea Mouse" and "Squealer" for a bird that is normally thought of as quiet. High-frequency noises may be the only way to be heard in an environment of rushing, crashing water.

In late April, after a coastal winter, Harlequins head inland, following rivers upstream to their nesting areas. The duck is a monogamous species that hides its nest under bushes, rocks and tall vegetation, small islands being particularly favored as nesting sites. The male tends not to hang around to help with incubation, but joins others of his sex and begins his molt. Later, the males head back to sea, leaving the females to follow on with the next generation of this very aquatic duck.

74. Greater Hoopoe-lark *Alaemon alaudipes*

A uniquely adapted and distinctive lark with a stunning display flight

Size: 19–23 cm (7.5–9 inches).

Distribution: Cape Verde Islands and east across northern Africa (south to Somalia) and the Middle East to Pakistan and northwest India.

Habitat: Desert, semi-desert, coasts, wadis, roadsides and other areas with sandy or soft soil, sometimes with stones.

Classification: One of 96 species in the family Alaudidae, and one of two in the genus *Alaemon*.

Population and conservation status: Not recorded, common in some areas. Least Concern.

Breeding system: Monogamous.

Nest and eggs: Twig nest (with softer lining) entwined in bush or on tussock, or in a shallow depression on ground. 2–4 eggs, 1–2 broods.

Incubation and fledging: 14 days. 12–13 days.

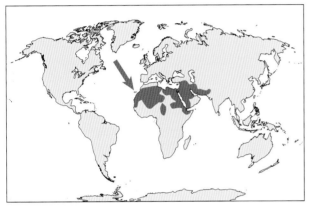

With its long, decurved, Hoopoelike bill, and a bold wing pattern that could trigger memories of that species, the Greater Hoopoe-lark has to be one of the easiest larks to identify. Its wing pattern is the most striking of any lark and may provide protection from predators, being obvious on a bird in flight but disappearing from view when the lark lands.

Despite living in some hot and arid habitats, this bird appears to be able to live without drinking. To survive in its thermally demanding environment, the Greater Hoopoe-lark concentrates its feeding in the early morning and just before sunset. As the day heats up, shadier feeding areas are used and foraging is interspersed with less demanding feather care or rest sessions. Researchers in Arabia found that this species spends more time resting than feeding. Activity during the heat of the day is avoided and shelter may be found by taking temporary residence in a lizard's burrow, sometimes remaining underground for over five hours a day. Temperatures in the burrows are a few degrees lower than at the surface and, as a result, water loss can be cut by 80 percent or more. As the day cools, activity levels rise again, with shady foraging areas being used first, and then more open areas for an hour or so before sunset.

When foraging, a Greater Hoopoe-lark will stop mid-stroll and, for no obvious reason, start digging vigorously with its bill. Digging may go on for several minutes, taking the search for food up to 5 centimeters (2 inches) beneath the surface. The success rate is high; many a beetle larva or antlion larva, and even the occasional gecko has ended its days inside a Greater Hoopoe-lark. Food may also be taken off the surface of the soil or off plants. Snails are dealt with in a manner that is at first reminiscent of a Herring Gull (*Larus argentatus*) trying to break into a mollusc: the victim is taken aloft, perhaps to 25 meters (82 feet), and dropped onto something hard. If this fails, it will use a rock as an anvil, much as a Song Thrush (*Turdus philomelos*) would do. While invertebrates make up most of the diet, some plant material is also taken.

Breeding depends on rainfall, with different breeding seasons in different parts of the bird's range. In some areas many pairs will not even attempt to breed when it is too dry (and those that do breed do not raise any young), deferring nuptials until conditions improve.

Courtship can be an extremely impressive affair, the male performing an aerial tumbling routine, with piercing, high-pitched whistles and a trill as vocal accompaniment. He lifts off from a bush or a rise in the ground, with tail fanned and wings quivering, going almost straight up for a few meters—sometimes as high as 10 meters (33 feet)—before flipping over, perhaps with a somersault, and descending beak first with wings held close until it seems almost too late, opening them just before re-landing on the launch pad. It is a stunning display—may it continue to impress the females for many years to come.

73. Pheasant-tailed Jacana *Hydrophasianus chirurgus*

The best-looking Jacana—a bird that "walks on water" and has a shocking sex life

Size: 39–58 cm (15.3–22.8 inches), of which the tail is 25–35 cm (9.8–13.8 inches).

Distribution: Asia—Pakistan east to Taiwan and Philippines; some winter further south to Java, also some in Yemen and Oman.

Habitat: Large freshwater lakes and swamps.

Classification: One of eight species in the family Jacanidae, and the sole member of the genus *Hydrophasianus*.

Population and conservation status: Estimated at 25,000–100,000 birds. Least Concern.

Breeding system: Polyandrous.

Nest and eggs: Platform of plant material on floating vegetation. Four eggs per clutch, about 10 clutches.

Incubation and fledging: Unknown, possibly 22–28 days. Unknown.

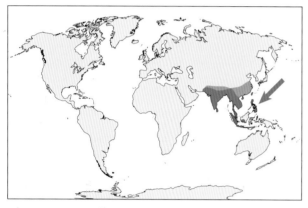

Taxonomically, jacanas, or lily-trotters, are thought to sit somewhere between the plovers (Charadriinae) and the sandpipers. This makes them shorebirds, which may surprise some readers. They are unusual birds and all bar one of the eight species have unusual breeding systems.

In every jacana species, the female is bigger than the male—a male can weigh less than half the weight of the female. In no other bird or mammal species do the genders differ in size as markedly. These surprising shorebirds are well known for their long legs, and load-spreading, stretched-out toes with stretched-out claws, which make almost gravity-defying lily-trotting possible, and can create a "walking on water" illusion when the plants that take the bird's weight are just beneath the surface of the water.

While jacanas as a group have their peculiarities, the Pheasant-tailed Jacana is unusual even by normal jacana standards. None of the Jacanidae changes its plumage with the seasons. None, that is, except the Pheasant-tailed Jacana, whose breeding plumage is quite different from its non-breeding plumage. Birds in breeding attire are smartly dressed, with dark underparts, a golden patch on the back of the neck and that pheasantlike tail. The tails of non-breeders are a lot shorter, their underparts are mostly white and much of the golden neck patch is lost.

While some other jacana species may move around within their range, none of them is a regular migrant. The Pheasant-tailed Jacana is, though admittedly not across its entire range—many northern breeders move south after the breeding season, and the species is recorded in some parts of Thailand, Peninsular Malaysia, Sumatra, Java and Borneo only during the northern winter. Small numbers also winter in the Arabian Peninsula. As might be expected for a migrant species, the Pheasant-tailed Jacana flies well, unlike other jacanas.

Its breeding behavior does comply with that of most other jacana species, though all but one do things very differently from most of the bird world. With the exception of the Lesser Jacana (*Microparra capensis*), all jacanas are polyandrous—that is, the female mates with more than one male.

The male Pheasant-tailed Jacana is the main nest builder and takes on sole responsibility for incubation and looking after the young, which may need his care for over eight weeks. The bulkier female will help to defend a territory, however, and may have her work cut out keeping other females out of three or more male territories. Typically, the nest is a platform of plant material, but occasionally eggs are deposited on a floating leaf. About 10 clutches are produced during the breeding season, totalling around 40 eggs, with all the hard work of parenting being left to the males. Eggs may be moved to a new nest site by the male, and when a chick emerges the eggshell is moved away from the nest, presumably to reduce the risk of predation. Not that many of the tens of eggs that a female produces in just one year achieve their potential, but clearly enough of them do.

72. Sinai Rosefinch *Carpodacus synoicus*

A rare bird of extreme habitats, with subtly glorious plumage

Size: 14.5 cm (5.7 inches).
Distribution: The Middle East in Israel, Jordan, Egypt and Saudi Arabia; parts of Central Asia and China.
Habitat: Arid, mountainous, rocky areas.
Classification: One of 179 species in the family Fringillidae, and one of 21 in the genus *Carpodacus*.
Population and conservation status: Not recorded. Least Concern.
Breeding system: Monogamous.
Nest and eggs: Basket-shaped structure of fine and coarse materials placed in a crevice. 4–5 eggs.
Incubation and fledging: 13–14 days. 14–16 days.

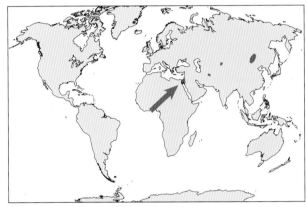

Some birds seem to fit perfectly into their habitat, and a good example of this is the raspberry-colored Sinai Rosefinch, a rare bird of sandstone cliffs and precipitous rocky slopes in several widely separated parts of the world. Amidst the color and grandeur of its arid environment, where the bright-plumaged male often sings from high up on a cliff face, it somehow looks just right. Its charisma is undoubtedly helped by some of the breathtaking places where it can be seen, such as the incomparable archaeological sites of Petra in Jordan and St. Katherine's Monastery in Sinai, notwithstanding the fact that it will stoop here to mix with the tourists and camels, drinking from leaking taps, scrabbling among rubbish bins and adorning holiday snaps and videos. It is a rare companion at rarefied locations.

The Sinai's Rosefinch's world distribution is indeed extremely odd. It occurs in the Middle East, then again in the Hindu Kush in Afghanistan and thence east to central China . . . And nowhere in between. The further east it occurs the higher it lives, from as low as 1,000 meters (3,280 feet) in Sinai and Jordan to as high as 3,050 meters (10,000 feet) in China, making its ecological

preferences hard to understand. It is as though it is trying to escape the typical high-altitude niche of its near relatives, and be its own bird, but hasn't quite managed it yet. However, wherever it goes there seem to be some precipitous rocks and ravines.

As befitting a finch, the Sinai Rosefinch is primarily a seed-eater, taking those of shrubs or herbs such as wormwood (*Artemisia* spp.) and spurge (*Euphorbia* spp.) although it will also tuck into other plant material, including fruit, buds and even leaves, which are shunned by many others in the family. It usually feeds on the ground and, not surprisingly considering its rather dry diet, is something of a water junkie. On hot days it has been known to drink 30 times an hour. On such days it will usually confine its bouts of feeding to the early morning and late afternoon.

The young are fed in the nest on a diet of seeds, a far cry from the seemingly more palatable insects fed to the nestlings of other passerines. This quirk of behavior has wide implications for the Sinai Rosefinch's social life: since it is not always possible to gather seeds close at hand—they tend to be found over wide areas—there is no need for this bird to hold a resource-filled territory. Thus pairs often nest close together and, even in the breeding season, unrelated birds commonly travel in small flocks to and from their feeding areas. Unusually among finches, both male and female share the responsibility of incubating the eggs.

After breeding, family parties stay together, and there are even records of small groups of apparently related birds remaining intact until well into the following spring. More typically, in the winter, parties coalesce and flocks become larger, and a couple of hundred may be seen together. So many flying raspberries all at once—that must be quite a sight!

71. White-plumed Antbird *Pithys albifrons*

The epitome of its family—a cover-hugging follower of ants, with unusual plumage

Size: 11.5–12.5 cm (4.5–5 inches).
Distribution: Amazonia and low Andean foothills.
Habitat: Humid tropical forest, evergreen forest and second-growth forest.
Classification: One of 213 species in the family Thamnophilidae, and one of two in the genus *Pithys*.
Population and conservation status: Not recorded. Least Concern.
Breeding System: Monogamous.
Nest: Cup of dead leaves, placed above ground. Two eggs.
Incubation: About 15 days. About 12 days.

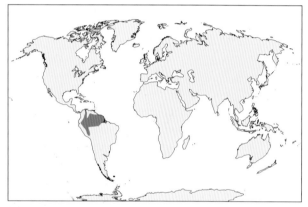

The perky White-plumed Antbird is not easy to see. In common with many species in its poorly known family, it is a shade-loving creature that is definitely not at home in bright sunlight. Indeed, for many antbirds, just to cross a river or even a road bisecting the dense rainforest where it lives is too much to contemplate—there is too much space and fresh air.

The Amazonian forest floor, with its enormous biodiversity, is full of feeding niches, but it is one of the better known and more fascinating of these that gives the antbirds their name. It so happens that the forest litter plays permanent host to nomadic swarms of army ants that periodically move in waves across the forest floor, terrorizing every small animal in their predatory path. These ants inadvertently provide food for a small club of followers, not by being palatable themselves, but by their actions, flushing out huge numbers of small litter-living animals—other ants, crickets, cockroaches, spiders—which normally spend their time concealed but, at the approach of the rapacious ants, are forced to flee for their lives. Unfortunately, their flight for safety often brings them straight to the hungry jaws of such birds as

White-plumed Antbirds, which wait for them at the front of the army ant column. It is probably a better death than at the hands of the ants, but a death nonetheless.

While many species of antbird will follow these insect armies to a greater or lesser extent, the White-plumed is highly unusual in depending completely on this feeding system—it is known as an obligate ant-follower. At any given time there is always a swarm somewhere, and this allows the species to eke out its living in this way every day. Just after dawn, it seeks out an ant column, both by checking the ants' overnight bivouac or previous centers of activity, or by listening for the excited calls of others of its species or other ant-followers. Once it has located a column, it works its way to the head and will often remain in the vicinity until the late afternoon. At first it feeds in almost frenzied fashion, darting from a horizontal or vertical perch down to the ground and back, avoiding not just the ants themselves but also larger ant-following competitors. But as it becomes satiated, its movements will slow down a little, and it will rest and preen.

There is no doubt that ant-following is a highly successful strategy for feeding; studies show that ant-followers can have a capture rate vastly exceeding those that scrutinize the litter in different ways, but it has its disadvantages. For one thing, it is not alone in being an obligate ant-follower, and has to fight against other, larger species, such as the Bicolored Antbird (*Gymnopithys leucaspis*), for the privilege of catching prey. Furthermore, most antbirds live as pairs and hold territories that, over the years, they get to know intimately enough to learn about all the food-providing hotspots. But White-plumed Antbirds live the life of the road, always moving about. They have to settle down for a while to breed, but they don't hold territories, and their partnerships don't progress beyond the raising of a single brood.

70. Greater Roadrunner *Geococcyx californianus*

An iconic species that can outrun any other flying bird

Size: Male 54 cm (21.2 inches), female 52 cm (20.4 inches).
Distribution: Southern-central and southwestern United States and much of northern Mexico.
Habitat: Open, dry areas with scattered scrub, including deserts; range expanding—
other habitats include woodland edges, dry grassland, juniper-strewn hills and farmland.
Classification: One of 144 species in the family Cuculidae, and one of two in the genus *Geococcyx*.
Population and conservation status: Estimated at 1.1 million birds. Least Concern.
Breeding system: Monogamous.
Nest and eggs: Twig platform with softer lining, including plant material, feathers,
snakeskin and bits of dung. 3–6 eggs.
Incubation and fledging: Around 19–20 days. 14–25 days.

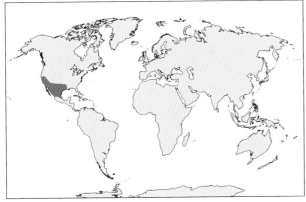

This bird features in folklore and fable, but for some readers it will be the well-known cartoon that first brought this cuckoo to their attention.

Roadrunners can fly, but seldom do and are more likely to glide than engage in sustained, powered flight, though may take to the wing to seek cover. Roadrunners are built to run; their leg bones are lengthened and their musculature differs from their tree-dwelling relatives. A running bird can exceed 30 kilometers (18 miles) an hour and sustain it—a speed of 42 kilometers (26 miles) an hour has even been claimed. At full pelt, it uses its long tail as a rudder. Roads, tracks and dried-out waterways are favored running tracks, where, on soft ground, the "x" marks of a Roadrunner's zygodactylic feet may be found.

Animals account for most of a Roadrunner's diet. Insects are especially important, but many other species are taken including scorpions, spiders, lizards, snakes, birds, mammals, eggs, centipedes and millipedes. When available, seeds and fruit supplement the meat-based menu. Roadrunners are not entirely likeable. Birds that come in to feeders, including hummingbirds (Trochilidae), may find themselves eaten rather than eating, and nest boxes are raided, as are mist

nets put up by bird ringers. When times are really hard, a Roadrunner may even devour its own offspring.

Prey is located by a strategy of stop and look, move, then stop and look again. A burst of speed will help a Roadrunner catch prey that is taking rapid evasive action. Roadrunners pick up scorpions by the tail, will despatch some mammals by whacking the victim's head with their bill, and larger animals by repeatedly bashing them on something hard.

Roadrunners are famous for eating snakes—even small rattlesnakes—swallowing a small serpent in around half a minute. A horned lizard (*Phrynosoma* spp.) is no easy meal, with real potential for the horns to avenge their owner's death as the reptile travels through the bird. To avoid this, Roadrunners orient the lizard carefully before swallowing.

Territories may be used all year round and are defended by both male and female, who revitalize their pair-bond with chasing, and by giving a stick or piece of grass to their partner. Other displays take place before mating. Nest-building is shared, the male collecting most of the materials and the female doing most of the building. If, for some reason, the twigs stop arriving, she "whines" to remind her mate of his responsibility. Both parents incubate the eggs, but will leave them for a while during the heat of the day.

Roadrunners are adapted to a desert environment in many ways, perhaps most remarkably with an ability to reduce their core temperature to save energy overnight. Birds that are incubating overnight, however (always the male), do not drop their core temperature. And, for an accelerated morning warm-up, Roadrunners raise their scapulars, exposing dark, heat-absorbing skin, which they line up with the sun.

The Greater Roadrunner is a fascinating bird with an expanding range and may actually be wilier than a Coyote.

69. Standard-winged Nightjar *Macrodipteryx longipennis*

A nightjar with very high standards

Size: 21–22 cm (8.3–8.7 inches).

Distribution: Breeds in a belt across much of northern hemisphere sub-Saharan Africa; most winter further north.

Habitat: Includes savannas, clearings, stony hillsides and pastureland.

Classification: One of 88 species in the family Caprimulgidae, and one of two in the genus *Macrodipteryx*.

Population and conservation status: Not recorded. Least Concern.

Breeding system: May be polygamous.

Nest: None, lays eggs on ground. 1–2 eggs.

Incubation and fledging: Both unknown.

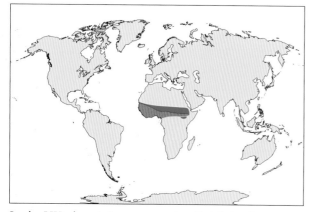

In the UK, there is just one species of nightjar. In the United States, there are nearer 10. Africa has 26 species and identification can be tricky. This one, however, is very easy to identify, or rather a male in breeding plumage is. During the breeding season, a male Standard-winged Nightjar is adorned with two of the most surprising and bizarre feathers in existence. The feathers in question are the second innermost primaries. These form the bird's "standards" and can be over 50 centimeters (20 inches) long; the bird's bill-tip to tail-tip measurement is just over 20 centimeters (7.8 inches). The only webbing that remains is at the tip of the otherwise naked shaft, creating a "flag" that the bird flies as part of his courtship rituals.

A Standard-winged Nightjar display is something to behold. A display arena provides the focal point for the action and will attract several males and females. To impress a would-be mate, males fly slowly around females, rising and falling on rigidly bent, trembling wings, and perhaps singing too. The wing trembling produces an up-current that lifts the standards, which fly over and to the rear of the amorous male. In the half-light, the shafts are impossible to see and a butterflylike illusion is created, further heightening the already dramatic effect.

These long, ridiculous feathers must be quite a burden. A resting bird lays them on the ground, at right angles to its body, and when their job is done their owner may break them off, or they may break of their own accord.

Nightjars are tricky birds to study and there is still much that we don't know about the Standard-winged. Unlike most nightjars, which are monogamous, Standard-winged may well be polygamous. They may be solitary breeders or breed semi-colonially but they have the simplest possible "nest"—their small clutch is laid straight onto the ground, often where it is sandy. The female is responsible for most of the incubation, but it is unclear how long this takes, and the same is true of fledging.

Like most nightjars, the Standard-winged feeds primarily on a range of nocturnal, airborne insects, including moths, mosquitoes, beetles and cicadas. Nightjars are very agile fliers, catching their prey and swallowing it in midair. They can open their mouths from top to bottom and side to side, thanks to an adaptation that allows the lower jaw to widen, giving them a very large gape. Their large eyes exhibit "eye-shine", resulting from a reflective layer at the back of the eye which improves low-light vision.

The Standard-winged Nightjar migrates within Africa, with a non-breeding range that abuts its breeding range. Birds may start their migration in April, or later— sometimes months later—and it may be that the wet season affects its migratory behavior. There are many gaps in our knowledge of Standard-winged Nightjars. One thing is certain, however—if you haven't seen one, this remarkable bird is definitely worth seeking out.

68. Golden-headed Manakin *Pipra erythrocephala*

A gem of the canopy with a sensational courtship display

Size: 8–9 cm (3.1–3.5 inches).

Distribution: South America, north of the Amazon.

Habitat: Forest and second growth woodland.

Classification: One of 44 species in the family Pipridae, and one of nine in the genus *Pipra*.

Population and conservation status: Not recorded. Least Concern.

Breeding system: Promiscuous; sexes meet only for display and copulation.

Nest and eggs: Small cup placed in fork in bush or tree. Two eggs.

Incubation and fledging: 16–17 days. Unknown.

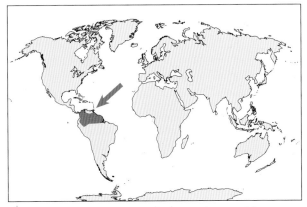

At first sight, the Golden-headed Manakin would appear to be about the most characterless bird in the world. The males are often colorful enough, but they seem to do very little. Tiny birds of the South American forests, they perch for minutes on end, motionless, in the canopy or sub-canopy. The highlight of their day would seem to be the occasional dart out from a perch to pluck a small fruit. They eat fruit almost to the exclusion of anything else, and have unusually wide gapes for the size of bird, so that they can swallow it whole.

But behind this cheerless veneer these are remarkable show-birds, with intricate relationships and quite astonishing courtship routines. If you really want to appreciate them, you need to leave the fruiting trees, where they are often seen, and follow them down to the lek.

The site for a Golden-headed Manakin lek is carefully chosen to catch beams of sunlight glinting through the canopy in the first hour after dawn and in the late afternoon, to show off the male's two-tone color scheme to best effect. When a female visits the lek, she will be greeted by the sight of up to 15 frenziedly displaying males. The sheer variety of the routines on offer must be bewildering for her. Some males will simply remain still in an upright position, clinging onto a vertical perch with their head up; others will perform astonishingly quick about-turns of the body on the perch, so fast that their leg movements are a whirr; others will fly madly between two perches about 1 meter (40 inches) apart, making their wings hum, and turning immediately after landing to face the direction from which they came; still others will fly between two perches up to 25 meters (80 feet) apart, approaching each landing with loud, accelerating calls; and finally, others will perform the remarkable "backward slide", in which a bowing bird on a horizontal perch will move backwards with such small, fast steps that it appears to be sliding.

Almost invariably, the female will choose the male holding court in the center of the lek; during the year, all the males fight for this most favorable court, so the incumbent, being centrally placed, has already proved his worth, and is a good bet for passing on a good set of genes.

Once the male and female have copulated, those genes, in the form of eggs and chicks, are the sole responsibility of the female. She builds the nest and carries out all breeding duties.

It has been shown that males spend 90 percent of their day at the lek, and are there throughout the year and throughout their lives, with short breaks for foraging excursions. At first it can be a frustrating experience, with all the female visitors bypassing them until they are old enough or strong enough to take possession of a central perch. Once there, however, they can be quite productive. It is what they aspire to as they spend those long hours perched motionless, contemplating the next gulp of fruit.

67. Bohemian Waxwing *Bombycilla garrulus*

A great-looking nomad that can still be elusive, despite occurring in towns and cities

Size: 18 cm (7 inches).
Distribution: Breeds in northern hemisphere at high latitudes; wintering areas vary, but south of breeding range, with some overlap.
Habitat: Breeds in taiga, winters in berry-rich areas, including in conurbations.
Classification: One of eight species in the family Bombycillidae, and one of three in the genus *Bombycilla*.
Population and conservation status: Estimated at 2.8 million. Least Concern.
Breeding system: Monogamous.
Nest and eggs: Twig cup with moss and grass and softer lining. 5–6 eggs.
Incubation and fledging: 14–15 days. 14–15 days.

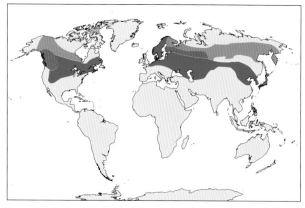

For most British and American birdwatchers, the Bohemian Waxwing is a bird that may or may not show up in the winter. It is a species that breeds in taiga forest in the north and may travel considerable distances to its wintering areas. However, its movements are not entirely predictable. Some areas are regularly used in the winter, including some parts of its breeding range, but others, including the UK and the United States, only irregularly host this exotic looking bird.

The Bohemian Waxwing is an eruptive species. When there are more birds than food, new feeding areas are sought, and a big waxwing year can see large numbers of European breeders reaching the UK, with some even reaching Iceland and Greenland. A big Nearctic irruption brings birds over the Canadian border into the United States, and waxwings may even make it to New England. Bohemian Waxwings can be great wanderers that are not site-faithful. One year's breeding location may be many miles from the previous year's, and the same is true of their wintering areas—one bird was in Poland one winter, and in Eastern Siberia, over 5,000 kilometers (3,000 miles) away, the next. Wandering winter flocks may be fairly small or may number hundreds of birds.

Berries and fruit are their main food, and they have a particular liking for Rowan (Mountain Ash—*Sorbus* spp.) berries. Bohemian Waxwings are not too fussy though, and will feed on juniper (*Juniperus* spp.), hawthorn (*Crataegus* spp.), rose (*Rosa* spp.), holly (*Ilex* spp.), ivy (*Hedera* spp.) and cotoneaster (*Cotoneaster* spp.) berries, as well as apples and pears. Their appetite for berries is substantial—a bird weighing 60 grams (2 ounces) might devour 180 grams (6 ounces) of berries in a day's feeding. Other winter sustenance is provided by flowers and buds, as well as a few invertebrates. They are also big drinkers and may flycatch snowflakes to help keep their fluid levels up.

As the winter fades, insects, especially midges and mosquitoes, become their supplementary nutrition in the breeding season, with most of their prey grabbed during flycatching sorties. Where there are good numbers, Bohemian Waxwings may build their nests reasonably close together, with perhaps 6–12 pairs in a fairly small patch of breeding habitat. The male woos the female by perching nearby and passing gifts to her—perhaps a flower, or a berry. The gifts are placed in her open bill and might be repeatedly passed from male to female and back again.

He leaves all of the incubation to the female, and goes out with the boys to feed. But when there are hungry young in the nest, he becomes a responsible parent and helps out with the feeding.

Waxwings are so named because of the red, waxy extensions on their outermost secondaries, though one of the three species, the Japanese Waxwing (*B. japonica*) has "wax-free" wings, as do some individuals of the other two species. What the wax is there for is unclear.

Seeing a flock of Bohemian Waxwings is a highlight of a winter's day of birding. If you are one of those birders who keep missing this stunning bird, keep trying. It will be worth it.

66. Crab Plover *Dromas ardeola*

A distinctive, idiosyncratic wader with a huge bill

Size: 38–41 cm (15–16 inches).
Distribution: Coastline around the Indian Ocean.
Habitat: Sandy areas for breeding; mudflats, lagoons, estuaries and coral reefs for feeding.
Classification: The sole member of the family Dromadidae and the genus *Dromas*.
Population and conservation status: Estimated at 60,000–80,000 birds. Least Concern.
Breeding system: Presumed monogamous, colonial.
Nest and eggs: Chamber at end of tunnel. One egg.
Incubation and fledging: Both unknown.

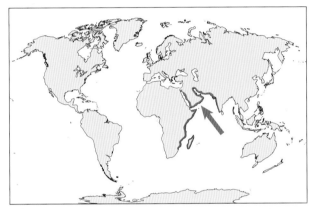

The Crab Plover is one of the world's more unusual shorebirds. It has a remarkable bill, lays its egg in a tunnel and is mostly nocturnal or crepuscular.

As you might expect from its name, it is a bit of a picky eater. It is a sociable bird that may feed in flocks, but doesn't always. Feeding is ploverlike, although the Crab Plover is not a true plover. The bird will move at a gentle pace until it sees a crab. A brief sprint then takes the plover to its mobile meal and the stout, black bill comes into its own—a "crab-stab" may be followed by some down-in-one nutrition if the crab is not too big, or a bit more preparation if the victim is too large to be swallowed intact. More substantial meals are given a good shaking to remove the appendages, and their transformation into more manageable pieces of bird food is accomplished by a serious battering from that crab-busting bill. Other invertebrates are sometimes eaten, but its crab-based diet is what defines the Crab Plover's feeding areas.

Crab Plovers are only found around the Indian Ocean, and are never far from the sea. They are colonial breeders and fewer than 15 colonies may account for the entire global population. Colonies range in size from sites that host around 20 pairs or fewer, to sites with hundreds, or sometimes over 1,000 pairs. Breeding colonies are always located on sandy areas, where, like no other shorebird, Crab Plovers dig impressive tunnels in which to lay their eggs. Presumably, these subterranean homes provide protection from predators; they may also protect young Crab Plovers from overheating. Going from tunnel entrance to nest chamber takes you downhill a little, perhaps around a few bends and finally, between 1–2.5 meters (3–8 feet) in, and after a final short incline, to the nest chamber itself. The chamber provides a home for the occupiers' single egg (occasionally two eggs)—a simple, unlined depression. Both male and female are thought to do the digging, using their bills and feet, and the same tunnel may be used from year to year.

No other shorebird lays a white egg, but clearly crypsis is irrelevant at the end of a tunnel and, where there is little light, a white egg may be easier for the parents to see. The uniqueness of the species among shorebirds is even more evident when the chick emerges. Walking is impossible at first and a very young Crab Plover must stay in the nest chamber waiting for a parent to appear with some mashed crab. As the chick becomes more mobile and ventures to the tunnel entrance, whole crabs are delivered to it, but the youngster will still be looking to its parents for some of its food several months later.

Crab Plover movements are not totally understood. At least some of them migrate and their winter range stretches to Kenya, Tanzania, Madagascar, India and even Thailand and Malaysia.

Go to the right place, and Crab Plovers are not too hard to see. They won't be hard to identify either—you just have to get there . . .

65. Broad-billed Tody *Todus subulatus*

A colorful Caribbean sprite with a character all of its own

Size: 11.5 cm (4.5 inches).
Distribution: Hispaniola and Gonave, in the Caribbean.
Habitat: Mainly arid woodland and scrub.
Classification: One of five species in the family Todidae and the genus *Todus*.
Population and conservation status: Not recorded. Least Concern.
Breeding system: Monogamous.
Nest and eggs: Burrow dug into a bank. 3–4 eggs.
Incubation and fledging: Both unknown.

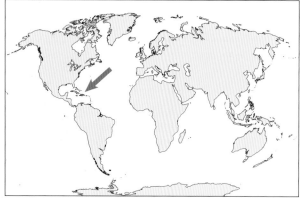

Forget beaches, rum punches and reggae; the best reason to visit the Caribbean, for the birder at least, has to be the opportunity to catch up with a unique and marvelous family found only on the Greater Antilles, the todies. These brilliant, green, gemlike birds look like a cross between kingfishers (Alcedines) and hummingbirds (Trochilidae), and by their abundance and effervescence, stamp their mark on the local avifauna. There are five species on four islands, and the most colorful and easiest to see is probably the Broad-billed Tody, of the island of Hispaniola.

Todies have a special style of feeding that quickly distinguishes them from other local birds. They sit on a perch, often at low or moderate levels within a forest or wood, and survey the scene briefly, bobbing up and down where they sit, in kingfisher fashion. They then take off on a darting sortie that has, as its target, the underside of a leaf. Having travelled upwards about 2 meters (6 feet), the tody will snap up an insect with its long, tweezerlike bill, perhaps hovering to steady itself, and will then return to its perch, having travelled no more than the 2 meters (6 feet) each way in the process.

It will then repeat the sortie routine incessantly throughout the day. Todies, indeed, are famous for their voracious appetites, taking thousands of insects during the hours that they are active.

These small birds, with their active lifestyle and tiny bodies, always struggle with the effort of finding enough food to keep themselves going, and they have come up with some innovative ways to save energy. The Puerto Rican Tody (*T. mexicanus*), for example, exhibits an astonishing ability to vary its metabolic rate, maintaining a body temperature of anything between 28°C and 43°C (82.5°F and 109.5°F), according to circumstance. Todies can also, it seems, descend into a state of torpor when it is cold, in order to avoid wasting energy, although it seems that only the female does this, when it is preparing for breeding.

The Broad-billed Tody, in common with other members of the family, lives in a small territory occupied throughout the year with a mate. Prior to breeding, the pair get into the mood by enacting courtship routines, such as aerial chasing, in which the wings might be flapped fast enough to make a rattling sound and the two birds pursue each other with astonishing vigor through the branches. They also enact a "flank-display", in which they ruffle the colorful pink feathers on their flanks, and flick their wings upwards, making their bodies look amusingly bloated and fluffy.

Preliminaries over, the two birds now dig a tunnel into a bank for their nest, using first their bills to carve out a depression, and then their feet to dig. The burrow can be 30–60 centimeters (12–24 inches) long, and the whole construction may take several weeks to complete, working for a short time each day. Some tody tunnel entrances are exposed to the full heat of the sun, and it has been postulated that this may help to keep away large spiders, which also live in burrows, but tend to shun the light.

64. New Caledonian Crow *Corvus moneduloides*

Not much to look at, but probably the most intelligent bird in the world

Size: 40 cm (15.7 inches).
Distribution: New Caledonia, in the southwest Pacific; introduced to Loyalty Islands.
Habitat: Woodland and open country with scattered trees.
Classification: One of 123 species in the family Corvidae, and one of 45 in the genus *Corvus*.
Population and conservation status: Not recorded. Least Concern.
Breeding system: Monogamous.
Nest and eggs: Platform of twigs placed quite high in a tree. 2–3 eggs.
Incubation and fledging: Both unknown.

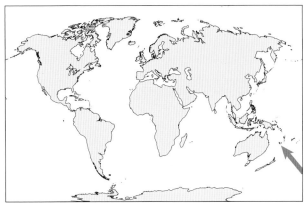

This dull black bird from an obscure corner of the southwest Pacific is an unlikely avian superstar. But recent research has demonstrated that that is what it undoubtedly is. Almost single-handedly, it has transformed our attitudes to the cognitive abilities of all birds.

What brought the New Caledonian Crow to the attention of scientists was its use of tools. Only a few bird species, including the Woodpecker Finch (*Camarhynchus pallidus*) of the Galápagos (see page 56), are known to use neutral objects to obtain food, so observations in the wild of New Caledonian Crows using thin twigs to impale grubs hidden in small holes quite naturally raised eyebrows. What nobody expected was the astonishing extent to which this behavior has developed among these birds—something that only later research revealed.

The first indications that the crow was something special occurred by accident. In an experimental investigation into tool-using, two captive crows were given lengths of wire to extract some meat from a pipe, one wire straight and one bent into a hook at the end. It was intended that the bird should choose one or the other, but one crow, named Betty, found itself with the straight wire and was evidently

not satisfied. By fixing one end of the wire and pulling it upwards, she bent it into a hook, which she then used to extract the snack by lifting a small bucket from a vertical pipe. Neither bird had seen wire before, so this turned out to be the first non-human example ever recorded of an animal intentionally manipulating material that it would not have seen in the wild into a purpose-built tool.

In further experiments, captive New Caledonian Crows were offered food out of reach, but given a stick that could be used to obtain a longer stick in another box. Several crows effortlessly worked out how one tool could be used to obtain the other, and successfully acquired what they wanted with the longer stick. This sort of problem solving is equal to the very best efforts that famously intelligent primates such as the Chimpanzee (*Pan troglodytes*) can achieve.

In the wild, New Caledonian Crows craft most of their tools out of the tough leaves of *Pandanus* trees. They tear off strips from the side of the leaf, and it has been shown that the specifications of the strips vary: some are wide, some are narrow and some are stepped. Evidently, the wide strip is the prototype, and the other types are modifications for slightly different tasks. The distribution of each type in the wild in New Caledonia strongly suggests that innovations have taken root in certain places and then spread to other parts of the island. This cultural transmission of ideas is similar to the flow of ideas seen in human anthropological studies.

Yet another indication of this bird's sophistication is that, on the whole, New Caledonian Crows are left-biased. Most prefer to tear strips with the left side of the bill, as opposed to the right. It is yet another amazing parallel with human society, in the life of what is turning out to be, just perhaps, the world's most extraordinary bird.

63. Desert Sparrow   *Passer simplex*
A scarce and erratic pastel-colored bird of the desert

Size: 13.5 cm (5.3 inches).

Distribution: Saharan Africa; also Uzbekistan and Turkmenistan.

Habitat: Sandy, desert regions.

Classification: One of 45 species in the family Passeridae, and one of 23 in the genus *Passer*.

Population and conservation status: Not recorded. Least Concern.

Breeding system: Presumed monogamous.

Nest and eggs: Oval or globular mass of grass and bark, interwoven into tree branches or placed in a hole. 4–5 eggs, fewer in dry years.

Incubation and fledging: 12–13 days. 12–14 days.

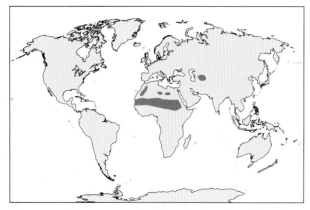

You can tell that a person is a keen birdwatcher when they get excited about sparrows, instead of being turned off by them. And the Desert Sparrow is a real birdwatcher's bird—intricately, if not spectacularly, colored, scarce in population, and also difficult to find because of its extreme habitat and essentially nomadic way of life. It is a challenge to find, and birders love challenges.

The Desert Sparrow is also something of a curiosity because it is found in two places of the world that are quite widely separated: the arid lands of Central Asia and, its core range, the mighty Sahara Desert. The birds from each place look pretty much identical, despite the vast distance between them. Some of this gap encompasses habitats that, to human eyes, look perfectly suitable for it, but ecology is in the eye of the beholder.

Everywhere it goes the Desert Sparrow likes sandy places. In the Sahara, this means picture-postcard arid-land scenes, such as large dunes, oases with palm trees, and buildings such as sharp-cornered forts. The sparrow is also highly tolerant of extreme temperatures and, in contrast to the effervescent House Sparrow (*Passer domesticus*), the Desert Sparrow tends to be a bit sluggish and shy, spending much

of its day hidden among the branches of palm trees, or among scrubby thickets such as *Tamarix* and *Acacia* spp. It is most active in the morning and evening.

All sparrows are seed-eaters and the Desert Sparrow follows the party line by scouring the arid ground for cereals and grass-seeds. In the Sahara, its main food is Awn-grass *Aristida*, a local speciality. However, it also seems to take far more animal food than most other sparrows, including caterpillars, beetles and spiders, as well as any scraps that it may find around human cultivation. Intriguingly, its gut is shorter than that of the House Sparrow, a sure sign that it is designed to digest more animal, and less tough vegetable food.

Another surprise is that, for a sparrow, it is a good songster. It dutifully chirps and cheeps, as it should, but will also enter into a spirited conversational twitter, with quite pleasing trills and musical phrases. Sometimes it will actually give this performance in flight, another departure from the usual sparrow way.

In the breeding season, Desert Sparrows build somewhat ramshackle nests out of coarse and fine grass and bark fibres. An inner dome, intricately woven, lies inside a sort of horizontal lobby with a sloping entrance, while the very outside covering is made up of loose plant fibres. Thus the nest has three separate sections, perhaps to keep out the worst of the sun. It is usually placed in a hole in a tree, or in the shaded side of the nest of a bird of prey—anywhere to keep out of the 40°C (104°F) heat. In common with other sparrows, the Desert Sparrow has a tendency to be sociable. It will sometimes nest in small colonies, in palm trees or in the nest of a large bird of prey, and outside the breeding season flocks of 200 have been recorded."

62. Little Forktail *Enicurus scouleri*

A delightful bird of rushing streams and rarefied high mountain habitat

Size: 12–14 cm (4.7–5.5 inches).
Distribution: Himalayas and China.
Habitat: Montane rivers and streams.
Classification: One of 294 species in the family Muscicapidae, and one of seven in the genus *Enicurus*.
Population and conservation status: Not recorded. Least Concern.
Breeding system: Presumed monogamous.
Nest and eggs: Cup of moss, leaves and grass placed in hole. 2–5 eggs.
Incubation and fledging: Both unknown.

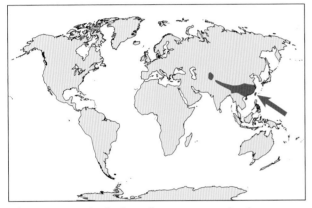

There are some birds that, if you were to take them away from their habitat, would be robbed of much of their appeal. Put a Little Forktail on a forest tree in the canopy and it may look a bit ordinary, if undeniably smart. However, put it where it belongs, beside a fast-flowing stream high up in some of the world's most scenic mountains, and to set eyes on it becomes an experience. It is a species inextricably linked, in fact and in the mind, with the places it dwells.

There are several species of forktail, and they are all, like the Little Forktail, birds of the sides of torrents and streams. Although they are all distinctive and clearly closely related, their affinities to other birds are less clear. At present they are grouped in with the flycatchers and chats, which is a bit embarrassing in one regard: in a family renowned for its exceptionally tuneful voices, the forktails sing hardly a note. But then, there is little point when any song would be drowned by the noise of the rushing water.

Instead, forktails communicate visually, and to this end their body movements are distinctly fidgety. They stand on rocks, wagging their rear ends in short bursts and, as an interesting embellishment, open and close the tail at the same time. To complete the effect the forktails flick their strikingly patterned wings. All this adds up to a sign language that everyone can understand, so that territories and other rights can be duly claimed without anyone raising their voice.

There are seven species of forktail, each with its own specific niche, and for the Little Forktail this means foraging from wet rocks, as opposed to, for example, the mud of the riverbank or the shallows. This confines it to the more vigorous stretches of water, where the rocks can be permanently splashed by rapids or, better still, waterfalls. Indeed, in some parts of its range the Little Forktail is very much a waterfall bird, and customarily builds its nest in the very safe space behind the actual fall. The nest itself is a compact cup, made up primarily of moss, but lined with leaf skeletons and rootlets.

The items that the Little Forktail eats are, quite naturally, minute, and usually include insect larvae such as caddisflies and mayflies. Various ants, beetles and flies have also been recorded in the diet, and these are occasionally snatched in a brief flycatching sally. This must relieve the drudgery of rock-picking, which is a pretty thankless activity. To acquire enough food, a Little Forktail has to take between 80 and 124 pecks a minute while it is foraging.

On the whole, the Little Forktail is very much a mountain bird, and its main altitudinal range lies between 1,800 meters (2,056 feet) and a lofty 3,300 meters (10,827 feet). It does make short migrations lower down in winter, down to only 1,000 meters (3,280 feet) above sea level, but on the whole, if you wish to catch up with this enchanting bird, you must head for the high hills.

61. Golden Swallow *Tachycineta euchrysea*

A swallow with stunning plumage and an increasingly precarious existence

Size: 12 cm (4.7 inches).
Distribution: Jamaica and Hispaniola, in the Caribbean.
Habitat: Montane forest, foraging over other habitats.
Classification: One of 86 species in the family Hirundinidae, and one of nine in the genus *Tachycineta*.
Population and conservation status: Estimated at 2,500–10,000 individuals. Vulnerable.
Breeding system: Monogamous.
Nest and eggs: Cup of vegetable fibres placed in a hole. Three eggs.
Incubation and fledging: Both unknown.

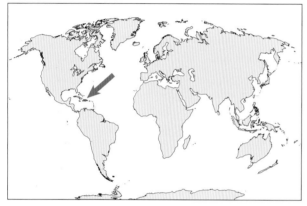

Various swallows and martins adorn the skies just about everywhere in the world, but no swallow is quite as special as the one found high up on mountains of the Caribbean islands of Hispaniola and Jamaica—the Golden Swallow. When the sun catches the back of this bird as it flies past, the golden iridescence is simply breathtaking; it is also a unique color among swallows. And as if to help birdwatchers admire it, this bird commonly swoops low to the ground to catch insects in midair, giving good views, so this is a species that rarely disappoints.

The sad truth, however, is that the Golden Swallow is in serious decline. It was once common all over the two islands, but that status, sadly, is ancient history now. Throughout the twentieth century it became progressively rarer on Jamaica. Now it is confined to just a single locality, and even here there have been no records for quite some years and it may already be extinct. So the highlands of Hispaniola are its probable last retreat and, although its decline has been just as dramatic overall on this island as on Jamaica, more suitable habitat remains as a lifeline to its survival.

The reasons for the Golden Swallow's plunging decline are surprisingly obscure. The foremost problem is likely to be habitat destruction, as mountain forests on both islands have been felled and degraded by shifting agriculture, but it is not clear what it is that these birds really need from the forest. In common with a number of their close relatives in the Americas, Golden Swallows usually nest in a hole in a tree, so perhaps the lack of nest sites is a problem. Yet these birds have also been recorded building in the eaves of houses and in rocky openings—even once in boulders near a bauxite mine—so that cannot be the whole story. At one time it was mooted that Golden Swallows may suffer from competition for nest sites with such birds as the introduced Common Starling (*Sturnus vulgaris*), but since that species tends to nest at lower elevations than the Swallow, this seems to have been ruled out. Perhaps the mountain air holds certain insects on which it specializes, for example beetles and parasitic wasps. But for now, at least, nobody seems to know.

At any rate, the Golden Swallow suffers from being very poorly known, and this doesn't help its conservation. It is known to nest mainly at elevations between 800 meters (2,624 feet) and 2,000 meters (6,562 feet), and, after breeding, will sometimes retreat lower down in winter, especially on Jamaica. The nest structure itself is made from fine fibres, such as cotton and silk, lined with some of the same materials, in addition to feathers, such as the green ones of the local parrots. Tucked safely into a hole, and with these super-soft furnishings, no young Golden Swallow can claim to have been brought up in anything other than luxury.

However, until its precise ecological requirements can be worked out, not even the best brought-up Golden Swallow will be born into a secure future.

60. Red Crossbill *Loxia curvirostra*

A specialist feeder with a tool for the job

Size: 16.5 cm (6.5 inches).
Distribution: Breeds at high latitudes in northern hemisphere, with some further south;
during irruptions, birds move into other areas.
Habitat: Conifer forests, especially spruce and pine.
Classification: One of 179 species in the family Fringillidae, and one of five in the genus *Loxia*.
Population and conservation status: Estimated at 15 million birds. Least Concern.
Breeding system: Monogamous.
Nest and eggs: Twig cup with moss, lichen, bark strips, wool and rootlets with finer lining. 3–4 eggs.
Incubation and fledging: 14–15 days. 20–25 days.

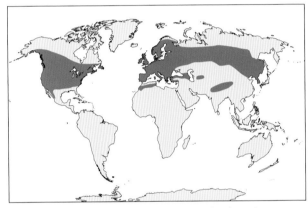

A bird's bill is its feeding tool, and one look at the eating apparatus of any crossbill would make those who didn't know wonder what a bird did with a bill like that, or even whether the bird were suffering from some kind of deformity! The bill, of course, is a very special tool that equips a crossbill to do something very impressive—specifically, to get seeds out of conifer cones.

It works like this. First, find your cone—Red Crossbills are great acrobats and they can move around twigs and cones with ease, holding on with their bill as required. When the cone is found it can be raided on the spot or removed for attention elsewhere. A Red Crossbill weighing 40 grams (1.5 ounces) has no problem airlifting a 40-gram cone to a more functional processing point. Next, get the seeds out. This is the really clever bit. With the right tool, difficult jobs are much easier—the tip of the bill slides in between two scales, levering them apart by a sideways bill movement, which makes enough space for the tongue go in and extract the seed. On really stubborn cones, a closed bill goes in and twists to make more space, and on other cones the bill itself is used to pull out the seed.

Red Crossbills will eat seeds of spruce (*Picea* spp.), pine (*Pinus* spp.), larch (*Larix* spp.), hemlock (*Tsuga* spp.) and Douglas-fir (*Pseudotsuga* spp.) and, when conifers are unavailable, they will eat insects and the fruits and buds of deciduous trees. Within the species some birds are bigger than others, and some bills are bigger than others, probably indicating some very finely tuned feeding preferences and raising questions of taxonomy. Red Crossbills need to drink a great deal of water, and will even ingest snow to take on fluid.

When food runs out, or perhaps after a particularly successful breeding season, Red Crossbills erupt, and may travel thousands of miles to find new feeding areas. Their flight call may well help them to locate other crossbills who have already found a food source. When suitable habitat is found, the nomadic crossbills will settle for a while, perhaps even breeding, but they don't normally take up permanent residence, although some in East Anglia are the legacy of a 1909 eruption.

Red Crossbill breeding is triggered by food supply. If there is plenty of food the breeding season can continue for nine months, and two broods can be raised. Conversely, if there is too little food, few or no birds will breed. Nests are built high up in a lone or forest-edge conifer, a spruce, pine, Douglas-fir or hemlock perhaps. The female (above) does all the incubation, but both birds look after the young.

Crossbill taxonomy is complex. Much work has been done in the UK to determine whether or not the Scottish Crossbill (*Loxia scotica*) is a species that can be differentiated from Red Crossbill; some North American thinking suggests that the Nearctic Red Crossbill may, in fact, be as many as eight different species, each with its own flight call. If that is the case, the nominate Red Crossbill will be a bit harder to see, and to identify!

59. Common Ostrich *Struthio camelus*

The world's largest living bird and a multiple record-breaker

Size: Male up to 2.75 m (9 feet) high and 150kg (330 lbs); female up to 1.9 m (6 feet) and 110kg (242 lbs).
Distribution: East, central, west and southwest Africa; feral population in southern Australia.
Habitat: Open arid and semi-arid areas including African plains.
Classification: One of two species in the family Struthionidae and the genus *Struthio*.
Population and conservation status: Not recorded, common in some areas. Least Concern.
Breeding system: Complex, including monogamy and polygamy.
Nest and eggs: Shallow scrape. 5–11 eggs from "major hen", 2–6 from each "minor hen".
Incubation and fledging: 42–46 days. 4–5 months.

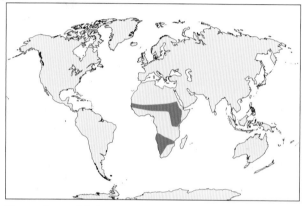

This is the world's biggest, heaviest bird species and, at up to 10 times the accepted weight limit for avian flight—around 15 kilograms (33 lbs)—it can't fly. But it can run faster than anything else with feathers. At a sprint, 96 kilometers (60 miles) an hour has been claimed, but it can't keep that up for long. In terms of stamina, however, the Ostrich can outperform the mammals, sometimes running at 48 kilometers (30 miles) an hour for around half an hour. Each of its long, strong legs has two toes, a toe-count unique among birds and an adaptation for fast running. The legs are also highly effective weapons: an Ostrich in defence mode can deliver a kick that can disembowel a man and has been known to dispatch Lions (*Panthera leo*).

Their size, long legs and long necks make Ostriches unmistakeable, high-contrast monochrome males being especially easy to spot. Ostriches have excellent eyesight and, at 5 centimeters (2 inches) across, their eyes are bigger than those of any other terrestrial vertebrate.

Breeding systems are complex. While some populations are monogamous, others are far from it. Large territories—up to 15 square kilometers (6 square miles)—are defended by "booming" territorial males. Unusually for birds, the male has a penis, which may be particularly obvious when a female is being wooed. After some impressive display, he mates noisily with one "major hen" who later lays 5–11 eggs in the scratched-out nest. Other polygamous females (the minor hens) also lay eggs there, and a single nest typically contains up to 40 eggs (78 in an extreme case). Carefree, territory-free males also mate, but have no parental responsibilities.

Eggs and young are tended by the territorial male and major hen, but this is not pure altruism. Somehow, the female can recognize her own eggs and positions them at the center of the nest. A sitting Ostrich can cover more eggs than the major hen laid, however, so that some "impostor" eggs are also incubated. Others are pushed out and create an outer circle that is easier food for predators. No bird lays a bigger egg (it equates to 24 hens' eggs) and getting into them is a challenge—one that the Egyptian Vulture (*Neophron percnopterus*) has solved by dropping rocks on to them. The egg is undeniably large, but relative to the size of the bird it is one of smallest in the avian world.

Young Ostriches may start life with the adults that incubated them but could soon find themselves in a crèche containing up to several hundred birds. Crèches are formed when one family party challenges another over ownership of the youngsters, the winning adults taking all the chicks.

The Ostrich's tough gut and grinding gizzard can cope with many different foods. Most of the diet is plant material, including *Acacia* seeds and figs (*Ficus* spp.), but insects, lizards and small tortoises (Testudinidae) are also taken. Sand and small pebbles are swallowed to help the gizzard grind up food—one bird even swallowed a shiny, red stone . . . revealing the location of a ruby mine!

Finally, just in case you were wondering, this giant bird has never been seen with its head buried in the sand.

58. Cutia *Cutia nipalensis*

A decidedly smart bird of high mountain forests that has an unusual way of foraging

Size: 17–19.5 cm (6.7–7.7 inches).
Distribution: Himalayas and some mountains of tropical Southeast Asia.
Habitat: Montane broad-leaved evergreen forest.
Classification: One of 281 species in the family Timaliidae, and the sole member of the genus *Cutia*.
Population and conservation status: Not recorded. Least Concern.
Breeding system: Presumed monogamous.
Nest and eggs: Cup of moss and pine needles, placed at junction of branch and tree-trunk. Unknown.
Incubation and fledging: Both unknown.

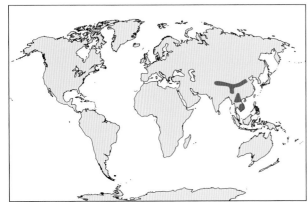

Not many people have heard of a Cutia, and not many people are familiar with the family to which it belongs—the babblers. Yet there are few more varied and beautiful bird families than the babblers anywhere in the world, and arguably they come close to rivalling even the more bejewelled families, such as hummingbirds (Trochilidae) and sunbirds (Nectariniidae), for boldness of pattern and color. The smart, colorful Cutia is just a star-studded example.

The Cutia lives in mature, evergreen broad-leaved forests in the babblers' heartland, Asia. It is rarely found below 1,200 meters (3,940 feet), and commonly reaches double that elevation, making it a familiar component of the Himalayan avifauna. However, in contrast to many Himalayan birds, it also makes it into the separate mountain ranges of Southeast Asia, including Vietnam, where the indigenous form, differing slightly in plumage from the Himalayan birds, is sometimes treated as a separate species.

Throughout its range the Cutia is decidedly difficult to see, mainly because of its habit of sticking to the tops of tall trees. However, in its favor is its rather un-

babblerlike manner of being somewhat sluggish and slow-moving, and its highly unusual mode of feeding also draws attention. For foraging it is strongly adapted to tearing bark off the limbs of trees to reveal the insects and other animals that lurk beneath, and in order to do this it clings to vertical stems, rather like a nuthatch (*Sitta* spp.). Its strong legs enable it to climb steep gradients and to perch in awkward positions. Occasionally, it will even descend head first, the only bird other than a nuthatch that is able to do this. With its strong bill, a foraging Cutia is able to deal with quite hard-bodied creatures such as beetles and small snails, as well as the usual range of more delicate insects. It will also sometimes take berries and the seeds from pine cones.

One babbler trait that the Cutia shows is sociability. It is commonly found in small groups of its own species, especially outside the breeding season, and it will also join mixed parties of other birds as they move through the forest. However, being slow and methodical, it does have a tendency to lag behind the main flock, seemingly having trouble keeping up. Another feature very typical of the family is that, in the times when finding food is not as urgent as usual, members of a pair will huddle together and preen one another.

Very little is known about the breeding biology of the Cutia, and this is often the case among the babblers. Only two Cutia nests have been found and described, both of which were rather bulky, open cups made from ferns, conifer needles and, probably, the roots of epiphytic plants. One example was placed within a bundle of leafy epiphytes, and the other at the junction of a branch and trunk. Although little information was gathered at the time about incubation and nestling periods, it was confirmed that both adults feed the young and brood them on the nest.

57. Giant Coot *Fulica gigantea*

A bad-tempered monster of the High Andes with an astonishing nest

Size: 48–64 cm (18–25 inches).
Distribution: Local in the High Andes, from south Peru to Chile and Argentina.
Habitat: High altitude (3,600–5,000 m) lakes and ponds.
Classification: One of 128 species in the family Rallidae, and one of 11 in the genus *Fulica*.
Population and conservation status: Not recorded. Least Concern.
Breeding system: Monogamous, pairing for life.
Nest and eggs: Huge cup of aquatic vegetation. 3–7 eggs.
Incubation and fledging: About 30 days per egg. Fully fledged at four months.

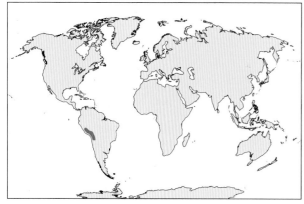

If, on the altiplano of the Andes, there is anything more intimidating than the formidable Giant Coot, it is the Giant Coot in a bad mood. It would be wise, therefore, to catch up with this bulky, black, goose-sized bird on a quiet day; but sadly, there is seldom such a thing. Irritation seems to be the Coot's default setting, and all the high altitude lakes where colonies occur seem to see foaming water stirred up by the birds' chases, kicks and splattering attacks. Coots are highly territorial and paranoid and the stealing of nest material is an endemic strife. Colonies resound to various complaining calls, including clucking hoots, growls and shouts.

The Giant Coot is a bird of dizzyingly high altitudes. The altiplano, where it primarily occurs, is a plateau running down from southern Peru, through Bolivia to Chile, the remnants of what was once a vast inland sea, and most of it is above 4,500 meters (14,764 feet). It is wild, cold, inhospitable open grassland ("*puna*") country, dotted with lakes that have snowmelt as their source, and are therefore very saline. Here, anywhere from 3,600 meters (11,810 feet) up to, remarkably, 6,540 meters (21,457 feet), Giant Coots can be found.

They have to survive the worst of the weather at these altitudes, for the super-sized adults are too heavy to fly and cannot easily disperse. Only when they are young, before the ravages of middle-age spread, can these birds take to the air.

The Giant Coot is invariably king of a castle—its remarkable nest. These birds are found only on lakes with an abundant supply of aquatic vegetation, because their nests are the center of their world, and need constant building up and refurbishing. Placed in a small territory occupied by the adults all year round, the nests are essentially rafts, built in water approximately 1 meter (3 feet) deep, with a high rim and a deep cup, and they are relatively enormous, sometimes large enough even to accommodate a sitting man. The largest, which are typically built up over a number of years, have been measured at 3 meters (10 feet) long. They provide a secure home for the youngsters, and the tall rim acts as an effective shelter.

Male and female Giant Coots pair for life and, in a good year, they can bring up two broods of young in their fortress. They generally nest in the austral winter, in June and July, but this is not a fixed rule. Not surprisingly, the cosseted youngsters are somewhat reluctant to face the outside world, and take as long as four months to fledge. Who can blame them?

The waterweed in the Giant Coot's wetlands also acts as its food for, like most coots, it is vegetarian. However, in contrast to the other species, this bulky bird is disinclined to dive for it. Instead, it just floats in the water and pulls food up often tossing it sideways with a flick of the bill. If it is feeling especially energetic it might occasionally up-end, but at these altitudes, there is no need for overexertion.

56. Pearled Treerunner *Margarornis squamiger*

A delightful bird of a special habitat, with an unusual feeding technique

Size: 15–16 cm (6–6.3 inches).
Distribution: The Andes, from Colombia and Venezuela south to Bolivia.
Habitat: Humid montane forest, occasionally higher altitude forest.
Classification: One of 248 species in the family Furnariidae, and one of four in the genus *Margarornis*.
Population and conservation status: Not recorded. Least Concern.
Breeding system: Apparently monogamous.
Nest and eggs: Ball of moss placed under a tree limb or rock. Unknown.
Incubation and fledging: Both unknown.

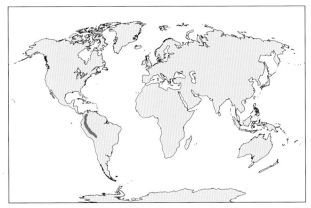

Some of the most exciting birding in the whole world is to be had in the humid montane forests of the Andes. Dawn in these forests is almost always met by a veil of thick mist but, as the light increases, the fog eventually burns off and reveals, little by little, a treasure trove of fantastic birds. This is a sumptuous habitat, with every square inch of tree festooned with epiphytes, including mosses, lichens and bromeliads, and this profusion, together with a thick understorey, gives the habitat an overgrown feel, like an opulently planted greenhouse.

One of the many species found in this rich habitat is the delightful Pearled Treerunner. This is an Andean speciality found mainly between 2,500 meters (8,200 feet) and 3,500 meters (11,480 feet) in altitude and, like the majority of the birds of the cloud forest, has a very specific niche. When foraging, it eschews normal perching in favor of scaling vertical trunks and branches, in treecreeper style. By moving upwards in small vertical hops, using its tail for support, the Pearled Treerunner can reach and locate animal matter that would be unavailable to competitors of similar size. The Treerunner can also profit by climbing right out to the slender tips of twigs and branches.

However, the Treerunner does share the tree-climbing habit with some other cloud forest birds, and to this end it has a further specialization. Close studies have shown that, 95 percent of the time, the Treerunner hunts by probing its bill among bundles of epiphytes, including clumps of mosslike material, rather than anywhere else. It also, in contrast to other birds foraging in similar places, confines its interest entirely to arthropods (insects, spiders and the like), and shuns seeds, molluscs or anything else. This fussiness is, apparently, a trait within its family, the ovenbirds.

Pearled Treerunners are hardly ever seen on their own. Not only do they usually stick together in pairs, or small groups, but they are also enthusiastic members of mixed feeding flocks. These flocks move through the cloud forest as a disparate group, dozens of brightly colored species associating together, each working its own niche but taking advantage of collective vigilance. In such flocks, Treerunners are often easy to spot, working the middle and upper levels of the trees. One study in Bolivia found that they foraged, on average, 2.4 meters (7.8 feet) from the top of the canopy. These flocks typically move on relentlessly throughout the day, remaining in view for only a few minutes at a time.

Although Treerunners are quite common and easy to see, they tend to be unobtrusive birds. When foraging they make soft, high-pitched "tsit" notes, sometimes elaborated into a trill, to make the song. Nevertheless, they make less noise than many other members of the flock.

Only a few Pearled Treerunner nests have ever been found. Those that have, however, are little balls of vegetation, with a side entrance. And, not surprisingly for a bird that spends most of its time among epiphytic clumps, the main building component is moss, a familiar and easy material for the bird to find.

55. Gyrfalcon *Falco rusticolus*

An iconic white killer and the world's biggest falcon

Size: 48–60 cm (17–24 inches).

Wingspan: 120–135 cm (47–53 inches).

Distribution: Circumpolar in northern hemisphere; some winter at lower latitudes.

Habitat: Taiga and tundra, especially on coasts and around rivers and mountains; some winter in more southerly open areas.

Classification: One of 64 species in the family Falconidae, and one of 38 in the genus *Falco*.

Population and conservation status: Estimated at 10,000–100,000 birds. Least Concern.

Breeding system: Monogamous.

Nest and eggs: Typically on cliff ledge—a scrape or reused stick nest of Northern Raven (*Corvus corax*), for example. 3–4 eggs.

Incubation and fledging: 34–36 days. 46–53 days.

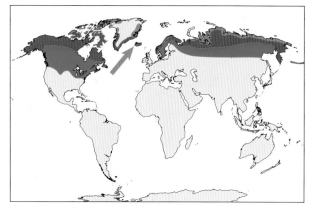

It's not just about seeing a Gyrfalcon. It's about seeing a white Gyrfalcon, and the whiter the better. Not all of them are white, of course; what was once thought of as a bird with three color morphs (white, intermediate or grey, and dark) is now regarded as a bird with continual variation in plumage from the whitest to the darkest birds. A trip to Arctic Greenland could make your white Gyrfalcon fantasy come true, or alternatively, a visit to Iceland, where white Gyrfalcons winter.

This is the world's largest falcon, but it varies in size—birds from continental Europe are smaller than those of Iceland and Greenland, for example. There is also great variation in size between the genders. On average, a male weighs in at 1.1 kilograms (2.5 pounds), whereas a female tips the scales at 1.7 kilograms (3.8 pounds)—over 50 percent heavier than the male. A really big female can weigh over 2 kilograms (4 pounds) and have a larger wingspan than some Rough-legged Buzzards (*Buteo lagopus*). A falcon this size is a formidable predator, capable of taking some sizeable prey, including Sage Grouse (*Centrocercus urophasianus*). In the north, however, while some concentrate on mammals or seabirds, Rock Ptarmigan (*Lagopus muta*) and Willow

Ptarmigan (*L. lagopus*) are their main food. The impact of a short stoop may be enough to kill a ptarmigan, but a lethal bite to the neck ensures closure. The slaughterhouse then becomes the kitchen, where the bird's feathers are removed, and finally the dining room. A ptarmigan that somehow manages to evade initial capture is not always let off the hook, and may be hounded relentlessly by a hungry Gyrfalcon, perhaps for as much as 10 kilometers (6 miles), until it drops from exhaustion and gives in to this Arctic killer.

When winter comes in the north, survival gets tougher, but most adult Gyrfalcons stay put. The juveniles can be incredibly mobile, however: in less than two months one radio-tracked bird left Alaska, flew to Siberia, then returned to Alaska before heading down to Kodiak Island. Typically, it is the young birds that are seen at lower latitudes in the winter but, when food is really hard to find, adults may be seen too. Gyrfalcon movements may also be influenced by a cyclical variation in prey numbers—when there is insufficient food, more birds may head south, and breeding may have to be postponed.

Gyrfalcons have been prized by falconers since at least 600AD, and were even flown at cranes (*Grus* spp.). Through history, many have been traded; over a 62-year period in the 1700s, more than 4,800 were exported from Iceland, to name just one country. It is still a bird of falconry but these days, thankfully, most falconers' birds are captive-bred.

The job of taxonomy is never done—captive-breeding and work with DNA may change our species list. It seems that the Gyrfalcon and the Saker Falcon (*Falco cherrug*) may be one and the same species.

But nothing can detract from the glory of this Arctic and sub-Arctic hunter. This is a bird that can stoop at 200–300 kilometers (125–185 miles) an hour. Do your best to see one—and preferably a white one.

54. Golden-winged Sunbird *Drepanorhynchus reichenowi*

A stunningly beautiful and highly specialized bird of the East African Highlands

Size: 14–15 cm (5.5–6 inches), up to 24 cm (9.5 inches) including tail.

Distribution: Highlands of East Africa.

Habitat: Forest edge, cultivations and gardens.

Classification: One of 131 species in the family Nectariniidae, and the sole member of the genus *Drepanorhynchus*.

Population and conservation status: Not recorded. Least Concern.

Breeding system: Monogamous.

Nest and eggs: A globular structure with side entrance, hung from a low branch. One egg.

Incubation and fledging: Both unknown.

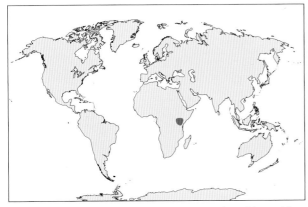

No hummingbird has ever made it over to the Old World under its own steam, but that does not mean that Africa or Asia is lacking in startlingly iridescent, brilliantly colored nectar-feeding birds. Far from it—they have the sunbirds, a family that is, in some ways, almost as glorious as those miniature hoverers from across the Atlantic. There are, indeed, striking similarities between the two families: both have long tongues for sipping nectar and both can be highly territorial around flower blooms. One other similarity is also noticeable, in some species at least: a bill shape that is in precise agreement with the bird's favorite flower blooms.

One such sunbird is the fabulous Golden-winged Sunbird, perhaps the most charismatic member of the entire family. Its bill is long for a sunbird, a little longer than the head, and it is curved down in exaggerated fashion. This enables it to feed from flowers that might be hard to reach for other sunbirds, but also restricts it to its own narrow range of food plants.

One very popular plant for the Golden-winged Sunbird is the Lion's Ear (*Leonotis nepetifolia*), a member of the mint family that can grow to nearly 3 meters (10 feet) tall. This plant has clusters of tubular blooms of perfect shape for the sunbird. Where the Lion's Ear grows in abundance, it may attract large gatherings of nectar-drinkers, sometimes 1,000 or more strong. In these circumstances, individual Golden-winged Sunbirds will often defend feeding territories against others of their own kind as well as other species of sunbirds. One study found that, when this happened, each bird attempted to defend up to 6,000 flowers, but usually between 500 and 2,500. Their efforts were not always successful, and at least a third of their blooms were lost to competitors.

Perhaps not surprisingly, considering its specialization, the Golden-winged Sunbird is quite rare. It occurs in the East African highlands, being recorded in Kenya, its stronghold, Uganda, Tanzania and DR Congo. As a breeding bird here it is seldom found below 1,800 meters (5,900 feet) and can be found as high as 3,400 meters (11,155 feet), for example on the slopes of Mount Kenya or Kilimanjaro, but its presence at such altitude is highly seasonal and reliant upon warm weather. Between March and September it retreats downhill and can make quite substantial altitudinal migrations: one bird, for example, was recorded moving over 100 kilometers (62 miles).

In the breeding season, the Golden-winged Sunbird builds an intricate nest, typical of the family. It is globular, with a side entrance, and suspended from the branches of a shrub. It is made up of fine pieces of grass and lichen, bound together with spider's web and lined with plant down.

Incidentally, it so happens that the Golden-winged Sunbird's favorite plant, the Lion's Ear, is popular with gardeners and has spread from East Africa all over the warmer parts of the world. This includes the Americas and, as an endorsement of the Golden-winged Sunbird's nectarivorous credentials, the plant is much loved in its new home by hummingbirds.

53. Blue-and-yellow Macaw *Ara ararauna*

A totemic species of the Amazon forest—big, loud and colorful

Size: 86 cm (2 feet 10 inches).

Distribution: Northern South America.

Habitat: Lowland forest, especially near water.

Classification: One of 359 species in the family Psittacidae, and one of eight in the genus *Ara*.

Population and conservation status: Not recorded. Least Concern.

Breeding system: Monogamous.

Nest and eggs: A hole in a tall tree, no structure. 1–3 eggs, usually two.

Incubation and fledging: 24–28 days. About 14 weeks.

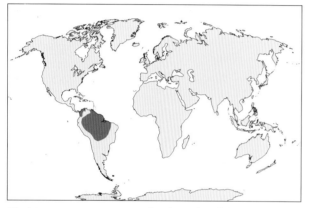

Nothing quite prepares you for the sight of the Blue-and-yellow Macaw in the wild. As one of the most common large parrots in captivity, and as an icon of the jungle, its image is used everywhere from movie posters to advertisements for safari parks. You will probably be familiar with the bird in the picture opposite. But release it into the rich Amazonian riverside forests where it belongs, and let it fly over the sun-kissed treetops with slow, imperious wing-beats, and it becomes simply magnificent.

Macaws are among the most conspicuous birds of South American forests. At dawn they make commuting flights between their communal roost sites, high in the trees, to feeding sites, which vary from day to day and can be some distance away. They often move in noisy flocks, making their famous guttural squawking which has been memorably described as sounding like a crow with a megaphone. Just before sunset they return, after a long day of feeding.

Macaws, in common with most other parrots, are vegetarians. They nonetheless have an extremely varied diet, which may include seeds, flowers, nectar and leaves. Despite the variety available to them, their large bills enable them to specialize in tackling large and slightly unripe fruit,

which is generally unpalatable or unavailable to competitors, including other fruit-eating birds, such as toucans, and primates. Such fruit is often high in tannin content, and may even contain slightly toxic compounds, which could explain the macaw's curious habit of regularly visiting mineral licks. These areas, which are often cliffs along riverbanks, are traditional sites hosting hundreds of birds at a time, all lapping up the neutral clay to ameliorate the effects of their potent diet. On the whole, however, the Blue-and-yellow Macaw is not as regular at licks as some of its close relatives.

Macaws breed in large holes high up in the canopy of very tall forest trees. In the case of the Blue-and-yellow Macaw, this is often a dead palm tree of the widespread genus *Mauritia*. Unfortunately for the macaws, which are such large and conspicuous birds, typical sites in distinctive trees are not especially difficult to find. Thus, almost wherever they occur, these birds suffer from the unwelcome attentions of humankind. Young in the nest are a valuable commodity, desired by unscrupulous dealers in the pet trade and, much as the collection and movement of macaws is forbidden by international law, there are always those willing to flout it for profit. As a result, macaws are often among the first birds to disappear from forests on the edge of human habitation.

The Blue-and-yellow Macaw is most closely associated with forest near water, for example gallery (riverside) forest, and in seasonally flooded growth (*varzea*). However, on the fringes of its broad range it is also found in some deciduous forest far from water, and in savanna. Intriguingly, in its core habitat it frequently coexists closely with other large macaws, including the Scarlet (*A. macao*) and the Red-and-green Macaw (*A. chloroptera*), sometimes mixing flocks, and the ecological differences between the three species have still yet to be worked out.

52. Azure Tit *Cyanistes cyanus*

A subtly-patterned sprite

Size: 13 cm (5 inches).
Distribution: Western Russia, through Central Asia to Mongolia and China.
Habitat: Deciduous woods, often near water; wetlands with osiers, *Phragmites* or scrub, for example.
Classification: One of 55 species in the family Paridae, and one of two in the genus *Cyanistes*.
Population and conservation status: Estimated at 5,800–22,000 birds in Europe. Least Concern.
Breeding system: Monogamous.
Nest and eggs: In a hole, often in tree; cup made of grass, moss, fur etc., with softer lining. 9–11 eggs.
Incubation and fledging: 13–14 days. 16 days.

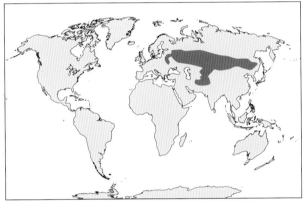

The Azure Tit is a very distinctive, attractive, blue and white tit, reminiscent of a Blue Tit (*C. caeruleus*) with some missing pigments. While it features in European field guides, most of its range is Asiatic, although there are Azure Tits in European Russia (its range reaches east of Moscow), some in Belarus and a few in Ukraine, where it may well be increasing in numbers. Broadly, where the Blue Tit's range finishes, the Azure Tit's begins, but there is a fairly substantial overlap.

Many Azure Tits are non-migratory, although in some parts of their range birds seek an easier life at lower latitudes during the winter months, sometimes coming into gardens. The scale of these movements is not predictable from one year to the next, but if the weather is colder, it is likely that more birds will move.

The species is also prone to periodic westward movements, most famously perhaps, and apparently in the biggest numbers, in the 1870s and 1880s. Birds were also on the move in the 1960s and 1970s, when Azure Tits reached Poland, Germany, Austria and the Netherlands. Vagrants have also delighted birdwatchers in France and Sweden.

When Azure Tits share habitat with Blue Tits, they may have more in common than similar nest sites and a similar diet. The pretty, pale easterners sometimes mate with the cheeky natives and produce hybrid young. The mixed-up offspring (Pleske's Tit) are more likely to be mistaken for Azure Tits than Blue Tits, but have less white in the wings and tail than a thoroughbred Azure, and a blue cap on what would otherwise be a white crown. There are records of Pleske's Tit from the late 1800s and, more recently, from the 1960s and 1970s. Clearly, this raises questions with regard to the specific status of the two congeners, and in the 1980s there was a school of thought that regarded them as a single species (*caeruleus*). Currently though, they stay apart, at least on the checklist.

Most Azure Tits nest in tree holes, although some races readily take to nest boxes and other holes, even holes in the ground. The female builds the nest and sits on the eggs, but the male participates in feeding the chicks. Information on their diet is incomplete, but their food includes butterflies and moths (from eggs to adults) and arachnids, with fruits, seeds and insect larvae helping them to survive the autumn and winter. Check *Phragmites* stems for Azure Tits during the colder months—these may well yield fly larvae, which can be welcome sustenance.

Most European birdwatchers think of the Azure Tit as a blue and white bird. It can be, but the reality is that it is a variable species. Two basic types are recognized: one has a white belly, and the other, found in parts of Central Asia and one Chinese valley, has a yellow belly. From above, it looks more like a classic Azure Tit, but its underparts are like those of a Blue Tit. Taxonomy may change, but it would still be good to see a (white) Azure Tit.

51. Eurasian Hoopoe *Upupa epops*

The original "punk" bird

Size: 26–28 cm (10.2–11 inches).
Distribution: Breeds in much of Europe and Asia and northern sub-Saharan Africa; northern breeders move south for the winter.
Habitat: Dry areas with short grass, bare soil or rocks, nest holes, shade and perches.
Classification: One of three species in the family Upupidae and the genus *Upupa*.
Population and conservation status: Estimated at 1.8–3.5 million birds in Europe. Least Concern.
Breeding system: Monogamous.
Nest and eggs: In a hole, nest unlined, or lined with plant material. 7–8 eggs.
Incubation and fledging: 15–16 days. 26–29 days.

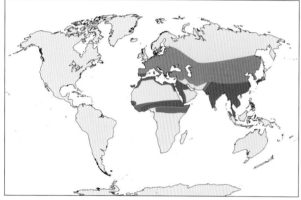

Surely Hoopoes are birds that anyone would want to see. When a novice birdwatcher leafs through a European field guide, the page with the Hoopoe on is likely to hold their attention for a while. The Eurasian Hoopoe is, quite simply, a remarkable looking bird, especially when its crest is up, or when it flies, showing off its broad, tropical butterflylike wings.

Despite their outrageous and seemingly highly conspicuous plumage, Eurasian Hoopoes are pretty good at disappearing into the background. Normally, the crest is kept down and a bird feeding on the ground can be surprisingly hard to see. If it senses danger, it stays still, taking to the wing only when the danger is very close. When it flies, it becomes very visible, but when it lands again normal crypsis is resumed, a strategy akin perhaps to that of color-winged grasshoppers, which use their brightly colored wings in a similar way to confuse predators.

Within its large range the Eurasian Hoopoe is a resident, a partial migrant and a migrant. Birds breeding at higher latitudes are migrants, the majority probably spending the winter months in sub-Saharan Africa (where other Eurasian

Hoopoes of a different race are resident) but not reaching right down to southern Africa. Portugal, Spain and North Africa are graced with Hoopoes throughout the year.

This species tends to eat alone and is particularly fond of insect larvae. A hungry Hoopoe ambles around a would-be feeding area, looking for food and poking here and there with its long, decurved bill. Animal dung can offer rich pickings—the Eurasian Hoopoe is well aware of this, and uses its bill to pick out juicy beetle larvae. Insects account for most of its diet, with caterpillars, pupae of butterflies and moths, beetles and beetle larvae being particularly frequent prey. Other prey includes locusts, ants and antlion larvae, and young Hoopoes have been fed the occasional adult butterfly as well as the more predictable insect larvae.

Eurasian Hoopoes make a noise that sounds like their name. Their song is a gentle, far-reaching "poo-poo-poo", used by the male to declare territorial ownership to those that need to know. When the continuation of his genetic line is at stake, a male will sing with great persistence. Tree-holes are frequently used as nest sites, often fairly low down, and from time to time, other sites may be used, including nest boxes. The female does all of the incubation and at least the majority of the brooding, but both male and female bring food to the chicks.

Often, when a Hoopoe is seen, its crest is down. An alarmed bird will raise its crest, but a better way of seeing the crest is to watch a bird in flight. Keep your eye on it just as it lands—that is when you will see this bird's "Mohican" glory.

The Eurasian Hoopoe is a bird that birdwatchers enjoy, and to non-Europeans is perhaps a bit of a surprise amidst the European avifauna. It is also a bird that has the potential to turn a non-birdwatcher into a birdwatcher. Why not try it?

50. Flock Bronzewing *Phaps histrionica*

A rarely-seen enigma of Australia's remote heartland

Size: 28–31 cm (11–12 inches).
Distribution: Inland Australia.
Habitat: Grassland, shrubland, plains.
Classification: One of 306 species in the family Columbidae, and one of three in the genus *Phaps*.
Population and conservation status: Not recorded. Least Concern.
Breeding system: Monogamous.
Nest and eggs: Small depression on the ground, sparsely lined with grass. Two eggs.
Incubation and fledging: 16 days. 10–14 days.

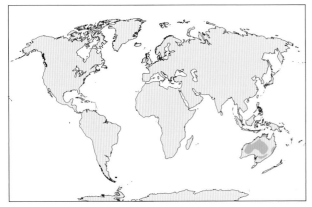

True to its name, this bird is a socialite par excellence, virtually never seen alone. In 1972 a single flock of 50,000 was counted in Queensland and in 1968 some spellbound observers watched a column 1 kilometer (0.6 miles) long, 100 meters (328 feet) wide and 10–20 meters (33–66 feet) deep fly over their heads. Moreover, in 1931 at least 100,000 Flock Bronzewings were recorded drinking at a single water hole, wave upon wave of birds each taking their turn, and even today it is possible to see tens of thousands at one time.

One might think, given these figures, that to see a Flock Bronzewing would be a matter of a quick drive to the arid heartland of Australia and a single scan with the binoculars. But that is a long way from being the case. For the Flock Bronzewing is something of an all-or-nothing creature: you see hundreds of them, or none at all. And these days, for Australian birders, that often means none.

Part of this is due to the Flock Bronzewing's unusual lifestyle. In common with many birds of the arid interior, it is essentially a nomad, following the availability of food—the seeds of various grasses and herbaceous plants. This means that it can disappear completely from a locality for long periods, sometimes decades, and then suddenly, particularly after a good spell of rain, it can appear again, in hordes, apparently from nowhere. This behavior gives the Flock Bronzewing something of a mysterious edge.

One of the few regular things in the bird's life is the need to find water. Living in the arid zone, it nonetheless has to drink at least once a day, and is therefore something of a commuter. Birds arrive at a watering place in the early morning or late afternoon, often homing in on one spot from all directions, whereupon they take their fill. Quite often, especially when thousands are using the same water source, birds at the front of the queue will be literally pushed into the water, whereupon they start to swim. In fact, birds will sometimes circumvent the rush and simply land straight on the water. They seldom have any problem taking off again.

The Flock Bronzewing's social habits extend to breeding, and nests are usually to be found in clusters or loose groups. Each nest is located on the ground under a bush, and holds the usual pigeon complement of two eggs. In such a vulnerable position the chicks waste no time in leaving the nest, often doing so before they are fully fledged.

Really big flocks of this species have now become much rarer, and for a while it was feared that the Flock Bronzewing was heading for extinction. However, it is now thought that the reduction may be due to dispersal rather than a dramatic decline. Over the years, as more and more of the center of Australia has fallen to human settlement, a larger number of smaller water sources have become available to the birds. So, much as the Flock Pigeon's future seems secure, it is still a pity that the truly enormous flocks of yesteryear will become a much less frequent sight.

49.Smith's Longspur *Calcarius pictus*

A smart bird of the North American tundra with a surprising breeding biology

Size: 14–15.5 cm (5.5–6 inches).

Distribution: Breeds in sub-Arctic North America, winters on the Great Plains.

Habitat: Forest/tundra interface; winters on short-grass prairie.

Classification: One of 167 species in the family Emberizidae, and one of four in the genus *Calcarius*.

Population and conservation status: Not recorded. Least Concern.

Breeding system: Males and females are both polygamous.

Nest and eggs: Open cup placed on the ground. Usually four eggs.

Incubation and fledging: 11–13 days. About 14 days, but the young leave the nest sooner.

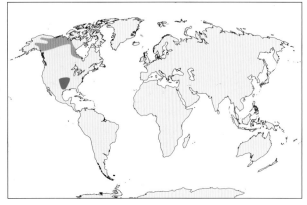

Every year, in the tundra of North America, something very odd happens among the population of an obscure seed-eater that hardly anyone has heard of. The Smith's Longspur, one of the least well known of America's much loved avifauna, practices a breeding system that is almost, but not quite, unique among birds.

The intrigue starts in March and April, when Smith's Longspurs, early migrants, arrive on their breeding grounds in the zone where the trees are replaced by open tundra. Almost immediately the attractively plumaged males begin to sing a pleasing high-pitched warble, advertising themselves in much the same way, seemingly, as every other small bird might do. But in fact, they are not singing to maintain a territory, which is the norm, and neither are they singing to acquire a single mate, which is also a departure from what you might expect.

Instead, Smith's Longspurs live in small communes, with several males and several females coexisting. They form no formalized pair-bonds but, essentially, just about everyone mates with everyone else heterosexually, so that a male may copulate with several females, and any given female will copulate with at least two or three males. It

is a very rare system known as polygynandry, and only the Accentors (Prunellidae) of Europe and Asia do likewise, as far as is known. Extraordinarily, at the height of the breeding season, before the eggs are laid, a female Smith's Longspur can expect to copulate about 350 times in a week.

Essentially, what is happening is that the males are competing to father the offspring of several females each, and it seems that most manage to get some genetic material spread around, for DNA studies on the broods tend to indicate multiple male parentage. Meanwhile, however, how can the system benefit the females? Well, it seems that, so long as a male achieves copulation with a certain female, he will then feel constrained to help with feeding the female's brood. Thus, while the males succeed in spreading their genetic material, the system ensures that the females can expect plenty of assistance when the young hatch.

In the majority of small birds the system is very different, with a single male and female conjoined as a pair. However, among Smith's Longspurs, polygynandry allows for each nest to be well equipped with helpers, which is probably why it works in the Longspurs' extreme habitat.

Having invested so much into the eggs and young, Smith's Longspurs, not surprisingly, protect them carefully. Besides building a reasonably well hidden nest, the adult female also has a distraction display, designed to lure predators away from the nest. The bird runs away from the nest, wings fluttering but apparently not working, as if it were injured.

Once breeding is long over, the Longspurs migrate to the short-grass prairie of the southern Great Plains, where they go about their business without the merest indication of their colorful life up north.

48. Northern Carmine Bee-eater *Merops nubicus*

A stunning bird that breeds in enormous, colorful, spectacular colonies

Size: 24–27 cm (9.4–10.6 inches) +10 cm (4 inches) with tail-streamers.

Distribution: A belt of Africa from Senegal in the west to Eritrea in the east.

Habitat: Open areas; in the breeding season, riverside cliffs.

Classification: One of 26 species in the family Meropidae, and one of 23 in the genus *Merops*.

Population and conservation status: Not recorded, but runs into millions. Least Concern.

Breeding system: Monogamous

Nest and eggs: Hole in sandy cliff, made by the bird. 2–5 eggs.

Incubation and fledging: Unknown. About 30 days.

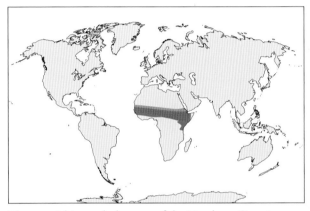

The astonishing red plumage of the Northern Carmine Bee-eater is such that even one of these birds makes a spectacular sight on its own, let alone hundreds or thousands of them in a colony. No wonder then that, at a number of places in Africa where these birds are known to nest in large numbers year after year, they act as a major tourist attraction. Few bird spectacles are quite as dazzling.

The Northern Carmine Bee-eater is just one of a number of bee-eaters in the world, almost all of which are startlingly colorful. Along with the swifts (Apodidae) and swallows (Hirundinidae), they are among the most aerial of all birds, making a living by snatching insects out of the sky. As their name suggests, most bee-eaters do indeed eat bees, along with a host of other small creatures with wings. However, the Northern Carmine Bee-eater is unusual in that, throughout its range, it has a special fondness for locusts and grasshoppers. Its complex migrations, which involve spending a few months of each year in three places, are partly geared to following the movements of these creatures.

All bee-eaters exhibit great expertise when hunting. Naturally enough, flying insects will perform various dodging maneuvers to avoid being caught. When a bee-eater is foraging, however, it won't simply trawl aimlessly through the air, but instead targets each particular insect, following its movements and hunting it down by following its twists and turns. Despite its slightly fragile appearance, the bee-eater's bill is strong, with sharp cutting edges, and it is often possible to hear the sound of a captured insect's exoskeleton breaking when the bird is processing it for eating. The largest prey is often beaten on a perch beforehand and, in the case of stinging insects, this serves to remove that potentially dangerous weapon.

Although Northern Carmine Bee-eaters capture their prey in midair, it doesn't mean that they remain aloft for hours on end. Much work is done in short sallies and, to this end, these birds have a highly unusual habit: they use living, moving animals as temporary perches. All manner of ungulates can be used for this, such as zebras (*Equus* spp.), Warthogs (*Phacochoerus africanus*) and Giraffes (*Giraffa camelopardalis*), as well as a number of birds, including Kori Bustards (*Ardeotis kori*), Ostriches (*Struthio camelus*) and several species of stork (Ciconiidae). There is a double advantage in using animals: not only do they provide an elevated lookout post, but they also disturb insects with their feet as they walk, flushing them into view and making foraging much easier.

Northern Carmine Bee-eaters begin breeding at the start of the rainy season, usually in May or June. Their colonies are almost invariably in cliffs by riverbanks (see above), where the soil is sandy enough to allow the birds to dig a burrow. Such places are at a premium, and thus it is not surprising that they tend to be densely pitted with burrows: up to 60 entrances per square meter (10 square feet) of cliff has been recorded.

47. Snowy Owl *Bubo scandiaca*
A great white hunter with "pussy-cat" looks

Size: Male 55–64 cm (22–25 inches), female 60–70 cm (24–27 inches).
Distribution: A circumpolar breeder in northern hemisphere; winters further south.
Habitat: Arctic tundra; in winter, open habitats further south, e.g. fields, plains, marshland and some coastal areas.
Classification: One of 187 species in the family Strigidae, and one of 18 in the genus *Bubo*.
Population and conservation status: Estimated at 290,000 birds. Least Concern.
Breeding system: Mostly monogamous.
Nest and eggs: Shallow scrape. 3–11 eggs.
Incubation and fledging: 31–33 days. 43–50 days.

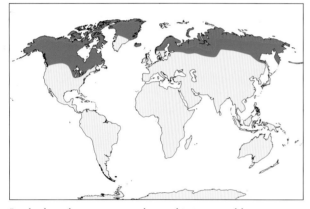

In the breeding season, at least, this is an owl best admired from a distance, despite what some describe as its "pussy-cat" looks. Snowy Owls breed in the Arctic tundra, where food supplies may vary from one year to the next. If they cannot find an area with enough food to support a nestful of Snowy Owls, breeding may be postponed, sometimes for more than a year. Little wonder then that, when they do breed, their young are defended with considerable enthusiasm.

When there is enough food to support breeding, the female creates a simple, unlined nest scrape. The selected site is typically a little higher than the surrounding terrain—it is therefore more likely to have lost its winter snow cover, and makes it easier for the watchful parents to keep a look-out. Courtship sees the male performing an up-and-down, flap-and-glide display flight, and passing food to his partner during the "angel display" or in a spectacular in-flight maneuver. Snowy Owls are monogamous, partners frequently remaining together throughout their lives. In bumper food years they lay 7–11 eggs, but only 3–5 in leaner years. Incubation and brooding are the female's job, with the male fetching and

carrying food for his mate and offspring. This can be quite a task—even with a large clutch, all the eggs may hatch, although success rates are variable.

When there are young to defend, Snowy Owls will dive-bomb interlopers, including people and wolves, to force a retreat, and may make physical contact during the attack. Injury feigning may be used as an alternative strategy. Skuas turn the tables though, and will fly at Snowy Owls, and there is a record of Pomarine Skuas (*Stercorarius pomarinus*) killing a bird on its eggs.

During the breeding season it is impossible for the Snowy Owl to hunt nocturnally—there is no "nocturne" in the Arctic summer. At this time of year, food is sought all day long, with perhaps a bit of a lull around midday and midnight. Lemmings are famous Snowy Owl food and one owl may eat more than 1,600 in a year, including a good number that were "safe" under the snow. Other mammals are eaten too, and bird prey includes shore-birds (Scolopacidae), wildfowl (Anatidae), auks (Alcidae) and ptarmigans (*Lagopus* spp.), and there are stories of Snowy Owls lying down beside water to fish! Carrion is sometimes exploited and ducks are a favorite food of Snowy Owls wintering along the western Canadian coast.

The dark Arctic winter may offer little food for resident Snowy Owls. Some remain, but many seek an easier life at lower latitudes. The scale and extent of their winter movements may vary from one year to the next, and may well be connected to the abundance or lack of prey in the north. Nomadic and eruptive movements may also occur, Eurasian birds occasionally showing up in the UK. In the United States, Snowy Owls often spend the winter near conurbations, delighting the locals. It is the wintering birds that most birdwatchers are likely to see—a trip to the Arctic is not essential to experience this huge, white owl.

46. Bee Hummingbird *Mellisuga helenae*

The world's smallest bird species

Size: 5–6 cm (2–2.5 inches). Weighs 1.6–1.9 g (0.05–0.06 oz).
Distribution: Cuba and Isle of Pines.
Habitat: Woods (especially coastal) or woodland edge; other habitats include gardens and swamps.
Classification: One of 347 species in the family Trochilidae, and one of two in the genus *Mellisuga*.
Population and conservation status: Not recorded, probably less than 2,500. Near Threatened.
Breeding system: Polygynous.
Nest and eggs: Thimble-sized plant-fibre cup with softer lining and adorned with lichens. Two eggs.
Incubation and fledging: 21–22 days. 13–14 days.

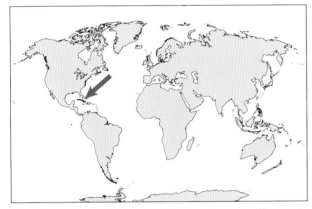

The Hummingbird Hawkmoth (*Macroglossum stellatarum*) is an insect often mistaken for a hummingbird. The Bee Hummingbird could easily be mistaken for an insect! This is the world's tiniest bird species, though its length doesn't communicate its minuteness—it is the bird's weight that tells you more. A male (males are smaller than females) may weigh just 1.6 grams (0.05 ounces). Compare that to the Common Ostrich (*Struthio camelus*) at around 150 kilograms (330 pounds) (see page 92) and you will see something of the amazing diversity of the bird world.

Bee Hummingbirds are endemic to Cuba and the Isle of Pines in the Caribbean. Sadly, owing to habitat loss and changing land use, what was once a common species has become rare, with a more fragmented distribution.

Although it will eat some insects, nectar is this bird's main food. Hummingbird bills come in different lengths and shapes, giving the family access to differently structured flowers. The Bee Hummingbird's bill is one of the less remarkable in the family—straight and not particularly long, but equipping the bird well for plundering energy-rich nectar from *Hibiscus*, *Aloe* and other flowering plants.

The hummingbird flying machine is, in some ways, more impressive than anything man has come up with. Hummingbirds can hover, fly backwards, and may even be seen upside down in midair! Flight is powered by the pectoralis major and supracoracoideus muscles; the former pull the wing down, the latter drive the upstroke. Most birds let the former do most of the work—in hummingbirds' powered flight, however, the division of labor between the two is much more equal. In a migrating bird these muscles might be as much as 20 percent of the bird's total weight. In a hummer, they are more than 30 percent. A hummingbird's keel is large and its skeletal structure allows an exceptional range of wing movement. It also has eight pairs of ribs rather than the more usual six, which provide a bit more stability for the airborne bird. Hummingbirds beat their wings very fast. Different sources quote different figures—smaller species can certainly achieve 70–80 beats per second. It has been claimed that the Bee Hummingbird can hit an astonishing figure of 200 beats per second. Whatever the truth, hummingbirds are masterful fliers. They are not good on their feet, however, which are good for little more than perching,

Typically, apart from mating, male hummingbirds avoid all parental responsibilities. The Bee Hummingbird's nest is built by the female (above). Perhaps not surprisingly, it is normally regarded as the smallest nest of any bird, being roughly the size of a thimble. Two eggs are laid, and these are claimed as the smallest of any bird. Their average length is 11 millimeters (less than 0.5 inches), though at their most extreme record-breaking, lengths of just over 6 millimeters (0.25 inches) are quoted. Once they have hatched, the chicks may provide a bit of ad hoc help to the female by eating any insects that come a bit too close.

Little is known of the Bee Hummingbird's movements—they are assumed to be sedentary, so if you want to see one, a trip to Cuba is your best bet.

45. Pallas's Sandgrouse *Syrrhaptes paradoxus*

An eruptive, flying water-carrier

Size: 30–41 cm (12–16 inches).
Distribution: A belt across Central Asia, some moving north to breed, some moving slightly south to winter.
Habitat: Dry, open areas including steppe and semi-desert.
Classification: One of 16 species in the family Pteroclidae, and one of two in the genus *Syrrhaptes*.
Population and conservation status: Not recorded. Least Concern.
Breeding system: Monogamous.
Nest and eggs: Shallow, unlined scrape. 2–3 eggs, 2–3 broods.
Incubation and fledging: About 28 days. Young feed themselves soon after hatching.

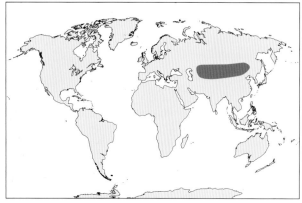

In 1863 something happened that has gone down in ornithological history. It happened again in 1888 and again 20 years later. Pallas's Sandgrouse were on the move. Wisdom has it that, if the weather closes in on the Central Asian steppes, Pallas's Sandgrouse must move or risk starvation. It seems that, when icy snow makes food too hard to find, the drive to survive triggers mass movement, although the triggering mechanisms are not yet completely understood.

Eruptions are irregular and unpredictable. Those of the 1800s were very impressive, with Sandgrouse in many parts of Britain including the Outer Hebrides, and some making it as far as Ireland. Small numbers of immigrant Sandgrouse attempted to breed in Britain, and young were seen near Elgin in Scotland in 1888 and 1889. The normal movements of Pallas's Sandgrouse are less remarkable; some push the northern boundary of their usual range during the breeding season and there may be a slight southward movement during the winter, which can be more marked if the weather is extreme.

As a group, sandgrouse are adapted for life in some demanding environments. The plumage of most of the world's birds grows in discrete tracts, with unfeathered areas in between. Sandgrouse have "downy underwear" which has no gaps and provides effective insulation against highly variable temperatures. There are feathers to keep unwanted particles out of the bird's nose too, and the plumage of Pallas's Sandgrouse totally covers its feet and legs, unlike most other sandgrouse species.

Pallas's Sandgrouse are sociable birds and may breed with just 5–6 meters (16–20 feet) between nests. Incubation is shared, but when the adults need to drink, the eggs may be abandoned for a while. Sandgrouse breed where water is not universally available and have to make periodic flights to established drinking places, sometimes over 30 kilometers (18 miles) away, where birds congregate. When there are young to look after, Pallas's Sandgrouse are normally nearer water: but they don't take their young to the water, they bring it to them. Sandgrouse have an innovative water-moving technique—the male's belly feathers are water absorbent. He flies to the watering hole and rubs his belly in the earth or sand to clean off any water-repellent oil. He then gives his specially adapted belly feathers a soaking. He carries the water home, the young birds get a drink, and another earth or sand bath completes the routine.

This species is primarily a seed-eater. Food may be taken off the ground, dug up or taken straight off the plant. Fresh plant growth is sometimes eaten, too, and rarely, insects. Small pebbles, sand and other grinding materials are also swallowed, as an aid to digestion.

No one knows if there will be another eruption to bring this bird into western Europe in numbers. It may be that the species' normal range does not reach as far west as it used to, sadly making an 1880s-style event less likely. Seeing a Pallas's Sandgrouse could be a challenge.

44. Capuchinbird *Perissocephalus tricolor*

A peculiar bird with a remarkable breeding system and an even more unusual call

Size: 34.5–35.5 cm (13.6–14 inches).
Distribution: A northern stretch of South America between the Amazon and Orinoco.
Habitat: Humid lowland forest.
Classification: One of 98 species in the family Cotingidae, and the sole member of the genus *Perissocephalus*.
Population and conservation status: Not recorded. Least Concern.
Breeding system: Both sexes promiscuous; no pair-bond.
Nest and eggs: Thin platform of sticks placed low down in tree. One egg.
Incubation and fledging: 26–27 days. Unknown.

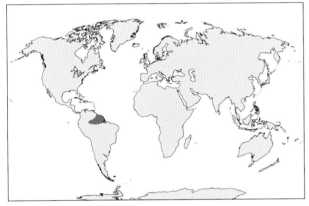

As you will see from the picture opposite, you don't have to be beautiful to get into this book. You do have to be extraordinary, however, and in this regard the Capuchinbird certainly fits the bill.

For much of the year, the Capuchinbird disappears into its forest home and is almost impossible to see. As a member of the cotinga family, it spends much of its time eating various sorts of fruit, often making aerial assaults to pluck hard-to-reach fruits. Less conventionally, it also has a taste for grasshoppers and crickets, and has been recorded catching and eating a bat. But what really makes the Capuchinbird odd is what it does in the breeding season.

You might first get an inkling that the Capuchinbirds are in the mood when you go into the forest and hear cows mooing up in the trees—an impossibility, of course. This extraordinary sound, which is really more like a cow with a sore throat, is made by male Capuchinbirds, and it is accompanied by a puffing up of the chestnut-brown plumage, the courtship posture. The birds don't display alone, but in groups. Males occupy different perches in the sub-canopy, and all display collectively in a lek, to which prospecting females are attracted.

Quite a number of bird species display in leks, an arena where females can compare and contrast the quality of available males in the neighborhood, and copulate with the one of their choice. They choose genetic quality over everything else, because they alone are responsible for all breeding duties after visiting the lek for their brief fling. However, the politics of a Capuchinbird lek are complicated, and unusual in many ways, showing fascinating differences from most other lek-using birds.

The Capuchinbird lek is a frighteningly efficient meritocracy. One male holds the central perch in the lek, and it is he who monopolizes all the available sexual encounters, while the rest of the males look on enviously. Fascinatingly, however, some of the other males actually try to usurp him in various desperate or devious ways. Some, for example, form teams of two, and spend the season sharing a perch and doubling up their displaying effort, vocalizing in turn, usually to no avail. Other males adopt femalelike behavior, making advances to the dominant male in an effort to set foot on his precious perch. The latter behavior is possible because, in considerable contrast to almost all other lek-using birds, the sexes of Capuchinbirds look alike, and are not instantly differentiated.

One might think that the sexual politics would be confined to the males, since the females have less to lose. However, it appears that the females often visit the lek in groups and, once they have discovered the identity and location of the dominant male, they all embark on an unseemly battle to copulate with the incumbent. Copulations for the contented dominant birds follow thick and fast.

All this, one assumes, must just make the subordinate males' eyes water. But that's life!

43. Red-cockaded Woodpecker *Picoides borealis*

An iconic American rarity, found in a cherished ecosystem, with unusual group-living behavior

Size: 22 cm (8.6 inches).

Distribution: Southeastern United States.

Habitat: Open mature pine woods.

Classification: One of 220 species in the family Picidae, and one of 14 in the genus *Picoides*.

Population and conservation status: Estimated at no more than 10,000 individuals. Vulnerable.

Breeding system: Monogamous.

Nest and eggs: Hole chiselled into living tree, no material. 3–4 eggs.

Incubation and fledging: 10–11 days. 26–29 days.

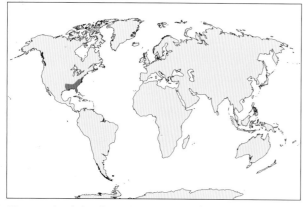

Here is a bird that lives the American dream—it works hard, has strong family values and has its roots set deep down in the soil. It also happens to be one of the best-studied woodpeckers in the world, and is a flagship species in nature conservation.

The Red-cockaded is a medium-sized woodpecker that lives in open pinewoods in the southeastern United States. Here it makes its living feeding primarily on arboreal ants, although it takes other arthropods too, including centipedes and scorpions. It specializes in stripping bark to reveal what is underneath, a difficult, time-consuming process, sometimes achieved by grabbing bark with its feet and flying off on a short sally. Interestingly, males and females often feed in different parts of the tree, the males on the upper trunk and branches, the females on the lower trunk.

When it comes to breeding, these birds turn their attention to another form of hard labor. In contrast to many woodpeckers, they make their nest holes not in dead trees but in live ones, and not just any tree, but a pine (*Pinus* spp.) selected especially for its high resin yield. Throughout the breeding season, the woodpeckers spend much time chipping away around the side of the nest hole, causing the tree to bleed its resin continuously. This, fascinatingly, is a highly effective form of defence: the smelly, gooey exudate keeps both predators and competitors away. Once selected, a nest hole may be used for over 20 years.

The chiselling job is not undertaken just by the pair of Red-cockaded Woodpeckers alone, but by helpers as well. For these birds live not as isolated couples, but as small groups of between three and six birds. Almost invariably the supernumeraries are male birds that are the pair's offspring from previous years, birds that have remained with their parents instead of dispersing. These birds throw themselves into the collective ethos, not just helping to keep the nest safe, but also feeding the young and dealing with fecal material. They will even help incubate the eggs, with the result that the next generation of youngsters will hatch in a mere 10–11 days.

Despite its collective approach to breeding, the Red-cockaded Woodpecker is suffering a severe long-term population decline throughout its range in the heartlands of America. The main problem is that it is very fussy indeed about its habitat: it will only breed in pine trees that are more than about 100 years old, and it requires the woodland in which it lives to have an open understorey maintained by regular wildfires. Although most of the remaining birds are found on federal land, the cost of restricting fires and allowing trees to grow so old is not consistent with the commercial constraints of timber production.

Thus the Red-cockaded Woodpecker, deprived of adequate protection, still declines in the world's richest country. It is a blot on America's reputation in the conservation world.

42. Crimson Chat *Epthianura tricolor*

A colorful resident of the Outback and one Australian that hardly ever drinks

Size: 11–13 cm (4.3–5.1 inches).

Distribution: Interior Australia.

Habitat: Arid and semi-arid shrublands and grassland.

Classification: One of 178 species in the family Meliphagidae, and one of four in the genus *Epthianura*.

Population and conservation status: Not recorded. Least Concern.

Breeding system: Monogamous.

Nest and eggs: Open cup placed in a low shrub. 2–4 eggs.

Incubation and fledging: 10–14 days. 9–11 days.

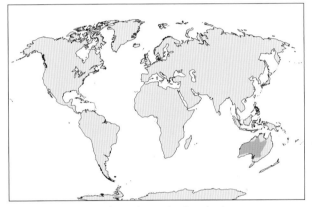

You have to be tough in the outback, whether you are a bird or a human being. So, despite its colorful appearance and gentle demeanor, you should not underestimate the Crimson Chat, a bird that lives its life in places where, if the temperature doesn't get you, the lack of water probably will. Go to see it at your peril.

The Crimson Chat is one of a small group of similar Australian birds with a demeanor all their own. Although some authorities lump the chats with honeyeaters on account of their brush-tipped tongues, an adaptation for sipping nectar, they are quite distinct. They are, for example, among the very few small birds that move on the ground by walking, rather than hopping, and they are somewhat robust and short-tailed, and travel with strong, undulating flight. And although they do sip nectar, this is not their primary food source; instead they wander along the ground searching for insects and other arthropods.

At heart, the Crimson Chat is a nomadic bird, highly unpredictable and difficult to find, and a problem for birdwatchers. Sometimes, for example, it will turn up somewhere after a long absence, or will occur in sudden abundance after several lean years. Furthermore, in common with other nomads, its breeding season is irregular. Nests have been recorded in every month of the year, and when conditions are especially suitable the Crimson Chat will motor through several broods in succession to maximize the opportunity for reproduction. Typically it is that precious commodity, rain, that is the trigger for breeding.

Wherever they are nesting, Crimson Chats are hard to overlook. That is because the colorful males indulge in a delightful display flight to beguile their mates and repel rivals, in which they take off vertically from a low shrub, stall, and then glide down to the edge of their territory, singing all the while. The accompanying song is not especially tuneful, a few clinking calls in succession followed by a whistle, but it is still a distinctive and far-carrying message. Once a displaying Chat has landed, it will often raise the colorful feathers of its crest.

That is not the only display that you might see from a Crimson Chat. A little later in the season, should the nest be threatened by a predator, both sexes can perform a conspicuous broken-wing routine, in which they appear to be struggling across the ground with terrible injuries, only to flit effortlessly away when the predator has been lured away. This sort of display is much better known among waders than it is among small passerines.

In the intense heat of their habitat, Crimson Chats need to have certain physiological adaptations to enable them to survive. One of these is the ability to live without water. These birds will drink when the opportunity arises, but if nothing is available they can either use water that is metabolized internally or, more often, obtain what they need from the body fluids of their insect prey.

Thus the Crimson Chat is a rare creature indeed—an Australian that hardly ever drinks.

41. Cape Sugarbird *Promerops cafer*

The perfect example of a special bird dependent on a unique habitat

Size: Male 37–44 cm (14.6–17.3 inches), female 24–29 cm (9.4–11.4 inches).
Distribution: Cape Province of South Africa.
Habitat: Fynbos scrub; gardens.
Classification: One of two species in the family Promeropidae and the genus *Promerops*.
Population and conservation status: Not recorded. Least Concern.
Breeding system: Monogamous.
Nest and eggs: Cup of dead twigs lined with plant down and fibres, placed in bush. Two eggs.
Incubation and fledging: 16–18 days. 17–21 days.

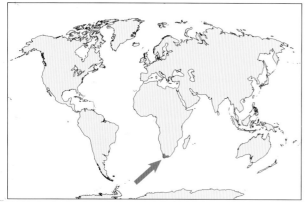

The photograph opposite may appear to be the ideal, well-planned, patiently-taken shot, captured just at the moment when the subject is conveniently perched on a colorful flower. But the truth is that, down in South Africa where the Cape Sugarbird occurs, it would be difficult to record an image of a sugarbird away from one of its beloved protea (*Protea* spp.) blooms, so close is the relationship between bird and plant.

The Cape Sugarbird is a South African icon, and there are several reasons for this. For one thing, it is pretty remarkable to look at, the male's outlandish tail being more than twice the length of the rest of the bird. The tail trails in unruly fashion behind its owner in flight, and even when the bird is perched, the merest breeze catches the long feathers and whisks them this way and that, even up and over the bird's head, adding to the exotic appearance. Another reason is that the sugarbirds, of which there are two species, are usually considered different enough from other birds to be placed in their own family: they have brush-tipped tongues for nectar-feeding, but are much larger and less colorful than sunbirds, for example. Thirdly, and perhaps most

importantly, the Cape Sugarbird is a flagship species for the fynbos, a vegetation type unique to South Africa.

The fynbos is the result of an explosion of plant speciation. The Cape is one of the world's great flower hotspots, with a mind-boggling 8,700 native species, and many of those are crowded into these riotously colorful scrubby communities. Proteas are major components of fynbos, and thus the sugarbird, too, tends to be a fynbos specialist. It is primarily a nectar feeder, and spends much of its time drinking from the inflorescences, but its dependence on the proteas goes much deeper than that. It forages on the invertebrates found in protea bushes, uses protea branches for the site of its cup-shaped nest, uses the same shrubs for general sheltering and loafing and, as a final touch, places the down of protea seeds upon a latticework of sticks to give its young a suitably designer-made platform on which to begin their lives.

Life for the Cape Sugarbird, therefore, is an endless series of visits to flower heads. But this does not mean that the birds stay in one place all year. Different protea species flower at different times, meaning that the birds follow the blooms around, making short migrations. Only in the early spring, from about March, do the birds settle down and this, the peak time for flowering, is also when they breed.

Quite frequently, a concentration of food will prompt the birds to breed together in loose colonies. Inevitably, this ensures that hormones pervade the atmosphere and, in order to protect both territory and mate, male Cape Sugarbirds feel compelled to make short display flights, launching themselves vertically upwards, along a bit and then just as steeply down. The sight of several of these birds, one after the other, fluttering over the brilliant blooms like small fireworks, tails trailing behind like feather dusters, is one of the great experiences of African birding.

40. Common Sunbird-Asity *Neodrepanis coruscans*

A fascinating oddity of the Madagascan rainforest

Size: 9.5–10.5 cm (3.7–4.1 inches).

Distribution: Eastern Madagascar.

Habitat: Rainforest.

Classification: One of four species in the family Philepittidae, and one of two in the genus *Neodrepanis*.

Population and conservation status: Not recorded. Least Concern.

Breeding system: Probably promiscuous.

Nest and eggs: Basketlike structure with side entrance, suspended from a branch. Two eggs.

Incubation and fledging: Both unknown.

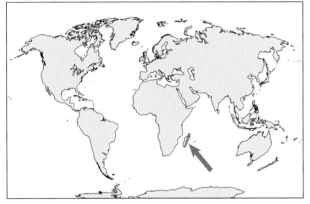

Islands tend to throw up peculiarities, and the landmass of Madagascar has managed to isolate more than its fair share. There are plenty of famous ones: cuddly lemurs and Hissing Cockroaches (*Gromphadorhina portentosa*), for example. But some of the lesser known anomalies are just as curious, and among these is a tiny group of forest birds known as asities.

The asities are unique in two main ways. Although they do not look especially unusual, all members of the family have brightly colored wattles on the face, which are most conspicuous in the breeding season. The color of these wattles is produced not by pigments, but by rows of collagen fibres, and this system of producing color is apparently not found elsewhere in the animal kingdom. Furthermore, the asities also share a highly peculiar quirk in their nest-building habits. In common with a number of rainforest birds, they build a globular, basketlike nest with a side entrance; however, instead of building the entrance into the overall structure, they apparently simply work their way into the weaving by inserting their bill and neck and pushing material aside, as if they had suddenly remembered that they needed

to get inside. This crude house-building method is also unique to the asities.

In addition to these quirks, the asities are also known to be highly primitive songbirds. In contrast to better-known small passerines, such as sparrows, thrushes and tits, the asities' voice-producing apparatus, the syrinx, is relatively simple, without the equivalent pairs of muscles that characterize more accomplished songbirds. This, the sort of thing to make museum specialists go weak at the knees, places the asities among a select band of primitive Old World birds, including pittas (Pittidae) and broadbills (Eurylaimidae).

Go into the rainforests of Eastern Madagascar and it is not difficult to see a Common Sunbird-Asity. As its name suggests, the species is numerous, and it will often allow a close approach, flicking its wings nervously as it checks the observer out. Sunbird-Asities cannot resist banks of flowering blooms, such as mistletoes and balsams, and this reflects their largely nectarivorous diet. With their long, curved bills they seek out forest blooms for much of the year, although in the cool season (June to September) they will also take large numbers of small insects, mainly searching for these among bark or hanging dead vegetation. At flowers, Sunbird-Asities often compete with the resident sunbirds, such as the abundant Souimanga Sunbird (*Cinnyris souimanga*).

Recent studies and observations suggest that, like its relative, the Velvet Asity (*Philepitta castanea*), the Common Sunbird-Asity is probably promiscuous, at least at times. Some males display "incomplete" breeding plumage, with reduced wattles, suggesting that there may be a hierarchy among males for access to females, rather than the usual monogamy. As yet this is unproven, but if it is, it would be another of the many singular anatomical and behavioral features of this obscure bird.

131

39. Ross's Gull *Rhodostethia rosea*

A stunning waif of the Arctic that is very rarely seen

Size: 29–32 cm (11.4–12.6 inches).

Distribution: Arctic seas and sub-Arctic tundra in Russia and North America.

Habitat: Breeds on tundra; winters at sea.

Classification: One of 100 species in the family Laridae, and the sole member of the genus *Rhodostethia*.

Population and conservation status: Estimated at 55,000–100,000 birds. Least Concern.

Breeding system: Monogamous.

Nest and eggs: Well-concealed cup of dry grass in tussock on island. Three eggs.

Incubation and fledging: 19–22 days. About 21 days.

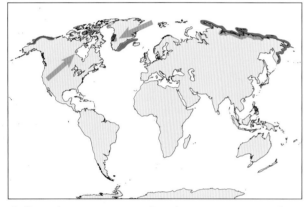

Gulls tend not to excite much enthusiasm among people, even birdwatchers, but there is one species that completely rises above such prejudice. It is Ross's Gull, a dainty, delicate gull of elegant demeanor, whose plumage, far from being dull grey, is washed through with the most perfect, subtle pink hue.

This is a rare species, hardly ever seen away from the remote sub-tundra of Russia and Canada, or from the winter pack ice of Arctic seas. Its beauty and rarity are powerfully beguiling and it seems that, almost from the moment that men first set eyes upon it, as recently as 1823, it has held birdwatchers in a kind of spell. Indeed, in the early days, when the breeding grounds were unknown (they were discovered in 1906), people would risk their lives to gather precious specimens. An expedition to the Russian Arctic in 1879 came to an abrupt halt when its ship was trapped and crushed by ice. The survivors had a desperate struggle to reach dry land, dragging the lifeboats over ice or rowing through treacherous waters before finally reaching Siberian soil many weeks later. Throughout this perilous 320-kilometer (200-mile) scramble to safety, the expedition naturalist protected three skins of the Ross's Gull under his shirt.

Even today, when we know where they breed, Ross's Gulls are still remarkably difficult to see. Their nests, although aggregated in colonies, are on average some 43 meters (140 feet) apart, so you do not see the ground covered with white bodies, as you would for other species. The nests, furthermore, are hidden in tussocks, usually on an island in a small tundra lake, and the birds are almost paranoid at the nest, making quiet, very subtle approaches when a member of the pair comes to bring in food or take an incubation shift. In common with some other Russians, Ross's Gulls have a habit of keeping bodyguards; they frequently nest close to Arctic Terns (*Sterna paradisaea*) (see page 10) and waders, making good use of their neighbors' general vigilance.

Of course, sometimes their cover is blown, and invaders steal into their territory and threaten the nest. If this happens, the gulls react according to circumstances. If they think the predator can be driven off, they will attack it without a trace of subtlety, but if more guile is required, they can adopt a suite of distraction displays. One of these, the "rodent run", is a bizarre behavior in which the Ross's Gull assumes the role of a vole or lemming, creeping hidden through the grass, squeaking in rodent language—in effect, doing an impression. The idea is to lead the predator off on a trail of possible prey—an alternative to the gull's eggs or chicks.

After breeding, these delicate gulls, whose young often die of hypothermia, make a bizarre migratory movement. Instead of moving south, as most birds do, they travel north instead. From the end of July onwards, they set off to meet the pack ice, where they will feed during the impossibly cold and inhospitable winter months.

38. Cock-tailed Tyrant *Alectrurus tricolor*

One of those hidden avian delights—an effervescent sprite with a wonderful display flight

Size: 12 cm (4.7 inches); male with tail 18 cm (7 inches).

Distribution: Central South America.

Habitat: Extensive tall grasslands.

Classification: One of 432 species in the family Tyrannidae, and one of two in the genus *Alectrurus*.

Population and conservation status: Not recorded. Vulnerable.

Breeding system: Not known for sure, but the males are suspected to be polygynous.

Nest and eggs: Cup of grass placed on or just above the ground. Unknown.

Incubation and fledging: Both unknown.

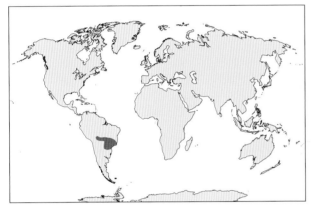

You have probably never heard of the Cock-tailed Tyrant, but this bird is an absolute gem. Perhaps, though, it should be called the Clockwork Tyrant, in honor of its remarkable, almost robotic display flight.

To see a Cock-tailed Tyrant, you have to visit one of the few remaining substantial grasslands of central South America, in Bolivia, Paraguay or Brazil. Here, in season, as the rains begin, this bold black-and-white character will adorn the tops of many a bush and tall-grass stem, looking suitably conspicuous, with a rather ridiculous tail sticking up behind its squat body. Those stiff, spread feathers, incidentally, are supposed to resemble those of a cockerel, hence the English name.

Every so often, one of these birds will quite suddenly take to the air, making an impressive, near vertical ascent on rapid, almost manically fast wing-beats. It will rise to some preferred height, which may not be much above the horizon, but can be substantially more, depending, one assumes, on the motivation of the performer—100 meters (330 feet) has been recorded. At any rate, as the bird rises slowly upwards, it can be seen to alternate its tail position from straight up to straight down, in

regular fashion, as if it were operating some pulley system to help its ascent. The overall effect is decidedly comical, and watching this earnest effort, it is hard not to acquire a soft spot for the bird.

Of course, for the Cock-tailed Tyrant, the display is deadly serious: there is a territory to defend and, more importantly, a female to attract. Or is that all? Recent observations suggest that males are not satisfied with acquiring just one mate, but will attempt to copulate with a succession of them, each of which builds a nest within the male's territory. The females, incidentally, completely lack any of the male's bold colors and ornaments, and are just everyday, streaky brown birds (see above).

Both sexes are, however, equally adept at catching their invertebrate food, which they do in some style. Most is caught during brief aerial assaults, when the rapidly beating wings make a short buzzing sound, as if imitating the prey. Cock-tailed Tyrants are also capable of hovering in front of leaves or grass stems for a brief moment before picking off some morsel, behaving like an outsize hummingbird. Curiously, for such an insectivorous bird, female Cock-tailed Tyrants have been recorded feeding fruit to the young in the nest.

Sadly, this delightful character is beginning to become very rare. Its habitat once covered a broad swathe across central South America, but much of this has now been converted to agriculture. Concurrently, the Cock-tailed Tyrant has declined alarmingly, its population has become fragmented, and it has almost certainly become extinct in Argentina since the last sighting in 1979. There is some hope for it, since the best populations are found in protected areas, but the days when these birds were common and widespread have most certainly gone forever.

37. Spoon-billed Sandpiper *Eurynorhynchus pygmeus*

An endangered shorebird, and the only one with a spoon-shaped bill

Size: 14–16 cm (5.5–6.2 inches).

Distribution: Breeds in small area of northeast Russia, winters in south and Southeast Asia.

Habitat: Breeds on coasts with sandy ridges, close to freshwater and on tundra; winters on coastal lagoons and coastal mud.

Classification: One of 91 species in the family Scolopacidae, and the sole member of the genus *Eurynorhynchus*.

Population and conservation status: Estimated at fewer than 2,500 birds. Endangered.

Breeding system: Monogamous.

Nest and eggs: On ground among sedges and mosses, etc. Four eggs.

Incubation and fledging: 19–23 days. Can fly at 15–18 days old.

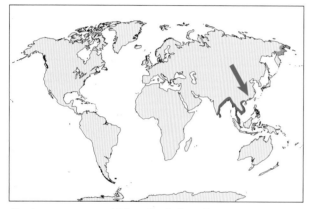

Getting to grips with shorebird identification is one of the trickier tasks in a novice birdwatcher's apprenticeship. Sandpipers can confuse, but this one has something that should make identification relatively straightforward. Its bill is unique among shorebirds, and even the chicks can be identified by the shape of their bill. There are some complications, however. First you have to find one. If you are looking for a Spoon-billed Sandpiper in winter, it may be tucked away in a big flock of other waders, and there are not many places where wintering birds can be seen. If you find one, you may not realize that you have—see one from the wrong angle and the bill shape may not be obvious, and, if you are successful, you should celebrate—there are not many Spoon-billed Sandpipers left.

This small wader is similar to the Red-necked Stint (*Calidris ruficollis*), though its bill is very different. Bills are about feeding and the Spoon-billed Sandpiper's techniques include a spoonbill-like sweeping, from left to right and back again, through water or mud, while moving forward, sometimes belly-deep in water. The "spoon" is extremely well endowed with touch receptors,

presumably making it much easier to find prey, which includes aquatic crustaceans. Land-based invertebrates are also taken, including flies, beetles and hymenoptera, and some seeds are eaten too.

After their northbound spring migration, many Spoon-billed Sandpipers return to the breeding area they used the previous year. The male courts the female with a display flight, using hovering serenades, among other tricks, to try to secure the deal. Both birds play a part in incubation and early chick-care, but after less than a week, and sometimes as soon as the birds are out of the eggs, the female heads off, leaving the male to do the work. Lemmings play an important part in the life history of several birds in this book, including the Spoon-billed Sandpiper. In this instance, lemmings provide a distraction: when there aren't enough of them, lemming predators target Spoon-billed Sandpiper eggs and young instead. That assumes, of course, that the predator can find them, something that is becoming increasingly difficult.

In 2007, BirdLife International believed that the Spoon-billed Sandpiper breeding population could be as small as just 100 pairs. This unique wader is being assaulted on several fronts. In the breeding areas local dogs have a carefree lifestyle—they disturb breeding birds and eat the eggs and chicks. Migration is much tougher than it used to be, too—the draining of the Saemangeum tidal flats in South Korea has wrecked a vital feeding area, and not just for this species. Climate change may also be playing a part, through the loss of permafrost.

Urgent action is needed to keep this species alive. Breeding sites need to be protected and local people are needed to work with their neighbors, to build pride in this unique bird, and to reduce the damage caused by dogs. There is still hope. Let us pray that it is not too late.

36. Hoatzin *Opisthocomus hoazin*

A bird that can hardly fly and cannot walk, though the young can swim

Size: 62–70 cm (24–27 inches).

Distribution: Northern South America.

Habitat: Trees by water in lowlands.

Classification: The sole member of the family Opisthocomidae and the genus *Opisthocomus*.

Population and conservation status: Not recorded, common in some areas. Least Concern.

Breeding system: Mostly monogamous, sometimes with helpers.

Nest and eggs: Stick platform. 2–4 eggs.

Incubation and fledging: 30–31 days. Can fly at 55–65 days old.

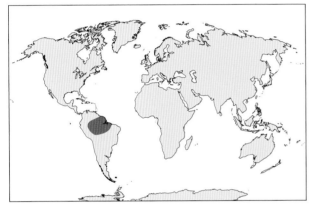

Hoatzins have strange looks and a strange lifestyle. They are birds that could easily pass themselves off as something from prehistory. Their plumage is often unkempt and they have staring eyes set in blue skin and a wild-looking crest. These are, indeed, curious-looking birds. They are not great movers either. For a Hoatzin, 300 meters (1,000 feet) is a long-haul flight, walking is impossible and, despite their preference for waterside homes, for adults at least, swimming is not an option—this is a very sedentary bird.

Hoatzins are tree- and bush-dwellers that clamber clumsily through thick foliage. They feed on leaves and do something that no other bird does—they digest their food like a cow. Leaves and buds make up most of the diet, and they are known to eat over 50 plant species, though in one area, just four or five species may account for most of their intake. They have a particular fondness for giant *Arum*, mangroves and legume trees, and deal with their vegetarian intake primarily at the front end of their gut, whereas most birds do the bulk of their digestive business further along the alimentary tract. Food ferments in the Hoatzin's crop and the adjacent part of the esophagus, which are

hard-wearing, squeezing, muscular food processors. It may take a Hoatzin two days to complete the processing, but it gets more out of its food than it would if it did things conventionally and this method of digestion may also help it to deal with the toxins in some of the leaves it eats. As far as we know, no other bird species works this way. There is a price to pay, however. Its "fermentation vessel" is large and heavy and limits the size of the bird's sternum. Because of this its flight muscles are smaller too, which is why the bird is no master of the air. When full, a Hoatzin is front-heavy and a lot of time is spent leaning on its sternum! It can be a smelly process, too—to Guyanans this is the "stinking pheasant".

Hoatzins are noisy, sociable creatures that normally breed monogamously in very small territories. Many pairs share the workload, though, and may have as many as six other Hoatzins helping out. These helpers are often their own offspring; the extra birds take on territorial roles but will also help with nest construction, sit on eggs and play a part in looking after the young. Where helpers are involved, young Hoatzins are quicker to leave the nest.

Life as a young Hoatzin does has its risks, including predators. The youngsters have a surprising survival strategy, however: they plunge into the water beneath the nest and swim (something that adults cannot do), sometimes underwater. After their daring escape, they clamber back up through the foliage, using two claws on each wing to help them on their way. The claws are temporary, and are lost when the birds are about 10–14 weeks old, but make comparison with creatures of prehistory even more likely.

Perhaps not surprisingly, the taxonomists struggle with Hoatzins—they just don't know where to put them.

35. Great Argus *Argusianus argus*

A shy species with the one of the avian world's most remarkable displays

Size: Male 1.6–2.0 m (5.2–6.6 feet); female 0.72–0.76 m (2.4–2.5 feet).
Distribution: Peninsular Malaysia, Sumatra and Borneo.
Habitat: Lowland forest.
Classification: One of 179 species in the family Phasianidae, and the sole member of the genus *Argusianus*.
Population and conservation status: Estimated at over 100,000 birds in 1994, but declining. Least Concern.
Breeding system: Male certainly polygynous; no real pair-bond.
Nest and eggs: No real nest; eggs placed on the ground or upon low tree-stump. Two eggs.
Incubation and fledging: 24–25 days. Unknown.

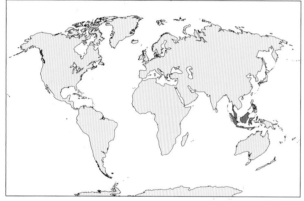

If there were a fair contest to find the finest, most spectacular and most ornamented display of any bird in Asia, the peacock would come a mere second. The winner would be the incomparable Great Argus.

The Great Argus is less famous than the peacock, partly because it is a shy, jungle bird that is difficult to see. It also flaunts its ornamentation less effusively, but this also explains the impact of the display. The presentation of the fan of feathers, somewhat similar to the peacock's, is far more of a thrill and a surprise.

The process begins any time between January and March, when fully-grown males return to a familiar spot in the forest where vegetation is naturally low. Here, often up a hillside or on some eminence, they clear a patch of ground that will become their displaying court, removing leaves and other debris. Immediately they combine their housekeeping with a regular succession of loud calls, claiming possession of their court and sending out invitations to females. The males work and call assiduously, spending on average 40 percent of the daylight hours at the court. The rest of the time they wander through the forest, seeking

out sumptuous insect morsels and choice fruits, or they simply stand still and rest from their exertions.

Moreover, by no means are all of the males in the population involved in this activity because many birds, especially younger males, cannot compete for a court and hold no prospects in any given season. And so, it tends to be the older, more experienced and most well-endowed males, in terms of their feathering, whose voices are heard.

The sequence of display, and its sheer opulence and intensity, is overwhelming; males have been seen displaying non-stop for a half-hour or more. Among the routines is a ruffling of the feathers, together with a thundering shake of the large (roughly goose-sized) body. Then, in courtly style, the male will walk past the hen, drooping the nearest wing to the ground as if presenting a cape like Sir Walter Raleigh, and lifting the farthest in a teasing show-off of the eye-spots (*ocelli*). He will follow this by bowing, stamping on the ground and producing a fizzing hiss. By this point the human visitor, if not the female, is spellbound.

But these displays are merely the support act. As a final flourish, the male Great Argus has more wonders in store. It leans forward and sweeps its wings forward, towards the female, and out, until their tips cross to the top and they scrape the ground below. As the fan is presented, the previously hidden, iridescent green ocelli are then revealed in their glory; widest towards the tips of the wings, they are arranged in rows, drawing the eye of the beholder inward toward the center, where the bird's real eye, shining with lust, pleads for copulation.

It seems highly appropriate that the advertising short-call of the male Great Argus is an exclamatory "Oh, wow!"

34. Ibisbill *Ibidorhyncha struthersii*

A bizarre, iconic and particular shorebird

Size: 39–41 cm (15–16 inches).
Distribution: Central Asia.
Habitat: Shingle river valleys.
Classification: The sole member of the family Ibidorhynchidae and the genus *Ibidorhyncha*.
Population and conservation status: Not recorded. Least Concern.
Breeding system: Monogamous.
Nest and eggs: Shallow scrape; may have pebble lining. Four eggs
Incubation and fledging: Unknown. 45–50 days.

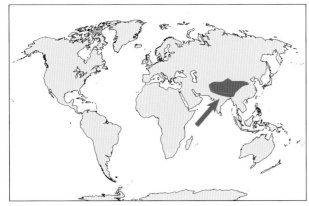

This is bird that has presented a challenge to taxonomists. It has been classified with the shorebirds for a long time, though it certainly doesn't match the image that most people have of a shorebird. In the classification that we are using for this book, it sits next to the Crab Plover, between the oystercatchers (*Haematopus* spp.), and the stilts and avocets (Recurvirostridae), a decision supported by DNA analysis which places this unusual bird very close to the Recurvirostridae.

The Ibisbill is a highly distinctive (but surprisingly cryptic) species that birdwatchers want to see. It's a bird that's "more unique than many" and one that lives in an impressive landscape that is not always easy to get to, making it an attractive proposition for the more adventurous.

To see an Ibisbill you need to get to a river valley in the Central Asian mountains. These are picky birds, though, and are consistently found in similar places, right across their range. Look for a wide valley—one between 100 meters (325 feet) and 1,500 meters (5,000 feet) from side to side. Make sure there are some sandy and silty areas. And if there are trees, or too much plant cover, move on

to the next valley. It needs to be a gently sloping valley—Ibisbills live around slow-flowing mountain waters, where they swim well. Faster moving waters are avoided—this bird is designed to feed where the water doesn't run too fast, and it knows it.

To peck, to probe or to rake—that's the decision facing a hungry Ibisbill, which has three main foraging techniques at its disposal. A pecking bird wades in up to its belly, loiters, and takes insects off the surface. Several hours may be devoted to pecking near rapids. A probing bird is more mobile but takes its time, moving slowly with the water lapping around its belly. It uses its long bill (the female's is longer) to search around underwater stones for something edible. Raking birds rake through stones, moving their bill from side to side in an attempt to bring hidden prey out into the open. Ibisbills eat mayfly and stonefly larvae, other insects, and crustaceans. Fish are taken too, especially in the winter.

Relatively little is known about the Ibisbill's breeding behavior. They get noisier in the spring, after a quiet winter. The combination of the male's calls and his vertical head movements may win him a female, and a simple nest is constructed for, typically, four eggs. The nest is not always right by the water and may be as much as 100 meters (325 feet) away. Mountain weather in Ibisbill country is not always kind, and an incubating bird (both sexes incubate) may have snow to contend with. After hatching, the young Ibisbills are given time to dry off, and are then escorted by the female to a new location, perhaps 100–200 meters (325–650 feet) away. The male is reunited with his family, and both adults look after the young.

Ibisbills are not long-distance migrants, but they are likely to move to lower altitudes for the winter, some birds moving just outside the breeding range.

33. Amazonian Umbrellabird *Cephalopterus ornatus*

A rainforest dweller with an umbrella

Size: Male 48–51 cm (19–20 inches); female 41–43 cm (16–17 inches).
Distribution: Northern South America.
Habitat: Forest near rivers and, at higher altitudes, humid forest.
Classification: One of 98 species in the family Cotingidae, and one of three in the genus *Cephalopterus*.
Population and conservation status: Not recorded. Least Concern.
Breeding system: Unknown.
Nest and eggs: Scant twig platform. One egg.
Incubation and fledging: Both unknown.

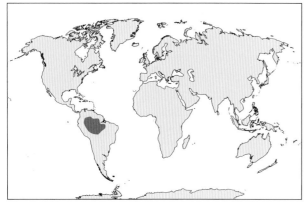

The Amazonian Umbrellabird is the world's biggest cotinga. At around 50 centimeters (nearly 20 inches) in length, and with an estimated weight of around 500 grams (1 pound), this is a very sizeable passerine. A first encounter with this parasol-toting bird may well be a view of one flying across a river, rising and falling on broad wings. To see the birds perched, however, check out riverside trees—*Cecropia* spp. are among their favorites. Look for one or two, sometimes a few more, large, blackish birds bounding around, perhaps near the canopy.

Amazonian Umbrellabirds are cautious characters that seem to be aware of what is going on. The male and female are similar in appearance, though the male is substantially bigger, with more "umbrella" and more wattle. When the umbrella is down, most of the bird's bill may be obscured. There may be 15 centimeters (6 inches) of wattle, but, perhaps surprisingly, it is not always obvious and there are no feathers on the back of the wattle. The black plumage has a bluish sheen and, in the male, the crest feathers have white shafts, which can be very obvious.

There is still much to discover about the breeding biology of the Amazonian Umbrellabird. Like other umbrellabirds, males gather at leks to display their wares. The proceedings may involve as many as six males, perhaps 10–25 meters (30–80 feet) up a tree. Lekking is both visual and vocal. It is time to put up the umbrella, pump up the wattle (the wattle is enlarged by filling it with air), and boom. The boom of a male Amazonian Umbrellabird has been likened to far-off cows and can be heard from quite a distance. They probably make this noise without opening their bill and the air in the puffed-up wattle may be an important part of the process.

After successful courtship and mating, Amazonian Umbrellabirds are believed to lay a single egg. The nest is a fragile-looking stick platform in a tree or sapling. It is a loose and "gappy" construction, so much so that the egg can be seen through the sticks. Larger trees seem to be avoided and nests have been seen at heights of 3–12 meters (10–40 feet), though it seems that only a small number of nests have been described.

Like most cotingas, Amazonian Umbrellabirds eat fruit, though insects are also taken and they are known occasionally to eat lizards. Beetles and orthopterans (grasshoppers, crickets, katydids, etc.) are frequent victims of this bird's grab-and-bash routine, while *Cecropia* trees, palms and other species make up the fruity part of their diet.

As far as we know, Amazonian Umbrellabirds are sedentary. Of the world's three umbrellabird species their range is the largest, and they also have the most favorable conservation status; both Bare-necked Umbrellabird (*C. glabricollis*) and Long-wattled Umbrellabird (*C. penduliger*) are listed as Vulnerable. So, if you want to see an umbrellabird, the Amazonian could be your best bet.

32. Southern Cassowary *Casuarius casuarius*

Physically, the world's most dangerous bird

Size: 1.3–1.7 m (4.3–5.6 feet).

Distribution: Northern Australia and New Guinea.

Habitat: Mainly dense tropical rainforest; some savanna woodland.

Classification: One of three species in the family Casuariidae and the genus *Casuarius*.

Population and conservation status: Not recorded. Least Concern, but rare and declining in Australia.

Breeding system: Pair-bond is short-term, and female will pair with several males in succession.

Nest and eggs: Simple depression on the forest floor. 3–5 eggs.

Incubation and fledging: Around 50 days. Chicks independent at nine months.

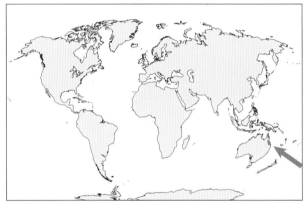

Birdwatching, on the whole, is not a very risky pastime. But if you are wandering through the forests of tropical northern Australia or lowland New Guinea, you may just stumble across a Southern Cassowary, and find yourself in unexpected danger. For this lumbering, heavy-legged forest monster is by far the world's most physically dangerous bird, and has been responsible for numerous human casualties. Back off and leave it alone, because it could seriously injure you, or even kill you.

Cassowaries are tall birds, reaching about the height of a human being; the three species are the largest wild land animals on the island of New Guinea. They have robust bodies covered with hairlike plumage, which is silky-black to keep them hidden in the shade of the forest undergrowth. The head is fitted with an extraordinary horny casque, or helmet, which is said to help the bird barge its way through thick forest undergrowth, although individuals have also been seen using it as a primitive implement for scraping the ground. The offensive weapons of a cassowary, however, are on its feet. The three claws are long and sharp, in particular on the inner toe, up to 17 centimeters (6.7 inches) long, and can be used to lash out at a potential enemy. In New

Guinea, where cassowaries range widely, human hunters are sometimes disembowelled by cassowary kicks. Normally, however, cassowaries are not especially bad tempered, and kick only when severely threatened.

In contrast to the world's other large flightless birds, such as ostriches and emus, cassowaries are extremely difficult to see, owing to their secretive nature, solitary existence and tall forest habitat. Males and females each have their own territory, in which they wander in search of their main food, the fruit of forest trees. Since they are ground-dwellers, this is a game of patience—they must wait for the fruits to fall. In northern Australia, they appear to be the exclusive dispersers of up to 70 plant species, whose seeds are too large for any other animal to eat. Thus, both here and in New Guinea, where there are no monkeys to rival their dispersing power, cassowaries are vital for maintaining the biodiversity of their forest habitat.

In the breeding season, males invite females into their territory for a few weeks, during which mating occurs. Females are larger and the dominant sex, so an interested male may need to pursue his intended for a while to reduce her instinctive aggression. Finally, he dances around her, inflates the colorful wattles on his head and neck, and makes a low rumbling call. This is enough to induce copulation, and the female then lays 3–5 eggs in a well-hidden platform nest. As soon as the egg-laying is over the male drives off the female, and is henceforth entirely responsible for egg incubation and the tending of the stripy young.

Unfortunately, the Southern Cassowary is in decline in many areas. In northern Australia, in particular, road casualties, attacks by dogs and creeping habitat degradation have reduced the population to few more than a thousand individuals. In New Guinea, too, forest destruction could become even more of a major threat in the future.

31. Golden Bowerbird   *Prionodura newtoniana*

A small, golden bird with big ideas

Size: 23–25 cm (9–9.8 inches).
Distribution: Northeastern Australia.
Habitat: Forests above 900 m (2,950 feet).
Classification: One of 19 species in the family Ptilonorhynchidae, and the sole member of the genus *Prionodura*.
Population and conservation status: Not recorded. Least Concern.
Breeding system: No pair-bond apart from copulation; male may mate with several females.
Nest and eggs: Deep, bulky cup, in tree fork or on the ground. Usually two eggs.
Incubation and fledging: 21–23 days. 17–20 days.

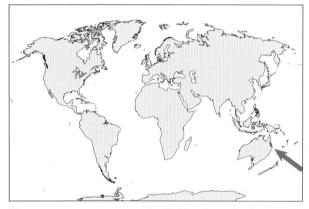

If you were to come across the Golden Bowerbird in the wild as it fed unobtrusively on fruit in the forest canopy, nothing would strike you as unusual. The Golden Bowerbird is an attractive enough species, and a rare one, occurring only above 900 meters (2,950 feet) in a tiny part of northeastern Queensland, Australia, but it is quite small, and really looks not very different from many other birds you might come across in such a place.

If you made a habit of wandering through these same forests of the Queensland Wet Tropics, you would probably come across something far more extraordinary and puzzling. In a cleared patch of forest, you could find yourself staring at an enormous double pile of sticks centerd around saplings, each pile up to 3 meters (10 feet) high. One of these "towers" would be taller than the other, and both would be constructed of interlaced components made into roughly the shape of a giant cone. The two towers would be 1 meter (3 feet) or so apart, loosely connected by a horizontal stick or roughly horizontal vine, and the whole combined structure strewn with strands of hanging lichen, fruit and small green and white forest flowers. Your immediate impression would be that it must have been built by human hand.

And yet, unbelievably, the two towers of sticks have indeed been constructed by the Golden Bowerbird. Some remarkable things have been made in the name of sexual attraction, but in the animal world few are quite as astonishing as this. The diminutive male is the sole builder, and it uses its own saliva as glue. The monument, known as a bower, towers over the architect, at almost 100 times its own height. The bower is not even a nest, of some practical use; it is made purely to attract and impress a passing female.

During the breeding season (September to January), the owner of the bower, a mature, full-plumaged male, will spend up to two-thirds of the day attending the bower, making sure everything is perfect for a female visitor. The male will also give a distinctive call, a loud rattle, to announce that he is in attendance. The frequency of visits should ensure that, should a female turn up, the male will be in place to display to her.

Needless to say, when a female does visit, the male goes into overdrive. The Golden Bowerbird has at least five courtship displays, each designed to show off his golden plumage. One display, a bow, draws attention to the brilliantly colored central crown crest, while another, the flight/hover, in which he might take a butterflylike flight from one perch to another, accentuates the brilliant tail margins.

If the male is impressive enough, the female will copulate with him, and that is the end of the relationship. From then on he will continue to attend the bower, hoping for another visit from a different female, while she will undertake all the breeding duties alone. It is quite a lot of hard work for the female, certainly, but it doesn't come close to all the effort and creativity put in by her hardworking mate.

30. Helmeted Hornbill *Rhinoplax vigil*

An amazing-looking forest bird, with highly unusual feeding and nesting behavior

Size: 1.1–1.2 m (3.6–3.9 feet).

Distribution: Peninsular Malaysia, Sumatra and Borneo.

Habitat: Primary evergreen rainforest.

Classification: One of 50 species in the family Bucerotidae, and the sole member of the genus *Rhinoplax*.

Population and conservation status: Not recorded. Near Threatened.

Breeding system: Monogamous.

Nest and eggs: Hole in tree, floor of wood chips. 1–2 eggs.

Incubation and fledging: Both unknown.

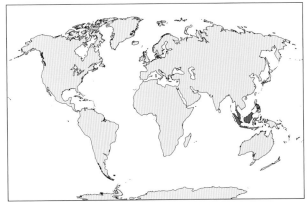

Movie-makers looking for a new design of monster to terrorize cinema-goers could do worse than visit the lush lowland forests of Malaysia and the Greater Sundas, where the Helmeted Hornbill lives. Here is a bird so bizarre and hideous that a beast based upon it would do an excellent job of scaring audiences.

As it happens, the Helmeted Hornbill is already a fearsome prospect, although admittedly only to other members of the forest canopy. Although the hornbills as a family are thought of primarily as fruit-eaters, they also indulge in some predation. And while the Helmeted Hornbill is enthusiastically frugivorous, with a severe weakness for figs (*Ficus* spp.), its menu also includes snakes, squirrels (Sciuridae) and even some birds, which have, on occasion, included smaller members of the hornbill family. So the Helmeted Hornbill is, it seems, a significant treetop predator.

The strange appearance of this huge bird is something of a mystery. The large casque, or helmet, on top of the bill and ending half way along, is the only solid casque within the hornbill family, the skull representing some 10 percent of the bird's entire weight. Presumably that could make it quite a powerful tool which might, for example, be used to hack bark or otherwise uncover prey. Whether it serves this purpose is not known, but one function is known for sure. In territorial disagreements, males clash casques, the sound of which can carry all the way to the forest floor.

It is almost impossible, in season, not to know that these huge birds are around, because they deliver one of the loudest and most recognizable territorial calls in the whole of Southeast Asia, with a voice that can carry for over 1 kilometer (0.5 miles) through the forest. The call is quite a performance, beginning with loud single hoots, which, over the course of a minute or more, accelerate. They soon progress into double notes and accelerate still more, until, with the notes almost tripping over themselves, they climax into a maniacal laugh.

Helmeted Hornbills, in common with other members of their family, have an unusual breeding arrangement. For nesting they select a large hole in a tree in the forest canopy and then, strangely, the female enters the hole and settles in for a long stay by plastering the entrance to a narrow slit. In so doing she entombs herself voluntarily and also, it is to be hoped, protects herself and her nest against potential predators. Only when the young have hatched, or are ready to fledge, will she chip away the plasterwork to release herself.

This intriguing practice has several consequences. For a start, it gives a heavy workload to the free-flying male, who has to bring food to his mate for weeks on end. Secondly, it means that, since entombment takes place well before any eggs are laid, the female must store the male's sperm. And thirdly, throughout the time they are sealed in, the female and young have to perfect the uncertain art of defecating out of the narrow entrance slit. Such are the practicalities of keeping the young safe and sound.

29. Andean Cock-of-the-Rock *Rupicola peruvianus*

A species with stunning plumage, fascinating breeding and a highly unusual nest

Size: 30.5–32 cm (12–16.5 inches).

Distribution: The Andes, from Colombia and Venezuela south to Bolivia.

Habitat: Montane forest.

Classification: One of 98 species in the family Cotingidae, and one of two in the genus *Rupicola*.

Population and conservation status: Not recorded. Least Concern.

Breeding system: No formal pair-bond; sexes meet only for copulation.

Nest and eggs: Mud cup attached to a rock face. Two eggs.

Incubation and fledging: 28 days. 28–42 days.

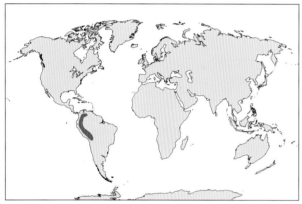

You would hardly expect a species with the name Cock-of-the-Rock to be a member of the "small brown bird" fraternity, and so it proves, for this scarlet-colored dandy is one of the most striking of all South American birds. Or at least, the male is; the female is clad cryptically in sombre reddish-brown, and thus never appears on stamps or holiday brochures, as does its iconic, marketable mate.

Such extreme sexual dimorphism is often a clue to an unusual breeding system. Males with excessively bright plumage may not be welcome around eggs and nests, where they might attract attention, and the development of brilliance is often the result of competitive sexual selection, in which winning the female is more important than any subsequent relationship. Thus it is no surprise that, in Cocks-of-the-Rock, male and female meet only for copulation, and the female performs all breeding duties unaided.

The meeting place of male and female is known as a lek, which is a communal display ground, where a sort of speed-dating occurs. The males dance and posture in close proximity to one another pretty much all the time (bowing, jumping, flapping their wings and uttering a moaning call), the female visits them (often several times over a few days), the female makes her choice from the available talent, and then she copulates with the winner. To make the female's choice quicker and easier, the males at the lek are spread out a few meters apart, each occupying a perch in the middle storey of the forest at some 4–6 meters (13–20 feet) above the ground, and it is the position they occupy that betrays the most information. Rather like the office of the chief executive in a company, the central perch is occupied by one individual at a time, but aspired to by the rest, sometimes over a number of years—young Cocks-of-the-Rock begin their careers on the outskirts of the lek and work their way inwards. This all-powerful position is the aphrodisiac, and the central male on the lek appears to win the lion's share of the copulations when the female visits the lek.

There is one curious quirk to this system in Cocks-of-the-Rock; some males share perches and appear to display in unison. They bow at each other in turn and would appear to be making a communal pitch, which may last the entire breeding season. Why they should do this is not yet known.

These birds get their name from their peculiar nesting sites, which are indeed usually on rock faces, especially along the edges of streams, something of a niche location for a forest bird. This helps to explain why the Andean Cock-of-the-Rock is mainly a bird of mountain slopes, between 500–2,400 meters (1,640–7,845 feet) in altitude, where such features, as well as caves, are more abundant. The nest itself is a cup of mud plastered to the wall up to 12 meters (39 feet) above the ground, and lined with coarse materials.

28. Superb Lyrebird *Menura novaehollandiae*

One of Australia's most famous birds, with its spectacular display and astonishing mimicry

Size: Male 1 m (3.3 feet), including tail up to 71 cm (28 inches) long; female 76–80 cm (30–31.5 inches).
Distribution: Southeast Australia.
Habitat: Moist forest.
Classification: One of two species in the family Menuridae and the genus *Menura*.
Population and conservation status: Not recorded. Least Concern.
Breeding system: Males may copulate with several females over a season.
Nest and eggs: Large domed structure of twigs, leaves and fern fronds, placed on or near the ground. One egg.
Incubation and fledging: 50 days. 47 days.

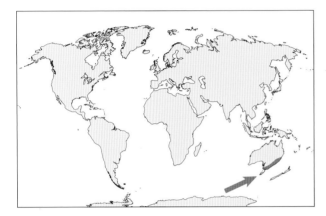

The Superb Lyrebird looks like the sort of species that any birder could see just by walking into the nearest patch of forest. But despite its size—about that of a Common Pheasant (*Phasianus colchicus*)—the Lyrebird is extremely shy and elusive, and the forests where it lives are often thick and dark, with a copious understorey. It can be many hours, or even days, before this iconic bird, with its fabulous train of lyre-shaped feathers, can finally be glimpsed.

It is certainly worth the effort, for the Lyrebird presents a startling sight, especially the male in full display. In some ways the male Lyrebird brings to mind a small, brown peacock, with the long train pulled up into a fan over the bird's head and back and ruffled as the bird does small circuits on the spot (see above). But the color and pattern are quite different, more subtle and a bit classier. Most of the 16 tail feathers (the "filamentaries") are thin and hairlike and, when spread, they look as though they cast a net curtain behind the bird. Meanwhile, the edges of the curtain are framed by the ornate, pale, brown-banded feathers (the "lyrates") that end in a lyrelike curve.

Impressive though this undoubtedly is—and the males

show themselves off to good effect by standing on an earth mound they have constructed, 1–2 meters (3–6 feet) across—it is perhaps the vocal accompaniment to the display that is the most remarkable feature. It has certainly attracted the attention of scientists, largely because of its rich imitative element. The song is an apparently ramshackle medley of different noises, some pure and pleasing, others harsh and loud, but it is actually more organized than it seems. About three-quarters of all the sounds are fragments copied from the voices of other birds, while the remainder are specific to the lyrebird itself. Both the specific fragments and the imitations tend to be specific to the area where the individual is found, with different birds exhibiting regional dialects. However, the exact song is unique to each individual bird.

On average, about a quarter of all the bird species of a given location will be imitated by the local Lyrebirds. There are consistent favorites, including the Laughing Kookaburra (*Dacelo novaeguineae*) and the Eastern Whipbird (*Psophodes olivaceus*), for example, but clearly, few sounds escape the birds' expert ear. On occasion, mammals such as the Koala (*Phascolarctos cinereus*) will also feature, and some captive or habituated lyrebirds have become famous for imitating human sounds, including the motor drives of cameras, chainsaws or steam trains. These, however, are exceptional individuals.

The astonishing vocal performance of the lyrebird puzzled the early settlers, who were initially convinced that this big bird with strong legs must be some sort of pheasant. But no pheasant could sing like this, and no pheasant could build such an elaborate domed structure for its nest. It was a long time before scientists reached the surprising conclusion that the lyrebird was a songbird, just like a sparrow or a tit. As such, it is one of the largest in the world.

27. Andean Condor *Vultur gryphus*

The world's biggest bird of prey—a spectacular species in a spectacular setting

Size: 100–130 cm (40–50 inches); male weighs 11–15kg (24–33 lbs), female 8–11kg (18–24 lbs); wingspan up to 3.2 m (10.5 feet).

Distribution: The Andes in South America, sometimes down to sea level.

Habitat: Mountains, plus remote, open areas for feeding; also forages on the coast.

Classification: One of seven species in the family Cathartidae, and the sole member of the genus *Vultur*.

Population and conservation status: Not recorded. Near Threatened.

Breeding system: Unknown.

Nest and eggs: Ledge in remote mountain cave. One egg.

Incubation and fledging: About 59 days. About six months.

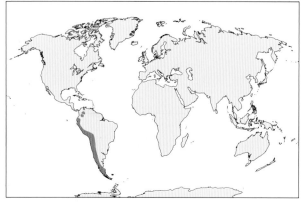

The Andes provide a dramatic backdrop for this most impressive raptor—the biggest there is, with the biggest wingspan of any landbird [although Africa's Marabou Stork (*Leptoptilos crumeniferus*) competes for that award].

Uniquely among the New World vultures, Andean Condors are sexually dimorphic—only the male has the comb and wattles on its bare head and neck. The condor's baldness has an obvious hygiene function—a feeding bird may put its head inside a bloody carcass—but all New World vultures are bald and only three of them do this regularly. The bare skin probably also plays a part in thermoregulation. Andean Condors fly high and fast in considerable wind-chill. Their plumage insulates the body well, but when they drop down to feed, things warm up. By losing heat through their bare skin, which has many blood vessels, overheating can be avoided. Cooling is achieved at the other end of the body too—Andean Condors urinate on their legs to lose heat through evaporation, a technique also employed by storks.

The Andean Condor eats large carrion including domestic animals, Guanacos (*Lama guanicoe*), Vicuña (*Vicugna vicugna*), and seals (Pinnipedia) and whales (Mysticeti and Odontoceti) washed up on the shore. In some areas flocks of tens of condors can be seen feeding at a single carcass, making a substantial contribution to the cleanup job. A condor may eat around 2 kilograms (4.4 lbs) in one sitting, sometimes becoming so heavy that it cannot take off. If a predator threatens it, it will vomit the meal back, so as not to exceed the "weight allowance" for its flight. In ideal circumstances, a condor will remain grounded for several hours before it can fly again. After a good meal, fat deposits are built up to get the bird through until its next meal—Charles Darwin believed they could survive a fast of five or six weeks.

To find carrion, the bird must cover great distances, sometimes 200 kilometers (125 miles) from the nest site, and to be energy-efficient condors must burn as few calories as possible in their hunt for food. They are, of course, supremely constructed for soaring, staying aloft on the ascending air as wind moves over mountains, or on thermals over the plains. Soaring is very energy-efficient and Andean Condors seldom flap. Once airborne, their white wing patches make it relatively easy for other condors to see them.

The breeding behavior of Andean Condors is not well understood. The breeding season is long and breeding seems to be biennial, or less frequent if food is hard to find. No nest is built but a single egg is laid on a ledge in a remote mountain cave. In different parts of their range they lay eggs in different seasons. Incubation probably takes over eight weeks and it is another six months before the young condor can fly, but the adults look after their substantial genetic investment way beyond this time.

Andean Condors are persecuted because they are perceived to be killers of livestock. They are a long-lived species that produce few young, and thus find it difficult to recover from persecution. Let us hope that current reintroduction programmes are successful.

26. Wandering Albatross *Diomedea exulans*

A legendary seabird with the biggest wingspan of any living species

Size: 1.07–1.35 m (3.5–4.4 feet). Weighs 6.3–11.3kg (13.8–24.9 lbs).
Wingspan: 2.54–3.63 m (8.3–11.9 feet).
Distribution: Circumpolar in southern oceans; northernmost parts of range reach southern tropics.
Habitat: Mostly seagoing; breeds on remote islands, often among tussock grass.
Classification: One of 13 species in the family Diomedeidae, and one of two in the genus *Diomedea*.
Population and conservation status: 28,000 mature birds. Vulnerable.
Breeding system: Monogamous.
Nest and eggs: Grass and mud heap. One egg.
Incubation and fledging: About 78 days. About 278 days.

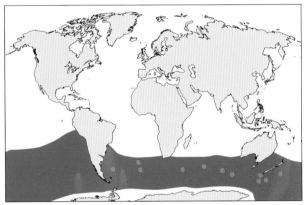

Albatrosses are renowned for their incredibly long wings and this species is the biggest there is. A wingspan of 3.63 meters (11.9 feet) has been measured and up to 4 meters (13 feet) may be possible. This is a big, heavy bird that flies over a big ocean. It is a bird of the air that rides the up-current from the wind hitting the waves and exploits the ocean's stratified wind speeds to travel great distances with minimal flapping.

Strong winds are no problem for an albatross, which is more likely to be grounded by too little wind than by too much. It needs moving air to fly and if it's not moving enough, getting airborne can be impossible. Very few southern hemisphere albatrosses cross the equator—the doldrums are a very effective albatross barrier. Their long, thin wings are very good for gliding but very poor for powered flight—a flapping albatross tires quickly.

Wandering Albatrosses have an average life expectancy of 30 or 40 years. Some may make it to 80, but this has yet to be proved. Most of their life is spent at sea, clocking up many thousands of air miles but, clearly, they have to come to land to breed.

No one would call a Wandering Albatross impetuous. Typically, they are 11 years old before they breed, some individuals holding out until they are 16. They are monogamous and form a very solid pair-bond that is broken only when a partner dies or after several failed breeding attempts. The male arrives at the colony first and defends the family patch, which extends just 1–2 meters (3–6 feet) from the nest. A little later, the female arrives. After some wing stretching, perhaps a bit of bill vibrating, and maybe a concluding noisy whistle and a sigh with bill pointed skyward, the birds mate. They then head out to sea to feed. On their return, the single egg is laid and the male starts to incubate. The female goes straight back to sea. His first egg-warming stint might last two or three weeks, during which time he neither eats nor drinks. As soon as the female returns, he is ocean bound, keen to replenish lost reserves before returning for his next incubation duty. And so it continues, through nearly 80 days of incubation, and up to five weeks of chick brooding. When brooding is no longer required, the chick is left unattended, and both adults feed it.

About nine months after hatching, while its parents are at sea, the chick uses its massive wings for the purpose they were made, and heads out over the southern ocean. With an incubation and fledging period totalling almost a year, it is little wonder that breeding is only attempted every other year.

In recent years many albatrosses have lost their lives to longline fishing. The long baited lines look like very easy pickings to a Wandering Albatross and many birds are hooked and drown. There are simple solutions to make longline fishing albatross-friendly and much is being done to change things before it is too late.

25. Diademed Plover *Phegornis mitchellii*

A poorly known but highly charismatic bird of bleak Andean habitats

Size: 16.5–19 cm (6.5–7.5 inches).
Distribution: Western South America.
Habitat: High altitude puna grassland.
Classification: One of 67 species in the family Charadriidae, and the sole member of the genus *Phegornis*.
Population and conservation status: Estimated at no more than 10,000 birds. Near Threatened.
Breeding system: Unknown. Probably monogamous.
Nest and eggs: On the ground. Unknown.
Incubation and fledging: Unknown.

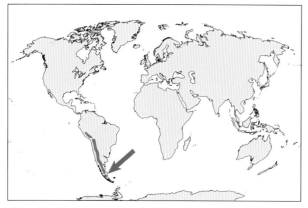

Ask a hardened veteran of South American birding what his or her most wanted or appreciated species of the continent happened to be, and you would be surprised how many would respond with the name of this highly obscure and somewhat mysterious bird. It is the classic enthusiasts' tick—rare, exceedingly difficult to find, exquisitely attractive and yet, at the same time, rather odd and individual: a great prize for a trip into rough and wild country.

The home of the Diademed Plover is the high altitude puna zone of the Andes, characterized by open ground dotted with bunched clumps of tough grass adapted to the cold and the dry. Within this zone the Plover is largely confined to bogs, fed either by snowmelt or ground water, and is rarely found below 4,000 meters (13,000 feet) in the breeding season. One of the many mysteries concerning it, however, is that although this habitat is abundant along the Andean chain between Peru in the north and Chile and Argentina in the south, the bird itself is both rare and localized. Birders on the trail of the Diademed Plover regularly comment that they can travel through miles of apparently ideal habitat,

before finally coming upon just another wetland among hundreds which, to the Plover's eyes, is special. Clearly, there is something within the bird's ecology that makes it especially fussy, and it has been suggested that it might need wetlands that are free from grazing or other physical disturbance. However, its true requirements remain a mystery and, until they are resolved, the Plover's rarity is both a puzzle and a concern. Largely through lack of information, together with the general perception that it has declined, the Diademed Plover is currently classified as Near Threatened.

Actually finding the bird, even when you have arrived at one of its few known sites, is by no means assured. It has an infuriating habit of simply remaining in one corner of a cushion bog for hours on end, feeding quietly and unobtrusively, just out of sight in a rivulet or pool. It is a small bird, about the size of a Common (*Actitis hypoleucos*) or Spotted Sandpiper (*A. macularia*) and, despite its colorful plumage, is not at all conspicuous.

Very little is known about the Diademed Plover's lifestyle. It is known to take insects in its diet, but exactly which ones is still a mystery. It has a longer, narrower bill than other plovers, and it is known to probe habitually into the water, but this quirk, quite distinct from the usual surface feeding of the rest of the family, yields as yet unknown results. For a long time scientists were not certain as to whether it was a plover or a sandpiper, but skeletal analysis of museum specimens confirms that it is a plover, albeit an odd one.

This is a bird in need of thorough study. All it requires is someone fit, dedicated, with built-in resistance to extreme cold and discomfort, who has a very good head for high altitudes, and a few free years to give to the conservation of a very special bird. Any offers out there?

24. Red-crowned Crane *Grus japonensis*

An elegant and increasingly rare icon of the East

Size: 1.5 m (4.9 feet).
Distribution: Breeds in Japan, China, Russia and Mongolia; also winters in Korea.
Habitat: Extensive marshes, bogs and wet meadows.
Classification: One of 15 species in the family Gruidae, and one of 11 in the genus *Grus*.
Population and conservation status: Estimated at 2,400 individuals, and declining. Endangered.
Breeding system: Monogamous.
Nest and eggs: Large pile of aquatic vegetation, placed on waterlogged ground. Two eggs.
Incubation and fledging: 29–34 days. About 95 days.

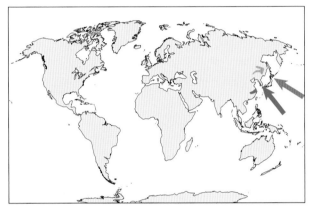

One of the bird wonders of the world is a winter gathering of Red-crowned Cranes. These superb, elegant, black-and-white birds seem perfectly at home in the snow, and the red on their heads seems to glow against the stark colors. Every line, every contour of a Red-crowned Crane seems aesthetically right and artistic. When many birds get together, as they sometimes do in their hundreds, they seem to paint their own pictures, both on the ground, where they are tall and slender, and in the air, where they are broad-winged and regal.

No wonder, then, that these birds have spawned a rich cultural history. They appear frequently in the art of Japan, Korea and China, their main centers of distribution. Intriguingly, they are often associated with longevity, presumably because, in recent history, these migratory birds would appear like clockwork at the turning of seasons, year after year—indeed, individual cranes were thought to live for a thousand years. These birds are also strongly associated with good luck and, in particular, happiness in marriage, being regularly depicted on bridal kimonos in Japan. This tallies well with the lives of the cranes, which, in the wild, embrace long-term pair-bonds. Moreover in Chinese art,

Red-crowned Cranes are often depicted transporting the souls of the recently departed to heaven, another allusion to their permanence in the landscape.

Ironically, this permanence is at considerable threat nowadays, and the Red-crowned Crane is in real danger of extinction. A resident flock at Hokkaido, in Japan, is reasonably secure, barring an outbreak of disease among this close-knit population. However, birds on the Chinese mainland, some of which winter in Korea, are under severe threat, mainly from destruction of habitat. Their population seems to dwindle annually and, at present, there is no sign of this trend reversing.

Red-crowned Cranes, in common with their relatives, show a very odd behavioral quirk that only adds to their considerable charisma. Long-legged and tall-necked, they seem quite unable to last long without breaking into a dance. Birds simply leap into the air, often with a flap of the wings, and they will also bow down or run about like exuberant schoolchildren. Birds of all ages perform these engaging rituals and their precise function is not entirely understood.

Another important aspect of the crane experience is to hear the birds calling. The sound is not especially musical—it is rather clanging in quality—but it is remarkable in its sheer volume, especially the unison call performed by male and female in sequence. Red-crowned Crane calls can be heard from several kilometers away, and the loudness is actually generated by an unusual arrangement of the crane's airways. The trachea is especially elongated and fuses along part of its length with the sternum, to make a series of plates that vibrate and amplify the sound, an arrangement unique among birds.

However, it is perfectly possible to envisage a time when these calls, for all their strength, are no more than a distant echo from a bird that has been lost.

23. Shoebill *Balaeniceps rex*

An intriguing bird with a truly outrageous bill

Size: 120 cm (3.9 feet).
Distribution: Central and East Africa.
Habitat: Swamps, especially papyrus swamps.
Classification: The sole member of the family Balaenicipitidae and the genus *Balaeniceps*.
Population and conservation status: Estimated at as few as 5,000–8,000 birds. Vulnerable.
Breeding system: Monogamous.
Nest and eggs: Flat pile of vegetation. 1–3 eggs.
Incubation and fledging: About 30 days. About 95–105 days.

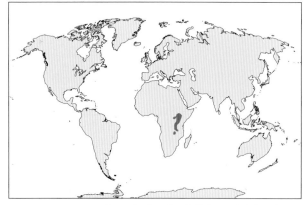

Taxonomists struggle with the Shoebill (or Whaleheaded Stork)—no other known bird species, either living or in ornithological history, has obvious close connections to this endemic African giant. It may end up somewhere near the pelicans, but links to storks have been suggested and there are also similarities to herons. Seeing one is not easy, which adds to their allure. They tend to be loners, and even paired birds forage in widely separated parts of their large territory, which can cover up to around 5 square kilometers (1.9 square miles).

The breeding season typically begins when the dry season starts. Lower water levels may make foraging easier, and the young birds fledge around the beginning of the rainy season. The Shoebill builds its nest on an island, or on a raft of plant material, with increasing quantities of plant material being added as the season progresses. The nest contains 1–3 eggs, though two is typical. Both parents incubate the eggs and look after the young. If the eggs need cooling, the shoe-shaped bill is used to bring water, and swamp plants may also be used to keep temperatures down. Water is also brought to overheating chicks and some of it may be drunk by the young Shoebills.

The outsized bill is much more than a water carrier, however. Shoebills are primarily fish eaters, and they need fishing tackle that can extract prey from a tangle of submerged vegetation. Their strong bill does the job well, even with fairly sizeable victims. Shoebills stand like statues on floating plants, waiting patiently, sometimes for over thirty minutes, their long toes spreading their heavy load (up to 6.7kg, or 14.7 lbs). The bill points at the water, so that both eyes can play their part, and the kill is a split-second move, a lunge with the bill followed by the rest of the bird, resulting in a "collapsed" Shoebill, hopefully with food in its bill. Its big wings push the bird back up to a more dignified position, with a bit of help from the bill perhaps.

Lungfish are frequent prey, but Shoebills are not exclusively piscivorous—they will eat snakes, lizards, frogs, mammals and young waterbirds. Food is swallowed head first, though some prey is first decapitated by the bird's sharp bill edges.

Shoebills can be prey as well as predator. Young birds may be eaten by crocodiles (Crocodylidae), though, in an ironic twist, young crocodiles are sometimes eaten by Shoebills!

For most of the year, Shoebills are solitary. But, if water levels drop and food has to be sought elsewhere, a few may gather where there are still fish to be caught, though they still try to give each other a fair amount of space. They soar well on thermals, but are sedentary and don't take to the wing lightly.

Shoebill numbers are in decline and their future is uncertain, threats to their survival including disturbance, habitat loss and hunting. Nests have been destroyed by grazing mammals, and birds are hunted for food and collected for zoos, with local people being made irresistible offers. Generating pride among local people for this ornithological marvel could be an important part of the Shoebill's future.

22. I'iwi *Vestiaria coccinea*

A stunning relic of the once incomparable Hawaiian bird community

Size: 15 cm (5.9 inches).

Distribution: Hawaii.

Habitat: Forests, mainly in highlands.

Classification: One of 23 species in the family Drepanididae, and the sole member of the genus *Vestiaria*.

Population and conservation status: Not recorded. Least Concern.

Breeding system: Monogamous.

Nest and eggs: Cup of twigs and mosses, lined with lichens and fibres, placed in crown of tree. Two eggs.

Incubation and fledging: 14 days. 21–22 days.

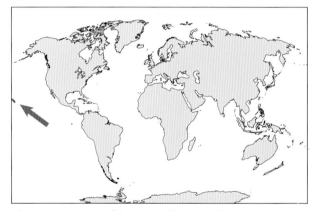

The very mention of the name Hawaiian honeycreeper inevitably arouses mixed feelings of wonder and regret. The wonder is in the sheer variety demonstrated within this family of birds, thought to have evolved from a single finchlike ancestor that pitched down on Hawaii some 5 million years ago. Through adaptive radiation, the Hawaiian honeycreepers have evolved a remarkable range of bill modifications and colors, more than enough to make the celebrated Galápagos Finches seem decidedly humdrum in comparison, with vibrant yellows, reds and greens to go with everything from heavy seed-splitting bills to the most delicate nectar-drinking, sickle shapes. The regret, however, is that, through various agencies, deliberate and accidental, we have decimated them.

No bird family has suffered such a catalogue of extinctions as the Hawaiian honeycreepers. Of the species recognized in historical times, half are already extinct and another half-dozen are well down that path, with one extinction—the Po'o-uli (*Melamprosops phaeosoma*)—known to have occurred in 2004. Some of the causes are deforestation, for example, and the introduction of harmful plants and animals. But another major problem has, if anything, been even worse: the accidental introduction of mosquitoes brought diseases such as avian pox and malaria, to which the honeycreepers had no defence. It destroyed the lowland populations, and if it were not for the fact that there are highlands on most Hawaiian islands, and that the mosquitoes cannot penetrate 1,219 meters (4,000 feet), it is doubtful that there would be any left at all.

But there are a handful of species remaining and one of these is the exquisite I'iwi. It has always been a widespread bird, being found on all the main islands and that, no doubt, has contributed to its survival.

The I'iwi's sharply curved bill fits neatly into the corolla tubes of some of the native flowers of the Hawaiian forests, and this bird could be considered primarily a nectar feeder. In some areas it seems to feed almost entirely at Ohi'a trees (*Metrosideros polymorpha*), but elsewhere it will also sup from a wide range of other native plants and, importantly, from a few introduced ones as well. If the bill doesn't fit, the I'iwi will sometimes use the sharp tip of its bill to pierce corolla tubes and thus to "rob" the plant of nectar without pollinating it. As another sideline, useful for survival, it also takes a few insects.

The recent history of the islands is permanently etched into the I'iwi's ecology. It is now the dominant feeder among native birds at most nectar sources in Hawaii, but was once subordinate to species that are now extinct. Yet it still behaves with caution, as if worried that its peers might turn up again. Furthermore, a common trick of subordinates at nectar sources is to incorporate snatches of its competitors' songs and calls into its own vocalizations, to fool them into mistaking its identity, if only for a moment. The I'iwi is thought to do this. So, if you should hear one singing, you may just be hearing voices from the past, whispers from long-extinct birds, and perhaps even some that were never seen by the eyes of man.

21. Emperor Penguin *Aptenodytes forsteri*

The biggest penguin and a breeder of the deep-freeze

Size: 112–115 cm (44–45 inches); weighs 19–46kg (42–101 lbs).

Distribution: Antarctica.

Habitat: Breeds on sea ice or coast, feeds offshore.

Classification: One of 17 species in the family Spheniscidae, and one of two in the genus *Aptenodytes*.

Population and conservation status: 270,000–350,000 individuals. Least Concern.

Breeding system: Monogamous.

Nest and eggs: None. One egg.

Incubation and fledging: 62–66 days. About five months.

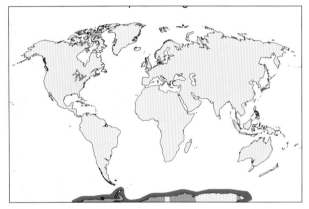

Life in the Antarctic is not easy. Winter temperatures may drop below –60°C (–76°F) and the wind can blow at over 300 kilometers (186 miles) an hour during day after day of darkness or semi-darkness. Amazingly, Emperor Penguins breed in the Antarctic winter.

The Emperor Penguin is monogamous, a male securing his mate by singing, face-to-face pair-bonding and their well-known waddling walk. With time, and after ceremonial bowing, mating takes place with the female on her belly.

Breeding is colonial and, uniquely among penguins, Emperors show no signs of territoriality, which enables them to huddle, even when incubating. Thousands may crowd together, with as many as 10 birds per square meter (11 square feet), creating a "huddle temperature" that can be more than 10°C (50°F) higher than the surroundings.

Colonies can be over 160 kilometers (100 miles) from the open sea and, therefore, from food. To survive the enforced fast of the journey to the colony, the long incubation and the journey back to the open sea, Emperors live off their fat. In the tightly-packed colony, effective communication is essential. Sound is important: males sound different from females, and individuals, including the chicks, can

be recognized by their voice. No nest is built and just one egg is laid, by which time the female may have lost 25 percent of her weight. The female passes the egg to the male and heads back to feed offshore. Males take responsibility for incubation, which takes over 60 days, although the female may return in time to play some part. He survives without food for around 115 days, sometimes longer, losing as much as 45 percent of his weight in the process.

The egg and chick are kept warm on the bird's feet. This keeps them off the ice and in contact with folds of highly vascular naked skin. If there is a chick to feed before the female returns, the male provides "penguin milk" from his digestive system, which can keep the chick going for as long as two weeks—no other penguin does this.

Emperors must also fast when they molt, as poor insulation and water resistance make fishing impossible. To minimize the impact of feather loss, molting happens just once a year during warmer weather (–5°C to 1°C/–23 to 40°F) and takes a mere month or so to complete. Whereas most birds lose a feather before replacing it, penguins keep the old feather until the new one has emerged. Penguin plumage also differs from that of other birds in that, brood patch excepted, feathers are spread evenly over the body (in most birds, despite appearances, feathers grow in distinct areas, with bald patches in between).

Emperor Penguins are supreme divers, staying underwater for up to 18 minutes and reaching depths of 265 meters (870 feet) or more, in pursuit of fish and squid. Their bones are solid rather than honeycombed—the extra weight makes swimming more energy-efficient. Under the sea, the bird "flies" through the water, the tail and feet acting as rudder. Our understanding of what their physiology should allow is a far cry from what we know this bird can do—there is still much to discover about this Antarctic champion.

20. Philippine Eagle *Pithecophaga jefferyi*

A flagship species for a severely threatened ecosystem, and one of the world's largest birds of prey

Size: 90–100 cm (35.4–39.3 inches).

Distribution: Philippines, mainly Mindanao.

Habitat: Undisturbed primary forest, mainly in mountains.

Classification: One of 242 species in the family Accipitridae, and the sole member of the genus *Pithecophaga*.

Population and conservation status: Estimated at 350–670 individuals. Critically Endangered.

Breeding system: Monogamous.

Nest and eggs: Huge platform of sticks, placed high in tall tree. One, occasionally two eggs.

Incubation and fledging: 60–64 days. 15–24 weeks.

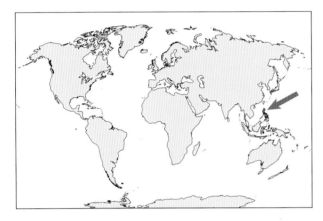

Not so long ago, this huge raptor was more commonly known as the Monkey-eating Eagle, and although monkeys are less important to its diet than other items, that epithet certainly conferred a unique sense of edge and danger to this mighty eagle, which is one of the three largest in the world.

It is certainly a predator at the very top of the food chain, catching and eating many of the medium-sized animals of the forest. Among its recorded captures are tree-squirrels (*Sciurini* spp.), various rodents, young pigs (*Sus* spp.) and small dogs. When in the mood for reptiles it will ambush snakes and monitor lizards (Varanidae). It somehow manages to catch bats, and the many birds recorded include hornbills (Bucerotidae), owls and other birds of prey, all of which implies that, despite its size, it must be fast and agile in the air. Indeed, when seen in flight, the long wings and tail are far more reminiscent of fast-moving ambush killers of confined spaces. such as the *Accipiter* hawks, than of other large predators.

Despite the obvious variety in the Philippine Eagle's diet, it actually predates on two particular animals above all others. These are the Palm Civet (*Paradoxurus hermaphroditus*) and the Philippine Colugo (*Cynocephalus volans*), two canopy-living mammals which, intriguingly, both tend towards being nocturnal. The latter is a curious mammal which glides from tree to tree on a membrane that surrounds its body completely, and it has been estimated that, in places, this cat-sized glider could constitute up to 90 percent of the Philippine Eagle's diet.

And then there are monkeys, of course. Although these animals are seldom taken, when they are on the menu the eagles snatch them in style. A pair has been observed hunting a troop co-operatively: one member of the pair perched near the monkeys in full view, to distract them, the other swooping in unnoticed, and lethal.

As befitting a large, dangerous predator, the Philippine Eagle builds an enormous nest high in a tree, as if it were a castle perched over a fiefdom. The platform can be as wide as 1.5 meters (5 feet) across, enough for a human to sit upon; but no human would be so foolish, given that it is regularly 30 meters (100 feet) or more above ground.

But when it comes to precarious positions, it is the Philippine Eagle that is in trouble. Relentless deforestation of the Philippine lowlands has already confined it to hills and mountains, while hunting and other disturbances are rife even there. Under such pressure, large birds with slow reproductive rates are bound to suffer, and the decline of the Philippine Eagle is looking increasingly terminal. Its populations on Leyte, Samar and Luzon may be so small as to be barely viable, while the population on Mindanao is just about holding its own. This species has been written off several times over the last 30 years, so perhaps there is hope, but the sad probability is that the Philippine Colugos will have fewer worries in the future.

19. Oilbird *Steatornis caripensis*
A nocturnal, echo-locating, fruit-eating troglodyte

Size: 40–49 cm (15.8–19.3 inches).

Distribution: Parts of southern Central America and northern South America; Trinidad.

Habitat: Caves, normally in forested mountains—some by the sea; feeds in forests.

Classification: The sole member of the family Steatornithidae and the genus *Steatornis*.

Population and conservation status: Estimated at 100,000–500,000 birds. Least Concern.

Breeding system: Monogamous, colonial.

Nest and eggs: Tapering pile of fruit stones, fruit pulp, excrement and spit, topped with a shallow depression. 1–4 eggs.

Incubation and fledging: 32–35 days. 88–125 days.

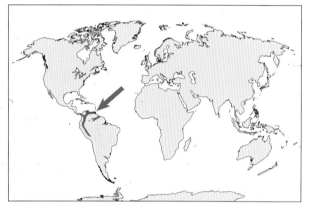

Oilbirds live in some disgusting places. Imagine a deep, dark cave, pitch-black perhaps. Regurgitated fruit stones are piled high on the ground and the place is crawling with a variety of six- and eight-legged creatures. Entering would not be a good idea. Your presence would trigger an onslaught of horror-movielike screeches and screams and you may even be putting your health at risk—catching histoplasmosis is a possibility in there, which can be dangerous and could even kill you. And, besides this, you would disturb the Oilbirds.

Oilbirds are fascinating creatures that spend the daylight hours in caves or gorges, coming out at night to feed on fruit. Life in a dark cave poses some challenges. In the darkest caves, Oilbirds find their way about by echolocation—their "technology" is less sophisticated than a bat's, but does the job well enough. When darkness falls, foraging begins, and Oilbirds fly through the growing darkness to their feeding areas. Once they are out of the cave, their sonar is switched off and they use visual clues to find their way. Oilbirds have lines of white spots on their wings and tail, which probably act as markers, to stop the birds flying in to one another.

Oilbirds eat nothing but fruit and will fly up to 150 kilometers (93 miles) to find it, though most travel no more than 40 kilometers (25 miles). Palm fruits are a staple and over 80 other fruits are also eaten. Their wings are adapted for slow flying, slow hovering and load-lugging. They feed in groups, hovering near treetops and ripping off whole fruits, which are gulped down in one piece. Many of the fruits they eat are scented; Oilbirds probably have a very good sense of smell and are able to sniff out at least some of their food. When feeding is done, the fruit-laden birds return to the cave, with neighboring birds from the colony arriving back at the same time.

Oilbird nests in Trinidad are used for roosting or breeding all year round, while others are used only in the breeding season. The nests are on high ledges and have the same occupiers from one year to the next, becoming progressively taller as their owners add new material. Regurgitated fruit is all the chicks eat, but it is not long before they are swallowing whole fruits and coughing up the seeds, just like the adults. A fruit-based diet may sound healthy, but the chicks grow slowly, taking around 3–4 months to fledge. It is also an oily diet, and after 10 weeks the chicks are huge, and much heavier than the adults. The chick's weight reduces however, when it begins to grow "proper" feathers.

After breeding, adults may either continue to use the same cave or move elsewhere; different populations appear to have different strategies.

Eating too much oil can be bad for you. Oilbird chicks are full of oil and wherever there are Oilbirds, at one time or another the chicks have been harvested to provide cooking oil for the locals.

What a bird. Another good reason to visit Trinidad!

18. Regent Honeyeater *Xanthomyza phrygia*

A colorful remnant of an unspoiled southeast Australia

Size: 22.5 cm (8.9 inches).

Distribution: Southeast Australia.

Habitat: Eucalyptus woodland.

Classification: One of 178 species in the family Meliphagidae, and the sole member of the genus *Xanthomyza*.

Population and conservation status: Estimated at 1,500 individuals. Endangered.

Breeding system: Monogamous.

Nest and eggs: Open cup with thick walls, placed in tree canopy. Two eggs.

Incubation and fledging: 14–15 days. 16–21 days.

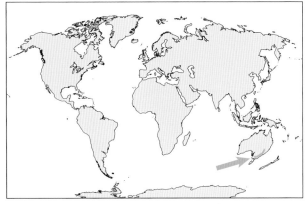

The Australian continent is dripping with honeyeaters, a varied and colorful family that dominates the nectar-feeding scene there. Many species are common and widespread and, on the whole, they have adapted reasonably well to the vast changes inflicted on the land over the years by human settlement.

But not all are prospering and, of all the species, the most urgent alarm bells are ringing for the Regent Honeyeater, a bird with smart dark plumage lit up strikingly by yellow scales. Its decline has been as insidious as it has been relentless, and, it has crept almost unnoticed into the Endangered category, making it one of Australia's most threatened birds. Once an abundant species of the southeast, which would turn up in thousands when nectar-feeding conditions were just right, it is now recorded in just a handful of places, and not necessarily every year. To make life difficult for conservationists, these favored locations are widely separated and the bird's movements, especially outside the breeding season, are very poorly understood.

The Regent Honeyeater's downfall seems to be its strong preference for certain types of nectar source, especially eucalypts known as box (especially Yellow Box—*Eucalyptus melliodora*—and White Box—*E. Albens*), and ironbark (especially Mugga Ironbark—*E. sideroxylon*). Forests dominated by these trees are found locally, especially in dry areas on the western slopes of the Great Dividing Range, but are nowhere near as extensive as they once were. Furthermore, to support Regent Honeyeaters, the trees have to be mature in order to produce the right concentration of nectar. This is why the degradation of woodlands, in which large trees die back or are removed, leaving only youthful stands, affects the Regent Honeyeater very badly.

Another, rather more subtle, problem also clips the honeyeater's wings. Being a nectar feeder, it inevitably faces competition from other honeyeaters, notably from more aggressive species such as the super-abundant Noisy Miner (*Manorina melanocephala*) and friarbirds (*Philemon* spp.). Once, this was not a problem, as these are typically edge species that used not to impinge too badly on the Regent Honeyeater's habitat. Nowadays, however, helped by the wide-scale felling of woodlands for agriculture and development, the populations of Noisy Miners, in particular, have exploded, and it is thought that they out-compete the Regent Honeyeaters for nectar and nest sites.

From a population of many thousands, therefore, and probably millions, the number of Regent Honeyeaters has now collapsed to no more than 1,000–2,000 birds. Some people may not think that this matters, but the species's problems have wider implications. On the face of it, southeast Australia still retains much natural habitat, with an impressive system of national parks and sparsely populated areas. But when a once common bird can sink here almost to oblivion, something deeper must be wrong; something that should make people sit up and take notice.

17. Wallcreeper *Tichodroma muraria*

Europe's butterfly-bird

Size: 16.5 cm (6.5 inches).
Distribution: Central Asia, plus some in Europe and Middle East.
Habitat: Rocky mountains, cliffs and crags; at lower altitudes in winter, including quarries and buildings.
Classification: One of 25 species in the family Sittidae, and the sole member of the genus *Tichodroma*.
Population and conservation status: Estimated at 77,000–200,000 birds in Europe. Least Concern.
Breeding system: Monogamous.
Nest and eggs: A cup of lichen and moss, grass, pine needles etc., with softer lining. 4–5 eggs.
Incubation and fledging: 18.5–20 days. 29 days.

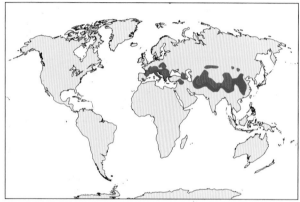

Any typical British birdwatcher who has not yet seen a Wallcreeper will be keen to see one, and anyone who has seen one will be delighted to see another! This is one of those birds that people *want* to see. From time to time, Wallcreepers do show up in Britain, but there is no point in being too parochial, and your chances of seeing them are much better elsewhere. You can find them in the mountainous parts of Europe or, at least, you can try. The breeding season may not be the best time to try; breeding Wallcreepers are often in places that are hard to get to, between 1,000–3,000 meters (3,280–9,850 feet) above sea level. In winter, however, they make it a bit easier for us and come down to lower altitudes. Cliff faces are worth checking out, including man-made ones in quarries. The birds are even seen on buildings and bridges, sometimes in cities, and may also put in an appearance on sea cliffs.

Wallcreepers hang onto rock faces and can be very hard to see—it is worth a good look but you could easily miss one. Catching a glimpse of a flying bird in its "red-butterfly" glory may be easier—the wonderfully marked wings betray the bird's presence to other Wallcreepers and

to birders. When it settles, keep an eye on the wings—Wallcreepers continually offer tantalizing glimpses of their hidden crimson by quick wing flashes—a habit that even very young birds have.

Wallcreepers track down most of their invertebrate prey in cliff-face nooks and crannies, but sometimes forage in other places, including streamside stones, and on buildings and trees. They will hover to grab a "perched" fly, bash caterpillars on rocks and pull the wings off moths before eating them. Their long list of prey includes damselflies, grasshoppers, bugs, beetles, spiders and centipedes.

After wintering at low altitude, Wallcreepers head back to their breeding areas. Returning early may be advantageous—it could be first come first served when breeding territories are in short supply. Pair-bonds last only for the breeding season, so building a partnership for the season ahead is a priority.

Wallcreeper song consists of simple, full-bodied whistles, and is likely to play a key part in securing a partner. The song may be delivered from midair during "nest-showing", when a male flies wild, unpredictable, dropping and rising circuits, from and back to the nest site. The nest itself may be set some way back in a crevice, and often has "his" and "hers" entrances, or one way in and another way out. Other nest sites include piles of rocks, and even buildings, and nests are often very near to water. Wherever they are however, the location must provide protection from mustelids in order to maximize breeding success. The male leaves the incubation and brooding of the young to the female, but helps to feed the chicks.

At the end of the breeding season most Wallcreepers abandon the higher altitudes, and some seem to be regular migrants, although not over great distances.

16. Helmet Vanga *Euryceros prevostii*

A puzzling oddity from deepest Madagascar

Size: 28–31 cm (11–12.2 inches).

Distribution: Northeast Madagascar.

Habitat: Primary rainforest.

Classification: One of 21 species in the family Vangidae, and the sole member of the genus *Euryceros*.

Population and conservation status: Estimated at fewer than 20,000 birds. Vulnerable.

Breeding system: Presumed monogamous.

Nest and eggs: Open cup placed in a tree. 2–4 eggs.

Incubation and fledging: 16–18 days. Not recorded.

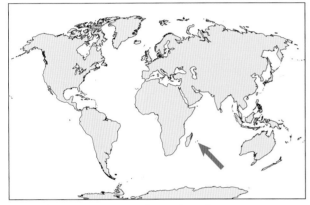

The Helmet Vanga is one of a number of species in Madagascar that are famously difficult to find. It is a largely quiet bird of the middle strata of thick primary forest, often sitting still for long periods, making it impossible to detect. So, despite its highly distinctive appearance, the Helmet Vanga melts into the forest and can turn up in certain places after what seems to be many years' absence. For example, at Mantadia National Park, not far from Madagascar's capital, Antananarivo, it remained a great rarity, scarcely ever seen, until a nest was discovered in the 1990s.

The obvious characteristic of the Helmet Vanga, its outsize arched bill of vivid blue, is an enigma. No one has yet seen the bird use it for anything other than reasonably routine tasks, such as snatching food from perch or air in the manner of countless other forest birds, so the possibility that it might be vital for opening up some kind of resource unavailable to other birds has not yet been confirmed. The fact that young Helmet Vangas do not have blue bills, but grey ones with a yellow rather than black tip, may at least suggest that the bill color is attractive to the opposite sex, but again, until somebody sees some courtship behavior and can come up with

concrete proof, this must remain a mere hypothesis.

The diet of the Helmet Vanga, however, seems to be largely composed of animal matter. It is most often seen catching large insects and other invertebrates during an operation known as sally-gleaning. In this technique, a bird takes off from a perch and snatches an edible item from a surface, such as a branch, while in flight, but does not catch it in midair. The Vanga also visits the ground and, as well as insects, has been recorded catching snails, lizards and crabs.

The habit of sally-gleaning clearly requires a bit of room to maneuver and, not surprisingly, the Helmet Vanga usually moves about in the airy mid-levels of rainforest. Here it frequently joins mixed feeding flocks of other rainforest birds, notably other vangas such as the White-headed (*Artamella viridis*), Blue (*Cyanolanius madagascarinus*) and Hook-billed Vangas (*Vanga curvirostris*). These move through the forest slowly, each species utilizing its own niche, while everybody benefits from the collective vigilance. The vangas, which are largely limited to the island of Madagascar, contain a variety of species of impressively different sizes, colors and bill shapes, analogous to more famous examples of adaptive radiation such as Galápagos finches or Hawaiian honeycreepers (Drepanidinae). They have not been as well studied as these other groups, but could easily prove to be as equally fascinating and instructive to scientists.

The Helmet Vanga remains a poorly known bird, with most details of its ecology still obscure. It is also rare, confined to primary rainforest below 800 meters (2,600 feet) elevation. The lack of records suggests that it maintains low populations over a wide area, and it is classified as Vulnerable. It is a highly charismatic, sought-after bird, and few species anywhere have such exciting potential for study.

15. Bengal Florican *Houbaropsis bengalensis*

An extremely rare Asian parachutist

Size: Male 64 cm (25 inches), female 68 cm (27 inches).
Distribution: India, Nepal, Cambodia, perhaps Vietnam.
Habitat: Lowland grasslands, frequently with bushes or trees.
Classification: One of 27 species in the family Otidae, and the sole member of the genus *Houbaropsis*.
Population and conservation status: Estimated at 250–999 birds. Critically Endangered.
Breeding system: Polygamous.
Nest and eggs: Scrape. 1–2 eggs.
Incubation and fledging: About 25–28 days. 4–5 weeks.

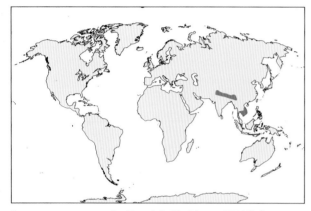

Imagine you are in the Royal Sukla Phanta Wildlife Reserve in Nepal, and the sun is just creeping over the horizon. It is late March, and there are more Bengal Floricans here than anywhere else in the country. This is a bird you have always wanted to see, but with so few left (just 100 or fewer in Nepal), time could be running out. Your telescope is trained on an area of short grass in the middle distance. That ridiculously early start is about to be rewarded. You hear the wing-clapping before you see the bird—you glance up, move your 'scope to the left and focus. The Florican is jumping up off the ground, rising to about 4 meters (13 feet), with puffed-up black feathers and bright white on its wings. The wing-clapping is noisy and easy to hear. He peaks, then parachutes down, but then, with trembling wings, goes up again before completing his fall to the ground. With luck, a female Bengal Florican will be as impressed as you are!

Bengal Floricans normally display at the beginning and end of the day. Once the mating is done, the female is left to her own devices and takes sole charge of incubation and looking after the young birds, which leave the nest shortly after hatching. Bengal Floricans are omnivorous, eating mostly plants during winter and spring but many more insects at other times. Their diet includes seeds, grass, berries and flowers, as well as beetles, ants and grasshoppers. There are records of vertebrates being taken too, with snakes, lizards and frogs on the menu.

This Critically Endangered species is found in two areas: Cambodia (and perhaps Vietnam), and India and Nepal. Wherever this bird is found, grasslands have been changed or destroyed, with obvious implications. The species' stronghold is now in Cambodia, where there are thought to be between 600 and 900 birds. Until 1999, no one knew that there were still Bengal Floricans in Cambodia, but even here numbers are falling fast. The area around Tonle Sap Lake is Cambodia's Bengal Florican stronghold. It is an area that has suffered massive losses, with perhaps almost 80 percent of the Floricans disappearing in just under a decade. Cambodian agriculture has changed; it is more intensive than it used to be and more land is being used to grow rice. As a consequence, a huge amount of grassland has been lost. Hunting has also played a part in the bird's decline, and is still an issue. In India and Nepal fewer than 400 Bengal Floricans survive, and perhaps as few as 250.

So what does the future hold for this great parachutist? Damaged grassland needs to be restored wherever possible, and grassland management in protected areas needs to be improved. One chink of light is the establishment of Integrated Farming and Biodiversity Areas in Cambodia, which may well benefit Floricans. The Indian and Nepalese population is patchily distributed, so enlarging and joining up protected areas could help. Fieldworkers need to keep looking for Bengal Floricans—there could be undiscovered populations out there, especially in Cambodia.

14. Gouldian Finch *Erythrura gouldiae*

A highly endangered and ecologically unusual bird of psychedelic plumage

Size: 13–14 cm (5.1–5.5 inches).

Distribution: Northern Australia.

Habitat: Tropical open grassy woodland.

Classification: One of 138 species in the family Estrildidae, and one of 11 in the genus *Erythrura*.

Population and conservation status: Estimated at fewer than 2,500 individuals. Endangered.

Breeding system: Monogamous.

Nest and eggs: Dome of dry grass placed in a hollow. 4–8 eggs.

Incubation and fledging: 12–13 days. 21 days.

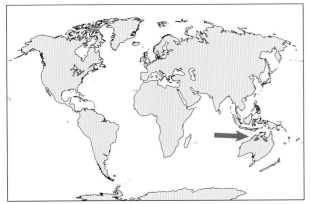

It is not just splendid colors that make the Gouldian Finch stand out; it is also the bold pattern and improbable design of the plumage, and the bird's consummate neatness, which never seems to slip. Intriguingly, the bird also comes in three color variants. All females and most males have smart black hoods, but a consistent minority (25 percent) of all males have red heads (see opposite), and one in 100 has an orange head. Nobody has yet worked out why these color morphs occur.

The species was first discovered by the English naturalist and explorer John Gould in 1844 and, as befitting something special, he named it in honor of his wife. At the time, it was an abundant bird of grassy areas of the tropical north, and was regularly seen in flocks of thousands. Now a thing of the past, it is hard to imagine what a wondrous sight they must have made.

The Gouldian Finch is very much a bird of hot, sunny climates; experiments have shown that its activity peaks at 38 to 42°C (100.5 to 107.5°F). However, it depends for breeding on the rains, which bring about the required abundant growth of seeding grasses, a vital component of its habitat. Thus, it is a bit fussy ecologically, needing just

the right balance of sun and rain to set breeding in train. In some areas, this necessitates a modest migratory movement to find the perfect location. The nest site, meanwhile, is highly unusual for an Australian "finch". Most of its relatives place their domed, grass structures in thick, thorny bushes, but the Gouldian Finch builds inside a cavity—either a hole in a tree or a crevice in a termite mound. The young hatch in the dark, their begging facilitated by iridescent nodules flanking their gaping mouths, reflecting light to guide the parents to the chicks' grateful jaws.

Although they eat some insects, and have been recorded launching into the air to snap up flying termites, Gouldian Finches are primarily seed-eaters. This is a very dry diet and, in contrast to most small birds, Gouldian Finches are able to suck up water. It is thought that this could be an adaptation to drinking from very small, shallow water sources.

Although grass does not sound like an exacting ecological requirement, the fine print of the Gouldian Finch's habitat is highly specific. It really needs a mosaic of open woodland with abundant grassy understorey, and it seems that this depends upon a regime of infrequent but regular fires. In recent years, unfortunately for the Finch, the fires have been too regular, resulting in a tipping of the balance towards unsuitable uniformity. This, together with the fact that cattle-grazing prevents the grass from seeding, has suddenly made the Gouldian Finch's precise habitat very scarce indeed.

And this is bad news. Already suffering from many years of trapping for the cage-bird trade, difficulties in the wild have sent the population of the Gouldian Finch into a sharp decline. Suddenly this bird is not just scarce, but endangered. The numbers are frighteningly small and, ironically, it may be that only captive-breeding, together with strict management, can save this bird for posterity.

13. Maleo *Macrocephalon maleo*

A colorful and highly individual bird with astonishing nesting habits

Size: 55–60 cm (21.6–23.6 inches).

Distribution: Sulawesi and nearby Buton Islands.

Habitat: Forest, beaches.

Classification: One of 22 species in the family Megapodiidae, and the sole member of the genus *Macrocephalon*.

Population and conservation status: Estimated at 8,000–14,000 birds. Endangered.

Breeding system: Apparently monogamous.

Nest and eggs: Burrows into warm substrate and buries eggs. 8–12 eggs over a three-month period.

Incubation and fledging: 62–85 days. Leaves nest once hatched.

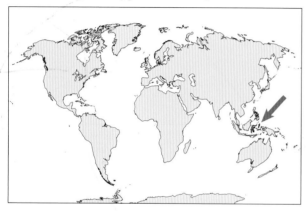

The image of a bird on its nest, incubating its eggs with its own body heat, is part of our universal understanding of birds' lives. In Australasia some birds build mounds, and tend them in order to keep the temperature constant. It is different, but at least it conforms to our notion of what separates them from the reptiles.

But on a few islands in the East Indies and beyond, a small band of species within one family of birds has entirely eschewed any parental care. These are the Megapodiidae, or megapodes, and one of the most distinctive members of the breakaway group within this family, endemic to the Indonesian island of Sulawesi, is the Maleo.

This bird, like a giant pheasant resplendent in light pink and black, with a horny plate upon its head that gives it a suitably reptilian look, places its eggs into warm soil. Its eggs are kept warm by the heat of the sun or by geothermal activity. In all, only 142 Maleo nesting sites have ever been found, many of them on beaches, others in forest clearings. They are used communally by dozens of birds at a time, of necessity cramming themselves into small, highly valued patches of ground.

Maleos are forest birds, living on the ground and eating fallen fruits and surface-living invertebrates. They can occur in hill forest at up to 1,200 meters (3,940 feet), but wherever they are they need reasonably close access to a breeding site. Throughout the year, females make the pilgrimage down to the soil, and make a burrow into which they lay one egg at a time. Over the years, entry burrows may become as much as 3 meters (10 feet) wide and penetrate 1 meter (3 feet) down into the ground. The eggs themselves are laid anywhere between 20–60 centimeters (8–24 inches) below the surface where, in theory, they should be safe. In reality, however, they suffer high predation from humans, pigs (*Sus* spp.), monitor lizards (Varanidae) and, discordantly for creatures that bury their own eggs in the same way, crocodiles (Crocodylidae).

The average Maleo egg may comprise as much as 16 percent of the female's total body weight and, by volume, contain 61–64 percent yolk. Every bit of this is needed, since the young Maleo hatches in a very advanced state, after some 2–3 months, and then has to tunnel its way to the surface. In contrast to the embryos of other birds, which have a modified bill to chip open their eggshells, Maleos and other megapodes kick their way out. Once out in the open, these remarkably precocious birds can fly almost immediately.

Its reliance on warm soil for incubation has made the Maleo extremely vulnerable to human activity. The eggs are nutritious and, of course, being confined to a few ideal sites, are easy to find. Of all the Maleo breeding sites known, only four are safe from persecution and, as a result of this, along with the fact that its entire population is confined to one island group, the species is classified as Endangered. Whether such a trusting bird can survive in today's world, only time will tell.

12. Resplendent Quetzal *Pharomachrus mocinno*

A remarkable cultural icon once worshipped by the Mayans and Aztecs

Size: 36–40 cm (14–15.7 inches), plus tail up to 65 cm (25.6 inches).

Distribution: Central America.

Habitat: Highland forest.

Classification: One of 42 species in the family Trogonidae, and one of five in the genus *Pharomachrus*.

Population and conservation status: Not recorded. Near Threatened.

Breeding system: Monogamous.

Nest and eggs: In a cavity in a tree, no lining. 1–2 eggs.

Incubation and fledging: 17–19 days. 23–31 days.

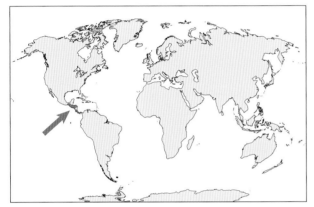

What would you make of a bird that, in order not to damage its splendid tail feathers, is compelled to fall backwards off its perch in order to fly? If you were a member of the Mayan or Aztec peoples of Central America, your answer would be to worship it. On appearance alone, the silky Resplendent Quetzal, with its narrow emerald train and scintillating colors, certainly dazzles all who set eyes upon it. No wonder that these two peoples wove it into the fabric of their cultural lives. Their god of good things, Quetzalcoatl, was depicted with the head of a serpent and the body of the bird and the head-dresses of rulers were always made from Quetzal plumes, plucked from live birds that were then released back into the wild.

Even today, the Resplendent Quetzal is revered. In Guatemala, for example, it appears on the national flag; even the official currency is called the Quetzal. Plumes were still collected widely in Central America until recently, and even now these feathers are thought to bring long life and prosperity. And, since the Quetzal itself brings ecotourists into its native countries in droves, perhaps the latter benefit is still true.

Although endowed with exceptional beauty, it cannot be described as the most effervescent or riveting of company. It spends much of its time just sitting on a perch, seemingly staring into space, and can turn its head through at least 180 degrees, almost as much as an owl. Except when breeding it has no need for feverish foraging; just a few successful helpings of fruit or snatches at flying insects will suffice for the entire day. Indeed, it has such small, weak feet that it has little gymnastic ability. But it can fly well and, astonishingly, those long feathers make barely a whisper in flight.

Extraordinarily, for a decidedly sedentary, apparently unimaginative bird, the Resplendent Quetzal has recently been found, in some places at least, to show complex migratory movements in response to supplies of fruit. In Costa Rica, where it breeds at altitudes above 1,500 meters (5,000 feet), it shifts downhill to the Pacific slope (1,100–1,400 meters, 3,600–4,600 feet) in July, slips over to the Atlantic side (700–1,200 meters, 2,300–3,900 feet) in about October or November, then returns uphill to breed again in January. This regular altitudinal displacement, confirmed by telemetry, was a complete surprise.

For breeding, Resplendent Quetzals select a tree cavity. Both sexes incubate, which presents difficulties for the male's extraordinary tail. When sitting, the male faces outwards and his tail curls round his body, past his head and sometimes out of the hole.

There is little extraordinary about Resplendent Quetzal nests except for their low level of sanitation. It is possible that this is a deliberate ploy, since predation of nests is exceptionally high (losses can be 80 percent). Faced with a chamber piled high with excreta, a predator might be put off! Nevertheless, had the Mayans and Aztecs been discouraged by such insalubrious habits, the Resplendent Quetzal's career as an icon might never have taken off at all.

11. Grey-necked Picathartes *Picathartes oreas*
An elusive and unusual African rarity

Size: 33–38 cm (13–15 inches).
Distribution: Nigeria, Cameroon, Equatorial Guinea and Gabon; may occur in Congo Brazzaville.
Habitat: Hilly rainforest with cliffs, caves and rocks.
Classification: One of two species in the family Picathartidae and the genus *Picathartes*.
Population and conservation status: Estimated at 2,500–9,999 birds. Vulnerable.
Breeding system: Monogamous, colonial.
Nest and eggs: Mud, leaves and grass cup attached to rock. 1–3 eggs.
Incubation and fledging: 21–24 days. About 24 days.

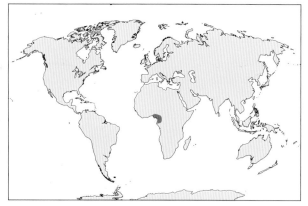

This strange bird helps to keep taxonomists in work. Over the years, it has been listed with the Old World warblers (Sylviidae), the flycatchers (Muscicapidae), the babblers (Timaliidae), the crows (Corvidae), and somewhere near the starlings (Sturnidae). Current thinking is that it may be close to the rockjumpers (*Chaetops* spp.). However it is classified, it is Vulnerable, as is the White-necked Picathartes (*P. gymnocephalus*), its closest relative. Both are birds of Africa, but their ranges are completely separate: White-necked is a West African species, whereas Grey-necked has a Central African distribution. Birdwatchers are used to reading depressing stories of birds in decline, but things may not be as bad for the Grey-necked Picathartes as current data suggests—breeding sites are still being discovered and conservationists are optimistic that there are Grey-necked Picathartes tucked away in Congo Brazzaville.

The Grey-necked Picathartes can be a tricky bird to understand and has not been the subject of much scientific research. It is a bird of untamed primary or secondary forest, and may live in inaccessible areas. If you are privileged enough to see one, it probably will be just one, or possibly two, on the ground in the forest, or moving from one tree to another nearby. They are wet season breeders and some pairs breed twice a year, depending on rainfall patterns. Picathartes are also known as Rockfowl and rocks and caves are important features of the bird's habitat—the concretelike mud nest is attached to the inside of a cave or on a cliff face, in a position that provides respite from rainfall and is inaccessible to predators. Where birds have chosen unwisely and not nested high enough, Drills (*Mandrillus leucophaeus*) and Chimpanzees (*Pan troglodytes*) may be a problem. When there are plenty of nest sites, Grey-necked Picathartes are solitary breeders, but when suitable rocks and caves are harder to come by, breeding is colonial. The colonies are not large, however, with perhaps 2–5 pairs sharing a cave.

Animals make up most of their diet, particularly invertebrates such as beetles, orthopterans, worms and snails. A column of ants may provide rich pickings and lizards and frogs may also be taken. They eat their greens too, including some fruit.

Typically, this is a bird of wild, forested areas—its habitat alone provides a certain amount of protection, but predictably, even some of these areas are being destroyed. Human activity in Picathartes habitat disturbs the birds, and clearly, infanticide is unhelpful in a declining species. Predation may well be an issue too, and in some areas unfortunate birds may be caught in traps intended for other victims. Some are deliberately taken for the bird trade.

BirdLife International has developed a species action plan for the Grey-necked Picathartes. We need to know more about its distribution and numbers. There is work to do to reduce disturbance. More areas need to be protected and habitat management must be improved. And as ever, there is work to do to engender support and understanding for this elusive, hard-to-classify bird.

10. Ribbon-tailed Astrapia *Astrapia mayeri*

A bird-of-paradise with a tail to tell

Size: Male 32 cm (12.5 inches); 125 cm (4ft 1in) including elongated tail; female 35 cm (13.8 inches);
53 cm (20.8 inches) including elongated tail feathers.

Distribution: Western Papua New Guinea.

Habitat: Upland moss forests.

Classification: One of 41 species in the family Paradisaeidae, and one of five in the genus *Astrapia*.

Population and conservation status: Not recorded, reasonably common in some areas. Near Threatened.

Breeding system: Polygynous.

Nest and eggs: Leaf and palm-frond cup, wrapped and lined with orchid-stems. One egg.

Incubation and fledging: 21 days. 22–26 days.

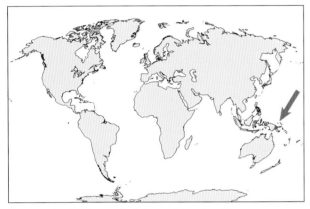

Despite the Ribbon-tailed Astrapia's scientific name, Mr. Mayer was not the first person to record this species. That honor seems to belong to a Mr. Hides, and it was the feathers he secured that aroused Mayer's interest. Those earlier feathers never resurfaced, and ultimately it was missionary work that led to the scientific description of *Astrapia mayeri*. Presumably, the missionary had a good relationship with the owner of the headdress that had been decorated with Ribbon-tailed Astrapia plumage. Whatever, feathers were passed to Mayer, and the rest is ornithological history. The Ribbon-tailed Astrapia joined the scientific record in 1939, but must, of course, have been known to local people for many generations.

The male (left) is a fantastic-looking bird. At his best, his head, throat and breast are richly iridescent, with a red-brown band underlining his glossy breast. His head is adorned with backward-pointing ear-tufts and a strange bobble at the base of the bill. But his most remarkable feature is his tail, or more specifically, the two innermost tail feathers. If you measure to the tip of his "normal" tail feathers, a male Ribbon-tailed Astrapia is similar in size to a Eurasian Collared Dove (*Streptopelia decaocto*)

or a Mourning Dove (*Zenaida macroura*). But if you measure to the tip of his extended white ribbons, his vital statistic can be increased almost fourfold. Each ribbon is tipped with a spearlike marking and, as he ages, the ribbons get longer and the other tail feathers get shorter, adding to the apparent length of his outsized rectrices. There are records of ribbons measuring from 66 centimeters (26 inches) to just over 1 meter (3.3 feet) in length—making it little wonder that they ended up in headdresses!

There are still things we don't know about Ribbon-tailed Astrapias. We know they are polygynous but we don't know whether the males show off to the females alone or with other males. The display involves leaping from branch to branch and back again, or perhaps, high in a tree, sideways jumps—left-right-left-right—swaying the ribbons. There may be a "ribbon-showing" display flight too, in which the Astrapia's wing rustling is more amplified than normal. The nest is often in a tree that is clearly detached from the nearby forest, which could make it less vulnerable to would-be predators, and all the incubation is left to the female (above). Ribbon-tailed Astrapias eat fruit and arthropods—*Schefflera* fruits seem to be particularly favored.

All of the Astrapia species are birds of high altitude. They have been described as a superspecies, each species normally being geographically discrete. There are, however, areas where the Ribbon-tailed Astrapia and Princess Stephanie's Astrapia (*A. stephaniae*) coexist, and where hybrids are frequent. An adult male Princess Stephanie's Astrapia has long, broad and dark innermost tail feathers—those of mixed parentage sport a tail that is intermediate in thickness between the two species, and black and white. Such birds are also known as Barnes' Astrapia.

9. Twelve-wired Bird-of-Paradise *Seleucidis melanoleucus*

A stunning bird-of-paradise with potentially seductive "wires"

Size: Male 33 cm (13 inches); female 35 cm (14 inches).

Distribution: Most of New Guinea, Salawati Island.

Habitat: Lowland forests.

Classification: One of 41 species in the family Paradisaeidae, and the sole member of the genus *Seleucidis*.

Population and conservation status: Not recorded, frequent in some areas. Least Concern.

Breeding system: Polygynous.

Nest and eggs: Cup set in top of large, messy construction of vines, bark and other plant material. One egg.

Incubation and fledging: 20 days. About 21 days.

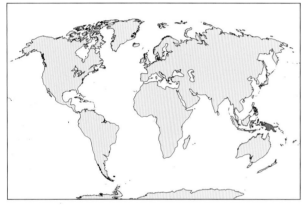

The male and female of this bird-of-paradise look very different. If you knew no better, and didn't see them together, you might not believe that the two belong to the same species. The female (above) is relatively drab— it is the much more flamboyant male (opposite) that most people will want to see. Adult males have very long, very yellow flank feathers whose shafts continue way beyond the main body of the feather to create the bird's twelve "wires". Fully "wired" males are not easy to see, however. You may hear one, but seeing one is tricky, and your best chance is when they are displaying, which, helpfully, occurs in seven or more months of the year.

When they display, they normally do it at the top of dead trees that stick out of the forest canopy. To see one, get out before sunrise, and listen. A male usually makes plenty of noise to announce his presence, moving around the top of a dead trunk and shouting out in all directions, with perhaps some wing lifting to show off his yellow sides to best effect.

Things get really interesting when a potential mate shows up. The male gives himself a very rapid makeover. Yellow hides black, he dons a jade-rimmed ruff and shows off his pink legs. His bill is an important tool of seduction—he plays with her bill tip, following her as she reverses down the trunk, perhaps corkscrewing after her, with plenty of bill contact along the way. She moves things on by going up to the top of the tree. He turns and moves towards her, for more "bill seduction", sometimes with a pulsating ruff, and this "foreplay" continues with pecks under her tail and then at the back of her neck.

His wires are about more than looking good and a female may find herself being stroked by them as the male swings leisurely from side to side, monitoring his own actions as his wires sweep across the female between bill and breast while making sure his yellow panels can be seen in all their glory.

When she stills herself for mating, his bill-work becomes increasingly intimate, as he works his way along her body, from the tip of the bill to under her tail, and then to the back of her neck, which, if she allows, is normally soon followed by coitus. It is the more cryptically colored female that constructs the nest and incubates the eggs, activities that are best not advertised by bright plumage.

Like some other birds-of-paradise, this species sometimes hybridizes with family members from other genera. The Wonderful Bird-of-Paradise is part Twelve-wired and part Lesser Bird-of-Paradise (*Paradisaea minor*), while Mantou's Riflebird is a mix of Twelve-wired and Magnificent Riflebird (*Ptiloris magnificus*).

Twelve-wired Birds-of-Paradise eat arthropods, fruit and nectar, and may have a certain penchant for *Pandanus* fruit, a foodstuff that may supply vital yellow pigment as well as nutrition. They are sometimes part of mixed-species feeding flocks which include other birds-of-paradise. Now there's something to dream about!

8. Long-tailed Ground Roller *Uratelornis chimaera*

A unique bird confined to one of the most astonishing habitats on the planet

Size: 34–47 cm (13.4–18.5 inches).

Distribution: Southwest Madagascar.

Habitat: Spiny forest.

Classification: One of five species in the family Brachypteraciidae, and the sole member of the genus *Uratelornis*.

Population and conservation status: Estimated at 10,000–20,000 individuals. Vulnerable.

Breeding system: Monogamous.

Nest and eggs: In a burrow in sand dug by the parents. 2–4 eggs.

Incubation and fledging: Unknown.

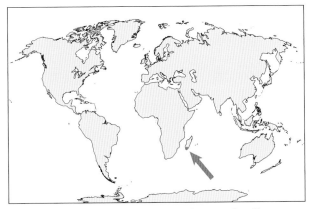

There is no doubt that the Long-tailed Ground Roller is a fantastic bird—a sort of Madagascan version of the Greater Roadrunner (*Geococcyx californianus*) (page 70), with strong legs, a long tail and a similar reluctance to fly. But what truly elevates it towards the upper echelons of star quality is the remarkable ecosystem to which it belongs, and from which it cannot be separated. See a Long-tailed Ground Roller in the wild, and you inevitably find yourself in one of the strangest landscapes on earth: the incomparable spiny forest.

What sets the spiny forest apart from other forests is the extraordinary nature of its component plants, which make it look like a set from a science fiction fantasy. One of the chief components is the Octopus Tree (*Didierea madagascariensis*), which looks like a cross between a cactus and an octopus, with flailing branches pointing in all directions, each equipped with spines. Other members of this tree's family, endemic to Madagascar, are equally weird, without the usual "branches" and "leaves" you might expect, but more pillar-shaped and skeletal. Add to these those famous baobabs (*Adansonia* spp.), which look like large trees planted upside down, and you might have some idea of this extraordinary landscape. Not surprisingly, the Ground Roller is only one of a number of birds unique to the area.

Within the forest, Long-tailed Ground Rollers are, as their name suggests, terrestrial feeders. They spend much time working the leaf litter for invertebrates, such as ants, beetles and cockroaches, but will also snatch food from foliage and chase butterflies, for example, in an upward jump. In common with other members of their small family, they have a stop-start approach to foraging, spending long periods standing still, interspersed with some surprisingly quick dashes after agile, tasty prey. Interestingly, there is much evidence to suggest that Long-tailed Ground Rollers may be semi-nocturnal, since they have been recorded hunting by night.

From about October onwards, male Long-tailed Ground Rollers put a little extra effort into foraging, and can be seen bringing offerings of food to their mates. This is a prelude to breeding, since the male's provision reduces the female's burden of food-finding at a time when she needs to devote her energies to egg-production. Nest-building coincides with the arrival of the rainy season, and in the Long-tailed Ground Roller's case it means digging a burrow in a sandy area that is relatively free of vegetation. The burrow goes down at a shallow angle for about a meter, with a chamber about 20 centimeters (8 inches) in diameter at the bottom.

At present the Long-tailed Ground Roller's status is listed as Vulnerable, but this could change in the near future. The spiny forest is a geographically restricted habitat, and the Ground Roller has always been considered rare. In contrast to the rest of Madagascar, there is little or no formal protection given to these amazing shrublands of the south, and the poverty of the population means that slash-and-burn agriculture for maize production, and the burning of wood for charcoal are among many threats to bird and habitat alike.

7. Southern Brown Kiwi *Apteryx australis*

The bizarre icon of New Zealand that its people are named after

Size: 45–55 cm (17.7–21.6 inches).

Distribution: South Island of New Zealand.

Habitat: Forest and shrubland, especially wet mixed hardwoods.

Classification: One of five species in the family Apterygidae and the genus *Apteryx*.

Population and conservation status: Estimated at around 27,000 birds, but severely declining on mainland. Vulnerable.

Breeding system: Monogamous.

Nest and eggs: In a burrow, chamber lined with ferns. 1–2 eggs.

Incubation and fledging: 85–92 days in the wild. Young leave burrow for the first time a week after hatching.

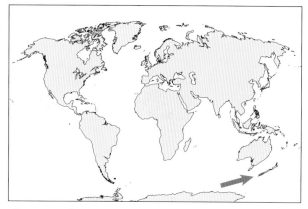

If you went to New Zealand today, you would be extremely hard-pressed to see a kiwi in the wild. This relatively small, very shy, nocturnal forest bird does its best to avoid people, and it seems incredible that the kiwi has acquired the status of New Zealand's number one natural icon.

But no other bird is quite as odd as the kiwi, and it is its uniqueness that clearly warms the heart of an isolated, fiercely independent nation. The kiwi—or kiwis, for there are five species—are among the world's few flightless birds, diminutive and distant relatives of the ostriches (*Struthionidae*) and Emu (*Dromaius novaehollandiae*). They are, in many ways, quite unbirdlike, with hairlike plumage, reduced wings covered by the plumage, and no tail. They creep along the forest floor like mammals, and make sniffling and shuffling sounds. In common with mammals, their world is more olfactory and tactile than visual. They even live in burrows, which they dig themselves, and come out at night.

One of the most distinctive features of a kiwi is its long, slightly curved bill, which is used to probe into the ground or search the leaf litter for worms, snails,

centipedes and other invertebrates. At first sight there seems nothing unusual about this, for plenty of other bird species have similar-shaped bills and use them in the same way. But the tip of a kiwi's bill is very different from that of other birds: the nostrils open out at the end, instead of just below the eyes, and this allows the kiwi to smell out food. Its sense of smell is exceedingly well developed, with just a few parts per million of a substance required for detection.

Kiwis also have a good sense of hearing, and their eyes enable them to see enough to run around in dense vegetation in the dark without blundering into obstacles.

In the breeding season their burrows, which may be up to 1.5 meters (5 feet) long and with a carefully concealed entrance, will be converted into nest sites. Kiwis are strongly territorial and monogamous, and will keep a number of suitable burrows within their borders for this purpose. Indeed, some burrows may be worked on for years before they are used. The female lays an egg which, famously, may account for one-fifth of her entire body weight. Remarkably, she may lay a second egg three weeks later.

Not surprisingly, after such an extraordinary investment of energy, the female then puts her feet up and the male, henceforth, is responsible for incubation and brooding. The incubation period, which occupies three months or more, is long, but the young have high food reserves in their enormous egg and eventually emerge well developed. Even upon hatching they still have plenty of reserves in a yolk sac and under the skin (they can barely stand up at first), and it is not entirely clear whether the father feeds them at all. Certainly, within a few days of hatching, they are out of the burrow, trying to fend for themselves.

6. Gurney's Pitta *Pitta gurneyi*

An exceptionally rare jewel of a bird, and subject of a massive conservation effort

Size: 21 cm (8.3 inches).
Distribution: Peninsular Thailand and extreme south Myanmar.
Habitat: Lowland semi-evergreen rainforest.
Classification: One of 33 species in the family Pittidae and the genus *Pitta*.
Population and conservation status: Estimated at 50–100 birds. Critically Endangered.
Breeding system: Monogamous.
Nest and eggs: Domed structure of leaves and sticks, placed low in tree. 3–4 eggs.
Incubation and fledging: Unknown. 14–15 days.

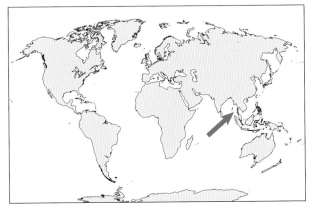

This is a bird that keeps coming back, albeit never very strongly. Having once been common in southern Myanmar, its epitaph had already been written when there were no sightings at all between 1952 and 1986, and it was presumed extinct. Then it was rediscovered in Peninsular Thailand and, amid much fuss, a reserve was created, money was poured in and the local people were educated about the Pitta's charms. It seemed to be doing well, in a precarious sort of way, with up to 45 pairs located in the late 1980s. Then, owing to the fact that most pairs were outside protected areas and that deforestation continued apace, its population collapsed to just nine pairs after 1997. However, in 2003, in the nick of time, it was discovered in four separate sites in Myanmar and now, with a world population of fewer than a hundred birds, it is still present and with us, and just about hanging on.

Gurney's Pitta has quite stunning plumage: striking yellow, blue, black and brown, all in bold arrangements. It is the sort of bird that makes an ideal flagship species, and the moderate and hard-earned success of the conservation project in Thailand is a worrying precedent, especially for less sensational species.

Despite its gaudy appearance, it is actually extremely difficult to see a Gurney's Pitta. The bird is extremely shy, and will often stand motionless for many minutes, sometimes on one leg. Its colors are rendered invisible by the shade of the forest floor, where the Pitta resides, and only show up when the birds strays into shafts of sunlight. Gurney's Pitta hunts terrestrially for worms, insects, slugs and the occasional small frog and, in this twilight world, it is known to use its sense of smell, as well as sight, to find its food. It works in stop-start fashion, tossing leaves aside dismissively with its bill, making a rustling sound that is often the only sign that it is there. Indeed, although it has a distinctive "Lilip!" song, Gurney's Pitta is notoriously difficult to census. An exhaustive watch at a Gurney's Pitta nest was a mainly silent affair, the male only bothering to sing nine times in 39 hours. It is hardly surprising, perhaps, that it was overlooked for 34 years.

Pittas are highly territorial birds, and it is unlikely that, once settled into their own patch, they ever stray outside their borders. It is important for a Pitta to know its surroundings well, so that it can learn the best places to hunt, roost (a spot above ground) and breed. The same stability also shows up in Pitta relationships. While DNA studies around the world show that extra-pair copulations are commonplace among a vast range of socially monogamous birds, not a single Pitta has been recorded indulging in extra-pair flings.

The outlook for this species continues to be grim. The lowland forest on which it depends has almost disappeared and, unbelievably, there is still apparently some pressure from the cage-bird trade in a fit of self-defeating madness. Thus, if you wish to see this bird in the wild, you may need to hurry.

5. Kagu *Rhynochetos jubatus*

A strange and endangered "spectral" species

Size: 55 cm (21.6 inches).

Distribution: New Caledonia, South Pacific.

Habitat: Remote forests and some bushy areas.

Classification: The sole member of the family Rhynochetidae and the genus *Rhynochetos*.

Population and conservation status: Fewer than 1,000 birds and declining. Endangered.

Breeding system: Monogamous.

Nest and eggs: Leaf nest on ground or no nest. One egg.

Incubation and fledging: 33–37 days. Independent after about 98 days.

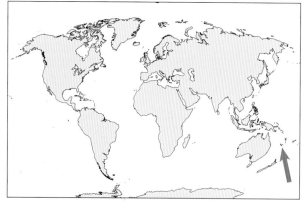

In the way it looks and moves, the Kagu is a cross between a heron (Ardeidae) and a crake (Rallidae). Taxonomically, however, it has no close relatives and may be best placed somewhere near the seriemas (Cariamidae) and the Sunbittern (*Eurypyga helias*).

Kagus cannot fly—their flight muscles are insufficiently developed, though they use their wings to glide downhill, and can run at quite a pace when required. Being flightless and not cryptically colored makes this "Ghost of the Forest", as some locals call them, vulnerable to predators, and this is part of the cause of their downfall.

Captain Cook arrived on New Caledonia in 1774 and introduced dogs to the island. Dogs have been used to hunt Kagus for food ever since and direct predation by dogs is still a serious problem. Introduced rats and cats also probably kill significant numbers of chicks, and Kagus have also been collected for the European pet market. Work to save the Kagu has been ongoing for many years and captive breeding plays an important part—released birds are known to have survived and bred with wild birds.

While a Kagu's wings may not help it to fly, they do have other uses. When they are opened, they reveal a bold pattern of black and white stripes on the primaries. In defence mode, a Kagu will open its wings to reveal these banded feathers, and raise its long crest a little (see above). If a chick is at risk, an adult may feign a damaged wing to distract a predator. When there is a mate to impress, or another Kagu to see off, Kagus stand erect, hold their wings like a cloak (with the stripes hidden) and show off a very impressive fanned-out crest while walking around each other. Their wings also function as "mobility aids" when there are tricky slopes to negotiate, or a predator to swiftly leave behind.

Kagus find their food by looking and listening, in a manner reminiscent of a thrush. Their large eyes are positioned for highly effective binocular vision and, if necessary, the bill is used to check under leaves or to dig for prey. Uniquely for a bird, Kagus have "rolled corns" which cover their nostrils and stop dirt getting in when the bird is digging. A Kagu's diet seems to be entirely animal-based, including worms, insects, snails and lizards, as well as some sizeable millipedes. Although millipedes produce chemicals that are meant to deter predators, they seem ineffective against a hungry Kagu.

Kagus are monogamous and defend a sizeable territory of 10–28 hectares (25–70 acres) throughout the year by singing duets (their voice is described as sounding like something between a rooster crowing and the bark of a young dog) and, if necessary, by scrapping with unwelcome Kagus, though neither bird comes to significant harm. A single egg is laid, typically in a nest of leaves on the ground, sometimes simply on a leaf or on the soil, and is incubated by both parents, with a daily change-over around midday.

This is an iconic bird for New Caledonia, appearing on souvenirs and logos. Hopefully, this role will help secure a brighter future for the Ghost of the Forest.

4. Kakapo *Strigops habroptila*

A extraordinarily unique and desperately endangered bird

Size: 58–64 cm (22.8–25.2 inches).

Distribution: New Zealand (now confined to small offshore islands).

Habitat: Forest edge, scrub, edge of tussock grassland, sea level to high altitude.

Classification: One of 359 species in the family Psittacidae, and the sole member of the genus *Strigops*.

Population and conservation status: None left in the wild; 86 birds translocated to predator-free islands. Critically Endangered.

Breeding system: No pair-bond apart from copulation; female undertakes breeding duties alone.

Nest and eggs: On ground in cavity. 1–4 eggs.

Incubation and fledging: 25–30 days. 10 weeks.

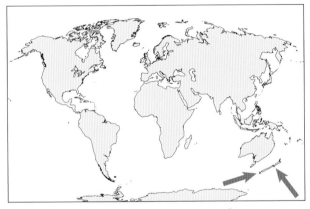

This is an extraordinary bird with an extraordinary story.

The Kakapo is a parrot, but no ordinary parrot. While not the largest in the world, it is by far the heaviest, weighing up to 3.3 kilograms (7.27 pounds). It is the world's only flightless parrot, yet its strong legs and rudimentary wings allow it to forage well above ground, often high in the treetops (it has been recorded at 30 meters/100 feet). It is one of a handful of parrots that are nocturnal, with a well developed sense of smell for tracking down its favorite plant foods. Its eyes are small, but are set forward on an owllike face, conferring some binocular vision. Its hearing is acute, but it makes one of the loudest bird sounds in the world. Although its digestive system is not that unusual, the Kakapo has a highly developed bill: the upper mandible has a finely grooved pad, against which the lower mandible works to crush and squeeze every drop of juice from every piece of plant matter, leaving the bird to ingest little more than mash.

The breeding system of the Kakapo is extraordinarily slow. Birds take up to nine years to reach maturity, and breeding can occur only when certain types of fruit (mainly Podocarps) are available in abundance, which might happen only once every six years. When conditions are right, males make loud booming noises at night, a sound that may carry as far as 5 kilometers (3 miles). Several males may boom close together, and the female selects her favorite boomer from the available birds. After copulation, the female carries out breeding duties alone.

The Kakapo's flightlessness and slow reproductive rate make it highly vulnerable to human interference and, although it once occurred throughout both main islands of New Zealand, its main decline began with Maori settlement about 1,000 years ago, widespread scrub clearance and burning. By the time of European arrival, introduced dogs and rats were already decimating its population, and it was confined to remote areas. Even as long ago as 1890, a visionary conservationist, Richard Henry, transferred 300 to a predator-free island to keep the species alive, but his efforts failed when introduced Stoats (*Mustela erminea*) invaded the island shortly afterwards. The beleaguered Kakapo did hang on in Fiordland, on the mainland, until 1989, but since the birds the were all mature males, extinction was presumed inevitable.

However, in 1977 a population of 100–200 Kakapos was discovered on Stewart Island, off the south coast of South Island and, happily, some were discovered to be females. This set in train an intensive effort to save the Kakapo, by introducing all the gravely threatened individuals to three offshore islands. The last truly wild bird was translocated from Stewart Island in 1992. Since then the population of living Kakapos has crept up from a low of 50 birds in 1995 to 86 in 2007. However, although the decline has slowed, the breeding birds are getting old and less fertile, and it is quite possible that the Kakapo will not last much longer. If that is so, it would be a tragic outcome, and the end of what is surely one of the most extraordinary birds on earth.

3. Marvelous Spatuletail *Loddigesia mirabilis*

A very rare hummer with a wonderful, mobile tail

Size: Male 15–17 cm (5.9–6.7 inches); female 9–10 cm (3.5–3.9 inches).
Distribution: Northern Peru.
Habitat: Forest edges, scrub and forest regrowth at 2,100–2,900 m (6,890–9,500 feet).
Classification: One of 347 species in the family Trochilidae, and the sole member of the genus *Loddigesia*.
Population and conservation status: Estimated at 250–999 birds. Endangered.
Breeding system: Polygynous.
Nest and eggs: Both unknown.
Incubation and fledging: Both unknown.

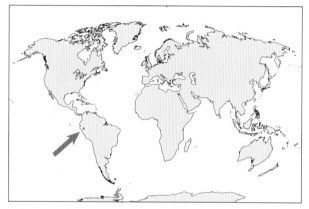

What is it about this 3-gram (0.1-ounce) bird that makes it such a desirable species to see? The answer is in its name, and is clearly visible in the photographs—what attracts people to this Peruvian gem is its marvelous tail.

Marvelous Spatuletail is not the only name that this bird has been known by. Andrew Matthews is credited with "discovering" the Spatuletail back in 1835 (though local people were surely aware of it long before that). Matthews' employer was George Loddiges, a British hummingbird enthusiast, and the provider of the bird's contemporary generic name, as well as part of another common name that has seen usage—Loddiges' Spatuletail.

Today, Marvelous Spatuletails can be found on the eastern side of the Rio Utcubamba Valley. There may be some at another Peruvian site too, but the truth is that of late, there is just one area in the world where this bird has been seen (near La Florida and Lago Pomacochus), and even here, numbers appear to be dropping.

The tail of an adult male is truly marvelous. Whereas all other hummingbird species have 10 tail feathers, the Marvelous Spatuletail has just four. The two "spatules" sit at the end of bare, bent, elongated shafts that cross over each other. In between the spatule bearers are two very long, fine, pointed and straight feathers. As if that were not enough to impress, the male also sports a blue gorget and crest.

The spatules are part of this bird's display kit and may be used against another male, or to impress a female visiting the lek. At rest, the spatuled shafts hang beneath the bird, one crossed over the other. But when he takes to the air to display, the male becomes a very different creature. He raises his bill to show off his gorget, which may look more turquoise than straight blue. His central, black belly stripe is conspicuous and his tail does something totally unexpected—the spatules are lifted high, one on each side of the bird, so high that each dark patch of spatule is significantly higher than the bird's head and a good way out to the side too. These are not just feathers that dangle or flap around, this bird has control of its spatulate rectrices, and a perched bird can flick them with speed and apparent purpose.

Their feeding technique may surprise you too. Marvelous Spatuletails are nectar feeders, and seem to find most of their nutrition in *Alstroemeria formosissima*, a red-flowered lily, though other flowers are visited. The classic image of a feeding hummer is of a bird hovering while it refuels. The Marvelous Spatuletail has a more relaxed approach, taking its nectar on board whilst perched nearby.

Forests are being cleared, but as this is a bird of forest edge, deforestation may not have the impact that it would otherwise have. More shockingly, this stunning bird is hunted because the heart of a male Marvelous Spatuletail is said to be good for your love life.

There are still gaps in our knowledge of this wonderful bird. Fieldwork may even reveal currently undiscovered populations. Now that would be good news.

2. Blue Bird-of-Paradise *Paradisaea rudolphi*

A gloriously iridescent beast that hangs upside down to display

Size: 30 cm (12 inches); male with tail 67 cm (26 inches).

Distribution: Central and eastern Papua New Guinea.

Habitat: Forest edge, forest and overgrown, neglected gardens, typically from 1,400 m–1,800 m (4,590–5,900 feet) in altitude.

Classification: One of 41 species in the family Paradisaeidae, and one of seven in the genus *Paradisaea*.

Population and conservation status: Estimated at 2,500–9,999 birds. Vulnerable.

Breeding system: Polygynous.

Nest and eggs: Various nests described of different shapes and materials, lined or unlined. One egg.

Incubation and fledging: Over 18 days. Unknown.

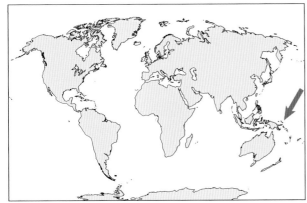

The adult male Blue Bird-of-Paradise (left) is arguably the most beautiful of all the birds-of-paradise. It is a stunning, mostly blue and black, or blackish, bird, with soft, blue plumes and two very long tail streamers. No illustration is likely to do justice to the bird's palette of iridescent greens, blues and purples. The "blue" that gives the bird its name is not just one blue, and may drift towards purple, and if illustration space is limited, the schizophrenic nature of its ornamental plumes may go unnoticed: viewed from the front or underneath, they are blue—viewed from behind or above, they are orangey-brown. The female (above) is visually less impressive but, once again, she is the one that builds the nest, incubates the egg and looks after the young bird-of-paradise.

This bird has a remarkable display. It is a polygynous species and a male may perform to an audience of four females at once. The star of the show does a bit of gardening before the performance, clearing leaves, perhaps to make sure everyone gets a good view. Normally, the inclined display perch is 1–3 meters (3–10 feet) off the ground and the show may be preceded by some more elevated singing. To impress his audience, the male hangs upside-down with his flank feathers fanned out, creating a wide shuttlecocklike shape, and with his tail streamers bending over into a curved "m" shape. The show may be enhanced by a range of visual treats, and he provides a rhythmic soundtrack too, which, on the approach of a female, changes to a noise like an electric-motor.

Lawes's Parotia (*Parotia lawesii*) is a bird-of-paradise that clears an area of ground to create a court to display in. This is a species that is known to hybridize with the Blue Bird-of-Paradise and, on at least one occasion, the latter's display perch has been positioned over the Parotia's court. Similarly, a display perch has been seen near the court of a Carola's Parotia (*P. carolae*), and hybridization with the Raggiana Bird-of-Paradise (*P. raggiana*) is also known.

The Blue Bird-of-Paradise eats a range of fruits and invertebrates, including figs (*Ficus* spp.), wild bananas (*Musa* spp.), cockroaches, orthopterans and ants, with fruit making up the bulk of its diet.

Taxonomically, the Blue Bird-of-Paradise currently sits with six other species in the *Paradisaea* genus, but it doesn't sit there entirely comfortably and some taxonomists believe that it merits a different generic status.

Hundreds of years ago, western wildlife "experts" examined legless bird-of-paradise skins, having never seen a living, wild bird. Their "logical" conclusion was that these creatures must spend their lives aloft in paradise, only contacting terra firma when they died. The local wildlife experts, of course, would have known differently, having hunted the birds for their amazing feathers for countless generations. Today, there is less habitat for the Blue Bird-of-Paradise than there once was, and hunters still seek this beautiful bird for its feathers. Thankfully, the landscape of Papua New Guinea is such that large areas are hard to get to and unpopulated, which should provide a measure of security for this inverted natural wonder.

1. Ivory-billed Woodpecker *Campephilus principalis*

A woodpecker to make history with . . . if it isn't history already

Size: 48–53 cm (18.9–20.9 inches).

Distribution: Southeastern Unites States and Cuba.

Habitat: Extensive old forests, including swamp forests and upland forests.

Classification: One of 220 species in the family Picidae, and one of 11 in the genus *Campephilus*.

Population and conservation status: Estimated at fewer than 50 birds. Critically Endangered (possibly extinct).

Breeding system: Thought to be monogamous.

Nest and eggs: Excavates hole in tree. 1–6 eggs.

Incubation and fledging: Unknown. About 35 days.

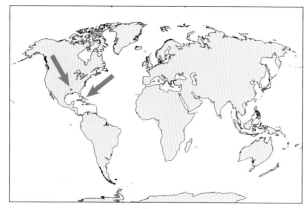

This book is full of remarkable birds, any one of which could make your day, but this bird is different. See one of these and you will remember that day for the rest of your life. See one of these and your name could appear in the world's annals of ornithological history!

This is a big, splendidly marked, black and white woodpecker with an ivory-colored bill and a large, impressive crest that is mostly red in the male and wholly black in the female. It is one of the world's biggest woodpeckers and, in its heyday, was a bird of big, old forests across most of Cuba and the southeastern United States, some even reaching Indiana, Illinois and Ohio.

Ivory-bills need very large forests, with big trees. One pair may occupy a home range of over 15 square kilometers (5.5 square miles). They also need enough dead trees to provide generous helpings of beetle larvae, especially those of longhorn beetles (Cerambycidae). A hungry Ivory-bill uses its "ivory chisel" to get the bark off dead trees, before feasting on the previously hidden beetle larvae. They are more than insectivores though and are known to eat seeds, fruit and nuts, including Hickory (*Carya* spp.) and Pecan (*Carya illinoinensis*) nuts.

When Europeans moved into the Ivory-bill's habitat, forest clearance began. Huge demands for timber after the American Civil War made things much worse, and twentieth-century conflicts have added to the bird's troubles. Forest was destroyed to build warships during World War One and, by 1939, the United States' population of Ivory-bills was estimated at fewer than 25 birds. The Second World War took yet more timber from Ivory-bills—some of which was used to carry tea to British troops. There are records of the birds in Louisiana in 1944, but it was six decades before any more American Ivory-bill claims convinced the ornithological establishment. Lowland forest habitat has been ravaged in Cuba too, and if any Ivory-bills survive there, they are probably in upland pine forest, though it is now over 20 years since the last definite record of a Cuban Ivory-bill.

Remarkably, in 2004, the Ivory-bill seemed to be alive and pecking in the middle of Arkansas. Tim Gallagher and Bobby Harrison saw one on February 27, 2004 in the Cache River National Wildlife Refuge. Not everyone is convinced, but BirdLife International and the U.S. Fish and Wildlife Service are believers. Since then, it has been a difficult game of finding needles in inaccessible, swampy haystacks. It is a game that is being played with twenty-first-century technology, equipment that can record what is seen and heard even when no one is there. Yet, at the time of writing, despite massive efforts searching across the southeastern United States, there is still nothing that thoroughly convinces the sceptics.

Of all the wonderful birds in this book, this regal woodpecker will certainly be the hardest to track down. While you're searching, listen for a noisy double tap and its famed "kent" call and, if you want your name in the ornithological history books, don't forget your camera.

We think it's still out there. Just imagine seeing one . . . or two.

Glossary

Advertising call—A vocalization given by a bird other than a Passerine, to declare ownership of a territory or to attract a mate.

Altitudinal migration—A seasonal movement not so much of latitude as of altitude, birds moving less between places than between heights.

Arboreal—Living in the trees, above ground.

Altricial—Helpless at hatching, with eyes closed. Usually naked or sparsely downy.

Aspect Ratio—A measure of flight performance defined by the length of a wing divided by its width.

Asynchronous hatching—Hatching that takes place over several days, leading to different ages within the brood.

Auntie—A bird enlisted to tend a crèche, which may or may not be related to any of the young.

Bigamy (Bigamous)—Breeding relationship in which one sex, usually the male, is paired to two of the opposite sex.

Binocular vision—A type of vision in which the fields of the two eyes overlap. Since the two eyes can see an object from two slightly different angles, binocular vision makes it easier to judge distance.

Boreal—Associated with the Northern coniferous forest belt.

Bower—A non-nesting construction built solely for the purposes of attracting a mate.

Breeding grounds—A broad term for the geographical range over which a species normally breeds.

Brood—A collection of young constituting a single breeding attempt.

Brooding—The act of an adult bird sitting on young, rather than eggs, to maintain their body temperature.

Brood parasite—A species that lays eggs in the nest of another species (interspecific) or individual of the same species (intraspecific). Intraspecific brood parasitism is sometimes known as egg-dumping.

Brood-patch—An area of skin on the belly that has lost its feather covering and can therefore be in contact with the eggs during incubation.

Brood-splitting—The act of assigning particular chicks within a brood to each adult, for their exclusive care.

Cache—A store of food, usually containing many items.

Call—Broadly, any bird vocalization that isn't a song. Calls are usually short (one or two syllables) and immediately address some sort of situation, such as alarm, flock contact.

Canopy—The more or less continuous network or branches and foliage forming the top vertical layer in a forest.

Carrion—The bodies of dead animals.

Cephalopods—A group of molluscs including squids, cuttlefish and octopuses.

Cere—A fleshy covering of the inner part of the bird's upper jaw (upper mandible).

Cloaca—The terminal opening of a bird's reproductive (and digestive) system to the exterior.

Clutch—A set of eggs constituting a full breeding attempt.

Cock-nest—A nest-structure, usually unlined, built by a male bird to show to a female as part of the pair-bonding process.

Colony—A clearly-defined gathering of pairs for breeding, each pair with its own small territory immediately around the nest.

Communal courtship—Courtship displays performed by several adults (usually males) at once.

Conspecific—A member of the same species.

Congener—A close relative, strictly a member of the same genus.

Cooperative breeding—A breeding system in which birds other than the parents help with feeding and tending the young. Helpers are often called supernumeraries.

Courtship—The act of performing ritualized, standardized displays to attract a mate or maintain a pair-bond.

Courtship-feeding—Provisioning of food by a male to an adult female. The offering helps to maintain the pair-bond, but also helps the female to keep in good condition while forming eggs.

Crèche—A gathering of unrelated young birds brought together for protection.

Crepuscular—Active at dawn and dusk.

Crypsis—The art of hiding by camouflage.

Cryptic—Colored, patterned or behaviorally inclined to be concealed.

Cursorial—Liable to run along the ground.

Decurved—Curving downwards.

Dimorphism—Exhibiting extremes within a species.

Distraction display—A stereotyped set of postures or behaviors performed by parent birds in order to distract the attention of a potential predator away the from nest or young.

Diurnal—Active by day.

Down—Small feathers characterized by their fluffy structure, found, for example, on chicks and on the breast of wildfowl.

Drumming—The sound made by the beating of a woodpecker's bill on wood for the express purpose of advertising; the vibration of a Snipe's outer tail feathers during display-flight.

Dust-bathing—A form of bathing in which a bird uses earth instead of water, to remove parasites, oil and detritus from the plumage.

Endemic—Found only in a specific geographical location; a species so restricted.

Eruption—The periodic but irregular arrival of a species or population well out of normal range, usually in response to overcrowding and/or lack of food. From the point of view of the areas that receive the visitors, it is known as an irruption.

Extra-pair Copulation (EPC)—Copulation outside the pair-bond in socially monogamous species.

False nest—A nestlike structure built or created for copulation or feeding the young, for example, rather than for incubating the eggs.

Family—A grouping of closely related genera and species.

Fingered—Refers to the tip of a wing in which the main flight feathers (the primaries) are spread out.

Fledge—The act of acquiring the first set of (juvenile) feathers, often a prerequisite to leaving the nest for the first time.

Fledgling—A bird that has fledged and left the nest.

Flight-song—A song that is specifically delivered as accompaniment to a ritualized display-flight.

Flush—To scare off a previously hidden bird or other animal.

Flycatching—Specifically, a food gathering technique involving short aerial sallies from a perch to catch prey in flight.

Fringing vegetation—Vegetation on the side of a water body.

Gape—The space created when the mouth is opened wide.

Genus (pl. genera)—A grouping of closely related species. In a scientific name the first word is the genus, and the second the species.

Gliding—The act of moving forwards in the air with the wings held still.

Gorget—A band of color on the throat or upper breast.

Harem—A collection of females bound by allegiance to a breeding male.

Herbivore (Herbivorous)—Having a diet composed of plant material.

Home range—An undefended area (thereby not a territory) where a bird lives and spends its time.

Hover—To fly on the spot, maintaining position over the same patch of ground, usually sustained by fast flapping flight.

Icterid—A member of the family Icteridae (the New World Blackbirds).

Immature—Any bird that has left the nest and has not yet acquired full adult plumage.

Incubation—The act of sitting on a clutch of eggs to warm them and allow them to develop.

Intertidal Zone—The ground covered by high tide and exposed at low tide.

Introduced—A non-native species that is present in the area as a result of man's activities, including deliberate release.

Invertebrate—A general term for the vast assemblage of animals that have no backbones (i.e. anything that isn't a fish, amphibian, reptile, bird or mammal). Includes arthropods such as insects and spiders, crustaceans, molluscs and worms.

Irruption—*See* Eruption.

Juvenile—A bird sporting its first set of true feathers.

Lek—A set of displaying males at a communal arena, gathered together for the purposes of mate selection by visiting females.

Littoral—Living by the shore of a lake or the sea.

Mandible—The jawbone of a bird, which makes up the bill.

Mandibulate—To work with the bill.

Melanistic—Having more black coloration in the plumage than usual, often owing to genetic or dietary defects.

Migrant—In one sense, a bird species that migrates; alternatively, an individual bird in the act of migrating.

Migration—A regular movement, usually seasonal, between one place or another carried out by a population of birds. Does not refer to daily movements or feeding trips for the young.

Monogamy (Monogamous)—A mating system in which one male is bonded to one female and both sexes have a role in the breeding attempt. In genetic monogamy the eggs are the genetic product of both parents only; in social monogamy the adults play their roles but may also indulge in extra-pair copulations.

Morph (*see* **Phase**)—One or more distinct and consistent plumage patterns or colors seen within a species, independently of an individual's age, location or sex.

Molt—The act of replacing worn-out feathers, usually carried out a specific time each year.

Molt migration—A journey undertaken to a special place with the express purpose of molting.

Mustelid—A predatory mammal of the family Mustelidae (weasels, stoats etc).

Mutual Preening—The act of preening another individual, usually, but not always, the mate. Often performed in pair-bond maintenance.

Nearctic—Found in North America and adjacent Mexico.

Neighborhood group—A group of pairs of birds whose territories are clustered more closely than would be expected by random dispersal, but do not form a colony.

Neotropical—Found in South America, the Caribbean and most of Central America.

Nestling—A young bird confined, by virtue of its early stages of development, to the nest.

Nocturnal—Active at night.

Nomad—A bird that moves in response to the availability, suitable breeding or feeding conditions, not normally predictably, and not necessarily returning to where it started.

Offal—Waste or rejected parts of a carcass.

Omnivore—A species that will eat any category of food, typically referring to both plant and animal matter.

Opportunist (Opportunistic)—A bird that can adapt to the immediate prevailing availability of food, rather than having specific limitations of diet.

Order—A high rank of classification grouping families together (*see* Family).

Orthopteran—A collective term for insects of the order Orthopetra (grasshoppers, crickets, locusts, etc).

Partial migration—Migration in which only certain individuals of a population or species migrate, while the rest don't.

Passerine—A member of the order Passeriformes, characterized by its foot arrangement (*see* Perching bird) and by its well-developed vocal apparatus, the latter giving the ability to 'sing'.

Perching Bird—A specific term sometimes used for members of the order Passeriformes, all of which have a foot arrangement (three toes point forward, one back), that aids perching.

Phase—*See* Morph.

Picking (surface-picking)—Obtaining food direct from a surface (mud, leaf, etc).

Piscivore—A fish-eater.

Plunge-diving—the act of diving into the water from any distance above the water, rather than from a swimming position.

Polyandry (polyandrous)—A mating system in which one female is mated with two or more males, either at the same time (simultaneous) or one after the other (successive).

Polygamy (polygamous)—A general term for a mating system in which a member of one gender is paired to two or more individuals of the opposite sex.

Polygynandry (polygynandrous)—A mating system in which the both birds forming a pair-bond may be polygamous at the same time.

Polygyny (polygynous)—A mating system in which one male is mated to two or more females (simultaneously or successive—*see* Polyandry).

Precocial—A chick that is well-advanced and mobile at hatching, usually downy, with eyes open; usually quickly self-feeding.

Probing—The act of searching for food below a surface (e.g. mud).

Promiscuous—A mating system with exclusively sexual, rather than social pair-bonds.

Quartering—The act of flying slowly and low above ground, searching for food below.

Raptor—A general term for a diurnal bird of prey.

Rectrices—The main tail feathers.

Regurgitation—The ejection of partially digested food from the crop or gizzard to feed to the young.

Reintroduction—A conservation measure involving the release of captive birds into the wild in areas where they have become extinct.

Relict—Generally refers to a population left isolated (from another) by the action of an ice-age or similar climatic or geological event.

Resident—A bird that remains all year in the same area.

Role reversal—A rare breeding system in which the males have taken on most of the duties often associated with females, such as incubating, brooding and tending the young, while the females often initiate display.

Roosting—A term referring in birds to sleeping and often also to those activities associated with sleeping.

Sahel—The region of Africa on the southern fringes of the Sahara Desert.

Scavenger—A bird that eats carrion or rubbish, typically not killing for itself.

Scrape—A shallow depression in the ground created by a bird for its nest.

Sedentary—Non-migratory (but the juveniles may disperse).

Semi-precocial—Having the characteristics of a precocial chick (e.g. well developed, downy) but remaining confined to the nest or nesting territory.

Skulking—Customarily remaining hidden low down in thick vegetation.

Sky-dance—An elaborate display-flight, usually referring to one carried out by a bird of prey.

Soaring—Flying upwards, usually in circles.

Solitary—Nesting in its own territory separate from other birds.

Song—A pattern of sounds, often repeated, that is used by a species to proclaim territorial ownership and/or to attract a mate. Usually longer and more complex than a call.

Song-flight—A stereotyped aerial routine for advertising purposes always accompanied by a song.

Species—A population of birds sharing a common phenotype (i.e. the same appearance and genetic make-up) and usually able to interbreed with one another but not with a member of another species.

Speculum—The colorful bar on the secondary flight feathers of a duck.

Staging area—An area, usually traditional, used by a bird or population of birds in mid-migration, often for refuelling, molting and fattening.

Steppe—Treeless and often waterless lowland grassland, typically found in Eastern Europe in a continental climate.

Stoop—Normally refers to a vertical or near-vertical dive in the air, usually for catching prey.

Stop-run-peck feeding—A method of feeding by sight employed by several birds, notably plovers, characterized by regular pauses while the bird is motionless scanning for food, followed by a run towards any prey sighted.

Subspecies—A phenotypically distinct population within a species that is usually defined by distribution but is not genetically isolated enough to be called a species.

Switchback flight—The name given to many display-flights, especially by waders, involving regular rising and falling in the air.

Synchronous hatching—A hatching in which all chicks are out within a 24-hour period, leading to all the brood being of roughly the same age.

Syrinx—The sound-producing apparatus of birds, located at the base of the trachea where the bronchial tubes are attached.

Taiga—The northern coniferous forest belt.

Talons—The feet of a bird of prey or owl.

Terrestrial—Primarily living on the ground.

Territory—An area defended by a bird or birds for breeding or feeding purposes, or both.

Thermal—A bubble of air heated by the sun and rising from the ground, composed of swirling updrafts that can be used by birds for lift.

Thermoregulation—The practice of regulating body temperature.

Tundra—The zone of low vegetation found beyond the tree-line at high latitudes and altitudes.

Up-ending—A feeding technique in water, in which the neck is immersed so far that the front of the body is immersed and the tail points up into the air, the position maintained by paddling with the feet.

Vermiculations—Dense patterns of fine, wavy lines.

Vertebrate—An animal with a backbone. Includes fish, amphibians, reptiles, birds and mammals.

Wader—Also known as a shorebird, a specific term referring to the generally long-legged birds of the sandpiper family (*Scolopacidae*), the plovers (*Charadriidae*), Oystercatchers (*Haematopodidae*), Stone Curlews (*Burhinidae*), Avocets and Stilts (*Recurvirostridae*), Pratincoles (*Glareolidae*) and Stone Curlews (*Burhinidae*). In contrast to the terminology used in North America, the term does not refer to the larger long-legged birds such as herons and storks—these are sometimes known as Wading Birds.

Wing loading—A measure of flight performance defined by the ratio of total body weight to wing area.

Wintering Grounds—The broad area where a species resides during the non-breeding season (also known as Resting Areas).

Zygodactylic—Having two toes pointing forward and two back.

Ranking Criteria

- Practical difficulty of seeing the species
- Rarity
- Conservation status
- Uniqueness
- Brightness and vivacity of color
- Plumage or boldness of shape
- The "X-factor"
- Level of habitat interest and how the species fits into it
- Behavioral interest
- Sounds made
- Cultural impact

Bibliography

Attenborough, D.—*The Life of Birds* (BBC Books, 1998)

Beolens, B. and Watkins, M.—*Whose Bird? Men and Women Commemorated in the Common Names of Birds* (Christopher Helm, 2003)

Birdlife International—*Threatened Birds of the World* (Lynx Edicions, 2003)

Brooke, M.—*Albatrosses and Petrels Across the World* (Oxford University Press, 2004)

Brown, L.H., Urban, E.K, Newman, K., Keith, S., and Fry, C.H. (Eds.)—*The Birds of Africa (Vols. 1–7)* (Academic Press/Christopher Helm)

Campbell, B. and Lack, E. (Eds.)—*A Dictionary of Birds* (T. & A. D. Poyser, 1985)

Cocker, M. and Mabey, R.—*Birds Britannica* (Chatto & Windus, 2005)

Cramp, S. and Simmons, K.E.L. (Eds.)—*Handbook of the Birds of Europe, the Middle East and North Africa: The Birds of the Western Palearctic (Vols. 1–3)* (Oxford University Press, 1977–83)

Cramp, S. (Ed.)—*Handbook of the Birds of Europe, the Middle East and North Africa: The Birds of the Western Palearctic (Vols. 4–6)* (Oxford University Press, 1985–92)

Cramp, S. and Perrins, C.M. (Eds.)—*Handbook of the Birds of Europe, the Middle East and North Africa: The Birds of the Western Palearctic (Vols. 7–9)* (Oxford University Press, 1993–94)

Davies, S.J.J.F.—*Ratites and Tinamous* (Oxford University Press, 2002)

Del Hoyo, J., Elliott, A. and Sargatal, J. (Eds.)—*Handbook of the Birds of the World (Vols. 1–7)* (Lynx Edicions, 1992–2001)

Del Hoyo, J., Elliott, A. and Christie, D.A. (Eds.)—*Handbook of the Birds of the World (Vols. 8–12)* (Lynx Edicions, 2003–2007)

Diamond, A. W., Schreiber, R. L., Attenborough, D and Prestt, I.—*Save the Birds* (Cambridge University Press, 1987)

Ehrlich, P.R., Dobkin, D.S., Wheye, D. and Pimm, S.L.—*The Birdwatcher's Handbook* (Oxford University Press, 1994)

Elphick, C., Dunning, J.B. (Jr.) and Sibley, D.—*The Sibley Guide to Bird Life and Behavior* (Christopher Helm, 2001)

Ferguson-Lees, J. and Christie, D.A.—*Raptors of the World: Helm Identification Guides* (Christopher Helm, 2001)

Fjeldså, J.—*The Grebes* (Oxford University Press, 2004)

Frith, C.B. and Beehler, B.M.—*The Birds of Paradise* (Oxford University Press. 1998)

Frith, C.B. and Frith, D.W.—*The Bowerbirds* (Oxford University Press, 2004)

Fuller, E.—*Extinct Birds* (Oxford University Press, 2000)

Gallagher, T.—*The Grail Bird* (Houghton Mifflin, 2005)

Gaston, A.J. and Jones, I.L.—*The Auks* (Oxford University Press, 1998)

Gaston, A.J.—*Seabirds: A Natural History* (T & AD Poyser, 2004)

Gill, F.B.—*Ornithology* (W. H. Freeman, 2006)

Gill, F. and Wright, M. (IOC)—*Birds of the World: Recommended English Names* (Christopher Helm, 2006)

Hayman, P, Marchant, J and Prater, T.—*Shorebirds, An Identification Guide to the Waders of the World* (Croom Helm, 1986)

Hilty, S.L. and Brown, W.L.—*A Guide to the Birds of Colombia* (Princeton University Press, 1986)

Kaufmann, K.—*Lives of North American Birds* (Houghton Mifflin, 1996)

Love, J.A.—*Penguins* (Whittet, 1994)

Marchant, S. et al.—*Handbook of Australian, New Zealand and Antarctic Birds (HANZAB) (Vols. 1–5)* (OUP, 1990–2003)

Martin, B.P.—*World Birds* (Guinness, 1987)

Michl, G.—*A Birders' Guide to the Behavior of European and North American Birds* (Gavia Science, 2003)

Newton, I.—*Finches: Collins New Naturalist Series* (Collins, 1972)

Perrins, C. (Ed.)—*The New Encyclopedia of Birds* (Oxford University Press, 2003)

Pratt, H.D.—*The Hawaiian Honeycreepers* (Oxford University Press, 2005)

Restall, R., Rodner, C. and Lentino, M.—*Birds of Northern South America.* (2 Vols.) (Christopher Helm, 2006)

Rowley, I. and Russell, E.—*Fairy–Wrens and Grasswrens* (Oxford University Press, 1997)

Schodde, R. and Tidemann, S.C.—*Reader's Digest Complete Book of Australian Birds* (Reader's Digest, 1986)

Sinclair, I. and Ryan, P.—*Birds of Africa South of the Sahara* (Struik, 2003)

Snow, D.W. and Perrins, C.M. (Eds.)—*The Birds of the Western Palearctic: Concise Edition* (2 Vols.) (Oxford University Press, 1998)

Turner, A. and Rose, C. – *A Handbook to the Swallows and Martins of the World* (Christopher Helm, 1994)

Tyler, S.J. and Ormerod, S.J.—*The Dippers* (T & A D Poyser, 1994)

Wells, D.R.—*The Birds of the Thai–Malay Peninsula* (2 Vols.) (Christopher Helm, 1999–2007)

Wernham, C., Toms, M., Marchant J., Clark, J., Siriwardena, G. and Baillie, S. (Eds.)—*The Migration Atlas, Movements of the Birds of Britain and Ireland* (T. & A.D. Poyser, 2002)

DVD–ROMs

Birds of the Western Palearctic interactive (Volume 2) (BirdGuides, 2004)

Web sites

BirdLife International Datazone (www.birdlife.org/datazone/species/index.html)

The Birds of North America Online (bna.birds.cornell.edu/bna)

Index

Acknowledgements

In one way or another many people have made this book possible. Without the skill and determination of many ornithologists and the people that have made their research accessible over the years, it would have been impossible for us to track down the facts that form the substance of the book. And of course, the book would be pretty lifeless were it not for the expertise and patience of numerous photographers.

Specific thanks are due to Ian Dawson and Lynn Giddings in the RSPB library, David Wege at BirdLife International, Abigail at the Galápagos Conservation Trust and Birgit Fessl out on the Galápagos.

Finally, a big thank you to Gareth Jones and Liz Dittner, Lucy Coley and Vicky Rankin, and Stephen O'Kelly at Carlton Books for being so easy to work with, and to our families for their support and understanding (again!).

Picture Credits

Species Checklist

100. Arctic Tern (*Sterna paradisaea*) ☐
99. Western Grebe (*Aechmophorus occidentalis*) ☐
98. Common Nightingale (*Luscinia megarhynchos*) ☐
97. Bar-headed Goose (*Anser indicus*) ☐
96. Vermillion Flycatcher (*Pyrocephalus rubinus*) ☐
95. Siberian Rubythroat (*Luscinia calliope*) ☐
94. Magnificent Frigatebird (*Fregata magnificens*) ☐
93. Angel Tern (*Gygis alba*) ☐
92. Rock Ptarmigan (*Lagopus muta*) ☐
91. Roseate Spoonbill (*Platalea ajaja*) ☐
90. Sociable Weaver (*Philetairus socius*) ☐
89. Indian Vulture (*Gyps indicus*) ☐
88. Red-billed Scythebill (*Campylorhamphus trochilirostris*) ☐
87. Common Cuckoo (*Cuculus canorus*) ☐
86. Paradise Tanager (*Tangara chilensis*) ☐
85. Snowy Sheathbill (*Chionis albus*) ☐
84. Greater Flamingo (*Phoenicopterus roseus*) ☐
83. Ruff (*Philomachus pugnax*) ☐
82. Tufted Puffin (*Fratercula cirrhata*) ☐
81. White-throated Dipper (*Cinclus cinclus*) ☐
80. Musician Wren (*Cyphorhinus arada*) ☐
79. Scissor-tailed Flycatcher (*Tyrannus forficatus*) ☐
78. Superb Fairywren (*Malurus cyaneus*) ☐
77. Woodpecker Finch (*Camarhynchus pallidus*) ☐
76. Montserrat Oriole (*Icterus oberi*) ☐
75. Harlequin Duck (*Histrionicus histrionicus*) ☐
74. Greater Hoopoe-lark (*Alaemon alaudipes*) ☐
73. Pheasant-tailed Jacana (*Hydrophasianus chirurgus*) ☐
72. Sinai Rosefinch (*Carpodacus synoicus*) ☐
71. White-plumed Antbird (*Pithys albifrons*) ☐
70. Greater Roadrunner (*Geococcyx californianus*) ☐
69. Standard-winged Nightjar (*Macrodipteryx longipennis*) ☐

68. Golden-headed Manakin (*Pipra erythrocephala*) ☐

67. Bohemian Waxwing (*Bombycilla garrulus*) ☐

66. Crab Plover (*Dromas ardeola*) ☐

65. Broad-billed Tody (*Todus subulatus*) ☐

64. New Caledonian Crow (*Corvus moneduloides*) ☐

63. Desert Sparrow (*Passer simplex*) ☐

62. Little Forktail (*Enicurus scouleri*) ☐

61. Golden Swallow (*Tachycineta euchrysea*) ☐

60. Red Crossbill (*Loxia curvirostra*) ☐

59. Common Ostrich (*Struthio camelus*) ☐

58. Cutia (*Cutia nipalensis*) ☐

57. Giant Coot (*Fulica gigantea*) ☐

56. Pearled Treerunner (*Margarornis squamiger*) ☐

55. Gyrfalcon (*Falco rusticolus*) ☐

54. Golden-winged Sunbird (*Drepanorhynchus reichenowi*) ☐

53. Blue-and-yellow Macaw (*Ara ararauna*) ☐

52. Azure Tit (*Cyanistes cyanus*) ☐

51. Eurasian Hoopoe (*Upupa epops*) ☐

50. Flock Bronzewing (*Phaps histrionica*) ☐

49. Smith's Longspur (*Calcarius pictus*) ☐

48. Northern Carmine Bee-eater (*Merops nubicus*) ☐

47. Snowy Owl (*Bubo scandiaca*) ☐

46. Bee Hummingbird (*Mellisuga helenae*) ☐

45. Pallas's Sandgrouse (*Syrrhaptes paradoxus*) ☐

44. Capuchinbird (*Perissocephalus tricolor*) ☐

43. Red-cockaded Woodpecker (*Picoides borealis*) ☐

42. Crimson Chat (*Epthianura tricolor*) ☐

41. Cape Sugarbird (*Promerops cafer*) ☐

40. Common Sunbird-Asity (*Neodrepanis coruscans*) ☐

39. Ross's Gull (*Rhodostethia rosea*) ☐

38. Cock-tailed Tyrant (*Alectrurus tricolor*) ☐

37. Spoon-billed Sandpiper (*Eurynorhynchus pygmeus*) ☐

36. Hoatzin (*Opisthocomus hoazin*) ☐

35. Great Argus (*Argusianus argus*) ☐

34. Ibisbill (*Ibidorhyncha struthersii*) ☐

33. Amazonian Umbrellabird (*Cephalopterus ornatus*) ☐

32. Southern Cassowary (*Casuarius casuarius*) ☐

31. Golden Bowerbird (*Prionodura newtoniana*) ☐

30. Helmeted Hornbill (*Rhinoplax vigil*) ☐

29. Andean Cock-of-the-Rock (*Rupicola peruvianus*) ☐

28. Superb Lyrebird (*Menura novaehollandiae*) ☐

27. Andean Condor (*Vultur gryphus*) ☐

26. Wandering Albatross (*Diomedea exulans*) ☐

25. Diademed Plover (*Phegornis mitchellii*) ☐

24. Red-crowned Crane (*Grus japonensis*) ☐

23. Shoebill (*Balaeniceps rex*) ☐

22. I'iwi (*Vestiaria coccinea*) ☐

21. Emperor Penguin (*Aptenodytes forsteri*) ☐

20. Philippine Eagle (*Pithecophaga jefferyi*) ☐

19. Oilbird (*Steatornis caripensis*) ☐

18. Regent Honeyeater (*Xanthomyza phrygia*) ☐

17. Wallcreeper (*Tichodroma muraria*) ☐

16. Helmet Vanga (*Euryceros prevostii*) ☐

15. Bengal Florican (*Houbaropsis bengalensis*) ☐

14. Gouldian Finch (*Erythrura gouldiae*) ☐

13. Maleo (*Macrocephalon maleo*) ☐

12. Resplendent Quetzal (*Pharomachrus mocinno*) ☐

11. Grey-necked Picathartes (*Picathartes oreas*) ☐

10. Ribbon-tailed Astrapia (*Astrapia mayeri*) ☐

9 . Twelve-wired Bird-of-Paradise (*Seleucidis melanoleucus*) ☐

8. Long-tailed Ground Roller (*Uratelornis chimaera*) ☐

7. Southern Brown Kiwi (*Apteryx australis*) ☐

6. Gurney's Pitta (*Pitta gurneyi*) ☐

5. Kagu (*Rhynochetos jubatus*) ☐

4. Kakapo (*Strigops habroptila*) ☐

3. Marvelous Spatuletail (*Loddigesia mirabilis*) ☐

2. Blue Bird-of-Paradise (*Paradisaea rudolphi*) ☐

1. Ivory-billed Woodpecker (*Campephilus principalis*) ☐